STORIES WITH A TWIST

Unexpected real-life stories to captivate the Jewish soul

Unexpected real-life stories
to captivate the Jewish soul

STORIES WITH A TWIST

Nachman Seltzer

A TARGUM PRESS Book

First published 2008
Copyright © 2008 by Nachman Seltzer
ISBN 978-1-56871-457-8

Published by:
TARGUM PRESS, INC.
22700 W. Eleven Mile Rd.
Southfield, MI 48034
E-mail: targum@targum.com
Fax: 888-298-9992
www.targum.com

Distributed by:
FELDHEIM PUBLISHERS
208 Airport Executive Park
Nanuet, NY 10954

Printing plates by Frank, Jerusalem
Printed in Israel by Chish

To my mother.
A very warm person, with a multitude of talents
and a desire to help as many people as she can.
Who has shown her love and concern for me as
long as I can remember and way before that.
Thank you, Mommy.

Contents

In Other Words

Just Part of the Plan

Acknowledgments

Once again to the *Ribbono shel Olam* for sending me the *siyatta diShmaya* to write another book that will, *be'ezras Hashem*, bring *chizuk* to *klal Yisrael*.

To my editor at Targum Press, Avigail Sharer, for doing such a great job. Keep up the amazing work! Thank you Mimi and Allison and everyone else. What a team! And especially good with names!

To Aliza and *kinderlach* for being the best family in the world! You are my inspiration.

Introduction

Why does everyone love hearing a story? Did you ever wonder about that? Allow me to answer this question with a story. A short while ago, I arrived at the Mir one morning and saw Reb Nosson Tzvi Finkel, the Rosh Yeshivah, standing at the doorway, instructing all the students in the yeshivah to make their way downstairs to the dining room. It seems that there was an inspection from the government office that pays a large portion of the students' paychecks: they had come to make sure that everyone was indeed *shteiging* away.

So, I go downstairs and get into line. Now, if you have had the occasion to visit the old Mir dining room, you will know that in all that large room, there are only a few small windows. True, there are fans, but they were not equipped to deal with the number of people in the room that morning. It seemed like the entire yeshivah was there (and in case you don't know, that's a lot of people, *baruch Hashem*).

I'm waiting in line and, since I'm waiting in line anyway, I figure that I might as well have a conversation with the guy standing next to me. We start talking and then someone else joins the conversation and he has a question about one of my latest stories. And before I know what's what and who's who, there is a whole group of guys discussing this *hashgachah pratis* story and that amazing *ma'aseh* and the *olam* is *chapping hispeilus* about Rav Chaim Kanievsky and it's just *lebedig*. And then, this *bachur* asks me where I get my stories from. I give him my standard line: "From people like you, of course." Then I ask him, "Do you have a story for me?"

And then he starts telling me not one, but three stories, all on the same theme. The line is inching its way to the front of the room, we're surrounded by hundreds of people, and the air is so thick we can barely breathe. But everyone is listening. And, nobody is thinking about the heat or the crush of the crowd or the fact that we are late for our *chavrusos*. Because the *olam* is in another world.

That is my point. A story allows us to reach places that are not in our normal realm. If the story is a good one, we will walk away feeling inspired and uplifted and exhilarated. We will want to know if it is true, because if it is true, then we have just experienced the *yad Hashem* in our everyday lives. And, as Yidden who live by His word, that is something very special for us.

So why does everybody love hearing a good story? Because a good story should — and usually does — bring us closer to Hashem.

If you have something that you would like to share, please don't hesitate to be in touch. My e-mail address is nachmans@netvision.net.il.

Nachman Seltzer
Ramat Beit Shemesh
Chanukah 5768

Twists and Turns

A Soul for a Soul

Winter in Eretz Yisrael can be the coldest of times, especially out, unprotected and vulnerable, in the frigid air of the Casbah. As Yoni patrolled the deserted streets and marketplaces, he felt a longing for the simple, uncomplicated existence he had enjoyed before being drafted to the Golani Brigade. He thought back to his high school days, to the summers spent at a little bungalow high in the hills of the Galil. He let his mind take him far away. Anywhere was preferable to where he was right now. "Any shadow could be a terrorist, every rock a mine waiting to be stepped on." Why, oh why, had he wanted to join an elite combat unit?

Although his mind was drifting, his feet stayed strictly on the course set out for the patrol, never once deviating from the route he was meant to follow. He passed the shuttered stores, metal awnings pulled down to the floor, Arabic graffiti scrawled over the soot-blackened facades. He had no doubt what the graffiti said, and his heart turned over in fear at the thought of what was going on behind all those closed doors. Recently, one of his fellow soldiers had followed a seemingly innocent Arab going about his seemingly innocent business, only to discover a highly efficient bomb-making factory by mistake. Although nothing was a mistake.

He passed the row of stores, passed the butcher shop, the asphalt outside still bloody from the fresh carcasses that had hung there only that morning. It seemed like a lifetime ago. He adjusted his helmet and pushed his gun up near his shoulder to a more comfortable position. Far away, someone turned up the volume of his radio, the Arabic music whiny and discordant against the midnight silence. Yoni felt very much alone.

◆　◆　◆

Not more than one hundred feet away, perched high in the minaret of the nearby mosque, Jamal steeled himself against the bone-numbing coldness of the damp stone wall. Next to him stood the rifle, snout poking through the small window high in the tower's side. He peered at his watch, a present from his uncle for his seventeenth birthday, and he knew that it would soon be time.

All those hours of target practice down in the quarry where his family eked out their meager living, all the time spent perfecting his aim until he could take out a target at 300 feet straight to the head. All of that leading up to this moment. Within the next three minutes, the Israeli soldier on foot patrol would be passing the minaret at the perfect distance and angle for his shot. There was time for only one shot, and he congratulated himself on being chosen for the task. It was a great honor — not only for him, but for his father as well, and, as every son, Jamal longed to bring honor and glory to the family name. As he put his eye to the sights, he mouthed a silent prayer, asking for divine assistance for his holy mission.

Wait! There he was, the Israeli soldier, out on the evening's patrol. Jamal's finger tensed, teasing the trigger, caressing it gently. As the Israeli soldier moved directly into his line of vision, equipment weighing him down, Jamal al Khadouri pressed down gently on the trigger, sending out a bullet which sped straight at the unsuspecting soldier. The bullet struck its target. The soldier crumpled to the ground, and Jamal knew that he'd been successful.

He quickly took apart his rifle, repacking it expertly in its case. Then he climbed down the minaret's winding staircase leading to the main body of the mosque. When he exited half a minute later, there was no sign of the rifle or of anyone resembling a youth. Instead, an elderly Arab man was shuffling home as fast as his ancient legs could carry him.

He needn't have hurried, however. The soldier was down and the night was as still as ever. Apparently, nobody had heard the shot. Never mind, they'd find out about it soon enough. His mind dreamed of the honor awaiting his family and the comfort of a warm shower.

◆ ◆ ◆

If there was one thing that Doron Halpern hated about being a soldier, it was the fact that the barracks were so crowded. It was too hard to find a little space for yourself in a room with so many other soldiers. Sometimes the only recourse was to get into his heavy army overcoat and go for a stroll outside. Just for a few minutes and not too far away — one never knew who was waiting in the dark streets and squalid alleyways.

There had been a special delivery of *shwarma* that evening, which one of the soldier's mothers had sent up to them from Tel Aviv, and the excitement was high, the mood festive. Their platoon had almost finished its time here, and the feeling of liberation was palpable. It was party time in the barracks and Doron wanted no part in the festivities.

He shrugged into his coat, slung his rifle over his shoulder, and prepared to brave the inclement weather. He opened the door leading to the street and left the building, strolling past the guardhouse where the soldiers stood alert and ready. He breathed in deeply, tasting the fresh night air and began walking down the quiet street in the direction of the Casbah, the city square. He had been walking for seven minutes when he heard the shot.

It came from somewhere to his left and his training kicked in immediately. Without pausing for a second, his rifle was off his shoulder and his eyes were sweeping from right to left as he ran in the direction of the shot. *They timed it well,* he thought as he ran. *No one was supposed to be out now.* On and on he ran, through the darkened streets and empty lots full of vandalized cars. And then he turned a corner and ran through the courtyard of the mosque and out through the parking lot. Doron nearly went flying over the prostrate form of the soldier who'd been shot.

Fresh blood gushed out of his wound, and Doron realized that time was of the essence if he wanted to save the young soldier's life. He dialed the base's emergency line, giving the soldier on the other end his location, and he then got down to work. First, he ripped a thick piece of material off his shirt and wrapped it tightly around the area of the wound, stanching the bleeding somewhat.

The soldier's face was turning paler and paler, and it seemed like forever before Doron heard the welcome relief of the sirens. The medics jumped out of the ambulance, pulled out the stretcher and practically threw the soldier inside. The doors slammed closed and the ambulance sped away to the nearest hospital, leaving Doron with torn clothing and bloody hands. With nothing more to be done, Doron ran back to the base, changed out of his clothes and, without telling anyone what had happened, went to bed and tried to sleep. He had never been one to boast.

And so, when the parents of Yoni Harel came to the hospital to visit their son — who was recuperating beautifully — and inquired as to the identity of their son's savior, nobody had anything to tell them. There were a few platoons stationed in the city, and there was no telling from which patrol Yoni's anonymous guardian angel had come. When a few more days had gone by and the brave soldier had still not come forward, the army gave up the search for the hero.

Yoni's parents, however, went home to the grocery store they owned in Kiryat Malachi and posted a sign on the wall with the date and details of the story. Israel is a small country, and they figured that sooner or later somebody was bound to walk in who knew the soldier, or who knew someone who knew someone who knew the soldier. But the sign hung there, month after month, with no one volunteering the information they sought.

◆　◆　◆

It was late December the following year when the woman walked into the store. She glanced around, as if to reacquaint her memory with her present surroundings, and she picked out a bottle of orange soda which she carried to the checkout counter. There were a number of customers in the store, and the woman had the chance to observe the owners in action. Every person was greeted as if he or she was a long lost friend. There were smiles, plenty of them, along with warm wishes and soothing energy. Small or large purchase, it mattered not; what was important was how each person was feeling.

As the woman waited in line to pay, she happened to glance at the old sign on the wall opposite the cash register. She scanned the bold, black print with obvious interest and, with mounting excitement, motioned at the owner's wife to come over to her. The owner's wife finished wrapping up a purchase and came over to the excited woman.

"Yes?" she inquired.

"This story," said the strange woman pointing at the sign, "I think it was my son. Yes, I remember, almost exactly a year ago, he arrived home from his army base for the weekend and told us the entire story. Wait," she whipped her phone out of her bag, "I'll call

Doron right now and ask him if this is the story."

She dialed the number and the storekeeper's wife stood nearby, watching intently.

"Doron," she began.

"Yes, Ima, what is it?" Yoni's mother could hear the voice over the phone as if he was right there in the store.

"Listen, Doron," said his mother. "I'm here in this grocery store in Kiryat Malachi and there's a sign on the wall..." She told him the entire story.

"That sounds like my story," Doron confirmed. "Tell them that I found the soldier lying wounded in the parking lot next to the Salheda ibn Salhera mosque." Yoni's mother heard every word, and tears began to well up in her eyes.

"That was the place," she confirmed through the sudden mist, and the two women suddenly discovered an intense bond between them and their families.

◆　◆　◆

The celebration party was set for the following *motza'ei Shabbos* at the home of the Harel family in Kiryat Malachi. Lights blazed from all the windows, and passersby wondered at the sounds of rejoicing coming from inside. The festivities were just beginning as members of the Harel family streamed to their home from all around the country, to meet the young man who had saved their son/cousin/brother or nephew. Trays and trays of luscious food kept on putting in an appearance, and the music was loud and heartfelt.

In the midst of all the goodwill and happiness, Doron's mother called Yoni's mother over to the side for a private chat. They strolled together outside behind the house and into the nearby park. After walking around the park for ten minutes, they sat down on one of the benches and Doron's mother began to speak.

"The truth is," she began, "that I didn't just happen to walk into your store. It wasn't just random."

"I know," replied Yoni's mother. "You live in Kfar Saba, and Kiryat Malachi isn't much of a tourist attraction."

"The truth is," said Doron's mother, "that I came especially to Kiryat Malachi to come to your store."

"Why on earth would you do something like that?"

"The reason for my visit to your store goes back many years," Mrs. Halpern said, and her eyes took on a faraway look.

"About twenty years ago," she continued, "a young woman walked into your grocery store. She had just happened to pass through the city and just happened to stop in your store for a drink. She was very troubled about something and it showed in her eyes.

"The woman behind the counter was very busy, but she became unbusy when she caught sight of the young woman's face. In a soft, caring voice, she began questioning the stranger, expertly drawing out her story. She was able to make the stranger feel comfortable enough to confide in someone she had never met before.

"The young woman related how she was expecting a child, but instead of joy, she felt only bitterness and heartbreak. Their desperate financial situation wasn't sufficient to support a larger family, and she and her husband had begun to argue over the upcoming child's arrival.

"All the fighting had made her sick, and the more the tension escalated, the more weak and frail she became. The doctors all concurred that the longer the situation stayed the same, the more danger she was in. They painted the blackest of pictures of what would happen to her if she continued with the pregnancy.

"The young woman found herself in the harshest of predicaments. On one hand, she was truly frightened over what would happen to her if she didn't listen to the doctors' advice. On the other hand, she couldn't imagine doing what they were advising her to do. And so, she was walking around torn from within, terribly sick from without.

"The store-owner's wife suddenly, miraculously, found herself without anything to do, and she bundled her young and troubled charge out of the store and into her home where, over hot coffee and fresh cake, they sat and talked, for what felt to the young woman like a few minutes, but what was in reality quite a while. And during the course of that conversation, her confusion lifted. The young woman suddenly knew that she was not going to listen to the doctors and their advice: she would find a new doctor who would support her in doing what felt right to her. The young woman's fresh resolve and newfound confidence was all because of that store-owner's wife, who saw a troubled soul and reached out to her in her time of need.

"Five months later," continued Doron's mother, "that young woman had a baby boy. His parents named him Doron."

As quoted on Arutz Sheva

The Rabbi and the Family

I t was late at night when he heard that the Rosh Yeshivah wanted to see him. When it came to a summons from Reb Aharon, it made no difference what time of the day or night it was — he ran. He had accompanied the Rosh Yeshivah to meetings all over the country and to fund-raising events where the Rosh Yeshivah had raised substantial amounts of money for the Jews of Europe. They were a familiar sight over on Capitol Hill, where they lobbied in support of their project and met with many influential American leaders of the day. Yes, Mr. Irving Bunim was the Rosh Yeshivah's right-hand man, and he relished every moment of his job.

It was a starry, chilling, mid-winter night as he left his home and got into his car. He started the engine and headed over to meet the Rosh Yeshivah. The house was shrouded in darkness, shades drawn across the windows, silent and still. There was a light burning in one of the back rooms, and that was where the Rosh Yeshivah led him, where they sat across from one another, where Mr. Bunim waited to hear what his mentor had to say.

The Rosh Yeshivah's face was luminous in the softly lit room, the whiteness of his beard offset by the creases in his forehead and the seriousness of his expression.

"My dear friend," he greeted Mr. Bunim, "we have a very pressing issue facing us right at this very moment!"

"What seems to be the problem?" inquired Mr. Bunim.

Reb Aharon stared straight into the eyes of his devoted friend and student, at the activist who didn't know the difference between day and night, and explained. "At this very moment," he began, "the Nazis are rounding up the not-so-large Jewish community in Italy and sending them off to the concentration camps. I have received a report that almost all the *rabbanim* in Italy have been taken into German custody. Their execution may be imminent." Reb Aharon's eyes were on fire as he spoke, as they were any time there was a mission to be done. "So, Irving," he said again, "what can we do to save them?" And Mr. Bunim thought. And when Mr. Bunim thought, he always came up with an idea.

"The Mafia may be the answer," he told the Rosh Yeshivah.

"What do you mean?"

"You see, it's like this," explained Mr. Bunim. "The Italian Mafia is extremely powerful and influential here in America. They control myriads of businesses all over the country from their strongholds in the Bronx, Bensonhurst, Cleveland and, of course, Chicago. They are the winners in every situation they find themselves in, and there are never any witnesses to anything they don't want people to see. They have a hand in everything illegal, from gun smuggling to gambling to race fixing. They have thousands of politicians on their payrolls, and they are the strongest loan sharks and usurers around. In short, if you are on their team, anything you need taken care of will be taken care of."

"Wait a second," said the Rosh Yeshivah. "If they are based in the United States, how does that help us? We need someone who can take care of things over in Italy."

"Yes, of course," said Mr. Bunim, "but they are based in Italy.

All these people were originally Italian immigrants, and they retain strong connections with their homeland until this very day. They speak the language among one another: they shop in Italian, sing in Italian, and conduct all their business in Italian as well. And, just as they are the leaders of the underground in this country, so their uncles and cousins lead similar businesses back in their homeland."

"Well, then," said the Rosh Yeshivah, "let us meet with them." And the die was cast.

◆　◆　◆

Through business connections that he had in the garment industry, Mr. Bunim was able to put the word out that he was looking to get in touch with someone from "The Family." It wasn't long before his messenger got back to him. Mr. Bunim was to go to the corner grocery store, go into the telephone booth, and wait for a phone call.

At three o'clock that afternoon, Mr. Bunim entered Rozelli's mini-market and drugstore and made his unassuming way to the telephone booth situated behind the pasta shelf. He closed the glass door and sat down on the scratched wooden seat as he waited for the phone to ring. At 3:15 on the dot the telephone rang. Mr. Bunim lifted the receiver to his ear.

A voice with a heavy Italian accent spoke quickly, and Mr. Bunim had to strain to hear every word. "Be at the Mayflower Hotel on Thirty-fourth and Sixth at seven fifteen tonight. Tell the concierge at the front desk that you have an appointment with Mr. Rigatti. He will show you where to go." The conversation came to a close before he was able to ask any questions. He arose, left the booth, and made his way out of the store.

◆　◆　◆

At seven fifteen that evening, Reb Aharon and Mr. Bunim made their way up the stairs, through the revolving doors, and past the uniformed doorman, into the opulent lobby of the classy hotel known far and wide for its upper-class service and expensive restaurant. Bellhops pushed luggage carts from place to place, and guests were constantly coming and going. The front desk was located at the far end of the lobby, and the sight of the venerable rabbi accompanied by the distinguished looking businessman made heads turn all over the lobby.

They approached the concierge and Mr. Bunim presented his message, quietly informing the nattily dressed man that Mr. Rigatti was expecting them. The concierge motioned for them to wait in the lounge. A few minutes later, they could see a most debonair-looking man moving quickly in their direction. He was tall, with shining black hair which he brushed straight back over the top of his head and deep-set eyes which looked like they had seen a great many things, many of them not worth seeing. He introduced himself as Frank Rigatti, telling them that the Boss would see them shortly.

They followed the man across the lobby and over to the elevator bank. The elevator boy gave Mr. Rigatti a deferential nod, and they proceeded upwards at a quick pace. They alighted on the highest floor of the hotel, and Rigatti knocked on the door immediately adjacent the elevator. It was opened by a man no older than twenty, who looked them over with a hawk-like gaze before allowing them into the suite. They entered a luxurious set of rooms and were again made to wait. They sat down on a set of beautiful leather couches. One entire wall was made of glass, giving them a view of the greater part of New York City.

Mr. Bunim was feeling just a tiny bit uncomfortable, knowing whose office they were currently sitting inside of, but the Rosh Yeshivah smiled at him and he felt better. The few men lounging around were dressed to the T, in three-piece suits, Borsalino hats, and suspenders. Two of them were heavily involved in a game of backgammon. After waiting for ten minutes, Rigatti came back and motioned for them to follow him down a long hallway, past numerous bedrooms, a kitchen, and a wood-paneled den. They halted outside a thick wooden door. Rigatti knocked and the door swung open, and again they were scrutinized before they were allowed entrance.

Sitting regally behind a roll-top desk was the Godfather of the Italian Mafia: Joe Bonanno. Mr. Bonanno was smoking a thick cigar, inhaling deeply from time to time, exhaling clouds of smoke. He was wearing a beautifully tailored suit of gray cashmere, and a tie with gray and burgundy stripes. He looked like a banker. The Godfather told Rigatti to leave the room. He did, leaving behind just one bodyguard at the door. Nobody spoke.

Finally, Bonanno looked at Reb Aharon and spoke in a gravelly voice. "Well, Rabbi, you wanted a meeting and you got one. What's on your mind?"

Mr. Bunim translated the gangster's words for the Rosh Yeshivah's benefit, then spoke to Bonanno. "Would it be okay it I serve as spokesman for the Rabbi?"

"Certainly," Bonanno replied.

Mr. Bunim then proceeded to explain the dire situation facing the twenty-four Italian rabbis. Bonanno listened carefully to the whole story, asking a question from time to time, but otherwise taking in every word.

When he finished speaking, the Godfather turned penetrating eyes on the Rosh Yeshivah. Then, looking at Mr. Bunim, he asked, "Who exactly is this old man sitting next to you?"

"This man," replied Mr. Bunim, "is Rabbi Aharon Kotler; the Godfather of the entire Jewish nation."

"All the Jewish people?" asked the Mafia chief in amazement.

"That is correct," Mr. Bunim replied.

"Tell him that I want a blessing," said the gangster, and Mr.

Bunim relayed Bonanno's request to the Rosh Yeshivah: "*Er vill a brachah fun der Rosh Yeshivah*," he told his *rebbe*.

Reb Aharon calmly inspected the notorious criminal sitting opposite him and said, "*Zog eim, er zol leben lang un shtarben in bet.*" Mr. Bunim translated the blessing into English for the Godfather's benefit: "The rabbi blesses you that you merit a long life and die in your own bed." The Mafia chief was visibly pleased with the Rosh Yeshivah's blessing and replied that that was more than sufficient. He then turned to the Rosh Yeshivah and promised to arrange complete release of the rabbis within the next two weeks. Reb Aharon and Mr. Bunim took their leave with good wishes all around, and they were escorted by Mr. Rigatti back through the suite and down to the lobby. And that would have been the end. Except that it wasn't.

◆　◆　◆

Twenty-five years later, a black stretch limo pulled up the drive into the parking lot of the Lakewood Yeshivah. The car came to a halt outside the building, and a young man wearing a leather trench coat and boots emerged, went around the side of the car, and opened the back doors for the two gentlemen who stepped out into the daylight. Both were dressed as if they had just been imported from Saville Row, in worsted suits and designer shoes. They wore sunglasses although the day was not an overly sunny one. Their hair was gelled and brushed into place and they sported Rolexes on their right arms. A student on his way from the dorm inquired if he could be of assistance; they requested to see the dean of the school.

Five minutes later, the Rosh Yeshivah emerged from the building and invited the men inside. He had never seen them before and was a little unsure of what they could possibly want. Once seated in the simple office, the older of the two came straight to the point.

"We," he began, "that is, my brother and I, are children of Mr.

Joe Bonanno of New York City. You may have heard of him." The Rosh Yeshivah nodded; indeed, he had most certainly heard of the infamous gangster.

"Recently," continued the man, "my father has retired from active business, and the company has been handed over to my brother and I. Our father is healthy and well although he approaches old age, something not too many of his contemporaries merited to see. He, on the other hand, has never even been shot. You might have seen the book he wrote where he details his life in the service of his country."

The Rosh Yeshivah shook his head and said that no, regretfully, he hadn't in fact had the opportunity.

"Anyway," the man went on, "my father always attributed his long and healthy life to one factor." Here, he paused significantly. "He attributed his long and healthy life to the blessing that he received from the dean of this school many years ago!"

The Rosh Yeshivah listened in amazement as the brothers related the story of how Reb Aharon and Mr. Bunim had come to see their father so many years before, and how Reb Aharon had blessed the Godfather with a long and healthy life.

"So now that we are taking over the family business," they went on, "we would really love to get a blessing for ourselves, as well."

The Rosh Yeshivah turned to them and said, "Gentlemen, that was my father who gave your father the blessing. I don't have that power — although I love the story."

He watched as they left his office, disappointed, and climbed back into the limo. He watched it drive off with a sigh of relief, and marveled at the number of people his father had touched while in this world.

The Power of Ma'ariv

I'm a *rebbi* in a yeshivah. It's not just any yeshivah, it's one of the most prestigious yeshivahs in the world, and I'm privileged to serve as a *rebbi* to anywhere between 100 and 200 boys a year. My connection with those boys doesn't end when they leave and go back to the States. I'm in regular contact with my former *talmidim* who reside all over the world. They update me on the events in their lives, and they come to see me when they are in Eretz Yisrael. They call me if they have a problem and I do my best to advise them. This is the case for the majority of my *talmidim*. Once in a while, however, I'll have a *talmid* who drops out of sight, out of my radar, though never out of mind. That was the case with Shaya.

Shaya wasn't just a *talmid*. Shaya was someone who used to come to my house to learn with me on those long Friday afternoons in the summertime and the endless Friday nights in the winter. We were really close, Shaya and I. That's what made the whole thing so strange. You see, Shaya had always been number one. Wherever he went, whatever he did, he finished first. His SAT's scores had been in the top five percent of the entire state of New York. Instead of going to college right away, he went to one of the most *chashuve* yeshivahs in New Jersey, where once again he was number one. He was considered one of the top *bachurim* in his yeshivah before arriving in Eretz Yisrael for a stint in the Holy Land.

He arrived at our yeshivah, joined my *shiur*, and became one of the boys. I enjoyed learning with him: his mind was alert and sharp, and he had a maturity unlike many of the other boys his age. He also had an innate, businesslike understanding of the ways of the world. He was attuned to things which other boys wouldn't have been able to grasp. That was Shaya. The more time we spent together, the closer we became. Then he went back to America for *shidduchim* and college.

Here, once again, Shaya was a number one. He was *redt* the best families, the most talented and goal-oriented girls, the richest fathers. In due course, Shaya got engaged.

He went to one of the better universities. It came as no surprise to me that he finished number one in his class. He had received offers for scholarships from almost every Ivy-league college in the country, and now the law schools began fighting over him. He had the pick of the crop, and he chose wisely. He was editor of the law review, the captain of the debating team, and the one who put in the most billable hours at the firm where he clerked during the summer.

He was still in his final year in school and hadn't even passed the bar when the mail started arriving. It seemed like every firm with class and old names on their letterhead wanted to hire Shaya. One firm offered a starting salary of $145,000 a year. The next firm was prepared to outbid them, and so on, until it was a war between the firms. Everybody wanted good old number one.

In the end, Shaya found a firm that he liked, and he accepted their offer. He bought himself a brand new car, as befitting a lawyer in the offices of Bradley, Yaxley, and Appleside, and he began working as a first-year associate. He was basically working round the clock, with time given off for breathing. And at that point, our relationship was kind of put on hold, since he had no time to call anyone. I wondered what was happening in his life from time to time, but there were many other *talmidim* to worry about and, before I knew it, I wasn't thinking about Shaya anymore, except once in a very long while.

◆　◆　◆

Five years went by. Five years of *shteiging*, five years of building my *shiur*, five years in which countless *bachurim* passed through the portals of my *shiur* and into my heart. And in all those years, there hadn't been any sight of the *bachur* whom I had been so very close with. And then, one day, in the middle of morning *seder*, Shaya returned. One second the aisle was empty, except for a middle-aged man with a potbelly and a *Ketzos* under his arm, and the next second, Shaya was striding down the aisle in a blue silk shirt, sunglasses clipped onto his pocket, shoes hand-sewn from some sort of leather that cost seventy dollars an ounce.

He was every inch the successful lawyer and, while I was happy at his apparent success, I was disappointed that Shaya, who had shown so much promise, had stabilized at this point. Where was the *ben Torah* who had learned with me for hours on end? Where was the pure yeshivah *bachur* I had cultivated, in whom I had instilled so much? Where had he gone?

Shaya approached me. He was ill at ease, knowing that he had been less than diligent in keeping up the connection. He sat down beside me on the bench and I held his hand in mine, like a long-lost friend who had suddenly surfaced from the ocean's depths.

"How are you, Shaya?" I asked him.

"*Baruch Hashem*," he replied.

"What brings you to Eretz Yisrael?" I continued my line of questions.

"You know, the usual. We're doing some touring, taking a vacation. Instead of going to Paris, we decided to come to Israel."

How very nice of you, I thought to myself.

"Anyway," he went on stiltedly. "I was hoping that we could get together, Rebbi, and talk."

Now I was surprised. "We are talking," I said.

"No. Somewhere private."

"What's going on?" I asked him, sharply this time, and I was rewarded with reddened cheeks and a drooping mouth. He looked at me straight in the eye, and I was suddenly faced by someone who was obviously very hurt, in a lot of pain.

"I need your help, Rebbi," he said. As he said that, I realized that I had known that all along. We left the *beis medrash* and found some private corner. And, as Shaya started to speak, all his pain came rushing out . They have no children, they've been married for five years already and nothing. Can I help them? The elegant lawyer, the suave, debonair facade has been stripped away, and there is nothing left. Nothing but the broken shell of a man who had everything going for him but remained with a life of emptiness.

"Tell me about your life," I commanded him gently, and he described the life of a couple in their social bracket. Business parties, trips to the Hamptons, cruises, pleasure joints to Miami to get away for a week. A lifestyle which, while most enjoyable, was not exactly the kind I felt was appropriate for a *talmid* of mine. We sat in silence. There were traces of tears on his cheeks. He was spent from crying, but appeared to be somewhat relieved at finally having gotten it all out. I was thinking, thinking.

"Listen," I said to him. "I want you to make a *kabbalah*. Take on yourself something difficult, something that will disturb this lifestyle of yours, but something that will have great merit in the eyes of Hashem."

"Anything."

"Okay," I said. "I want you to be *mekabeil* on yourself to make sure to always daven *Ma'ariv* with a minyan." He listened closely and I could see that he knew what that meant. Goodbye exotic vacations. Goodbye cruises to Alaska. Goodbye to those drives up to the Hamptons (unless Ralph Lauren is hosting a minyan). This meant that no matter how tired he was, no matter what time he got home from work, no matter how his week has gone, he will find a minyan for *Ma'ariv* whatever it takes.

I could see the resolution taking hold of him, the fire of the Shaya of old taking over, the dejected slump of his shoulders slipping away. A brand new Shaya sat up straight, knowing that this was the way out for them and willing to grab onto it with both hands.

"Remember," I warned him, "it's not going to be easy, but you can do it. You have the *ko'ach*!" We said goodbye to one another once again. But this time, we knew that I would be seeing him again soon, that we would stay in touch. I would be waiting for the good news.

I kept in touch with him over the course of the months that followed and, sure enough, there were positive developments. Almost nine months to the day after we met, Shaya and his wife were in the hospital awaiting the arrival of their son. I got a call from the hospital. Shaya was on the line. "Rebbi, what should I do?" he asked me. "I'm here at the hospital and it's all taking a long time. I'm afraid that I'm going to miss davening *Ma'ariv* with a minyan. What should I do? Should I go find a minyan or should I stay with my wife?"

"Shaya, you know the answer," I told him. "Off you go to the closest shul this second. This is the most important moment for you to be davening with a minyan. *Davka* now, while your baby is on the way. This is the perfect way to ensure that he will be born healthy and well."

He went to shul to daven *Ma'ariv* and the baby was born a short while later. A baby boy. Their *bechor*. They wanted to name him something to do with *Ma'ariv*, but Ma'ariv Goldstein just didn't have that ring to it. They thought and thought, and they couldn't come up with any ideas. Finally, they decided to name the baby after Shaya's grandfather. It was only after they named the baby Yaakov that they realized that it was Yaakov Avinu who was the originator of *Ma'ariv*. Yaakov Avinu, the man who made *Ma'ariv*.

◆　　◆　　◆

Months have passed since then, and I'm pleased to say that Shaya's life has changed for the better. He has reverted back to himself, back to the person he once was. They are a changed couple. I come to America for a visit and make it my business to stop by his house while I'm there. I enter his home. It's a beautiful home, furnished with class. But now, it's a Torah home once again. I can hear little Yaakov cooing as Shaya leads me into his study and tells me about the projects he's involved in these days. I watch him as he speaks. He is animated, full of life. He is in his element, finding creative ways to help other people, all without their knowledge. And then he relates how *Ma'ariv* has infiltrated his life, how its importance has penetrated his existence.

He shows me a business opportunity that he's heavily involved in. Explains to me where the potential lies in the project. How this will become the wave of the future. It's complicated, but I see that he knows what he's talking about. I have confidence in his business acumen. If he thinks something will be a success, then I believe in it, too. Then he tells me a story.

The previous month, there had been a convention for all those people involved in this investment. The convention was due to take place in Singapore: convenient for the Chinese, Japanese, and Korean businessmen, terribly inconvenient for those businessmen residing in America and Europe. But, that's business. Shaya made all his arrangements. He organized kosher meals for himself. He booked rooms in a hotel. He had all his flights in order. He was leaving in two days, when he realized that he had neglected to take care of one vital thing: he didn't have a minyan for *Ma'ariv*!

There was no way he was traveling to Singapore without having a minyan for *Ma'ariv*. He was just going to cancel the ticket. There would be other conventions, other opportunities for him to see and be seen. But he wasn't going to miss *Ma'ariv*; that was much too important. Then a thought struck him. Before giving up, maybe he should see if he could come up with a minyan for *Ma'ariv* near the convention. He began making phone calls.

"Hello, is this Dvir Yacobi?"

"It is."

"I was told that you spend some of your time in the Far East on business. Is that true?"

"Eh...usually, I'm there about once a month. Why do you ask?"

"Well, I wanted to know if you know anything about minyanim out there."

Silence.

"Mr. Yacobi? Are you still there?"

"*Minyanim*? I should think not! Sir, do you know what line of business I'm in?"

"No."

"I'm a missionary. I convert people. I most certainly do not daven *Ma'ariv*!"

Things went on that way, with Shaya phoning halfway across the globe and then halfway round the other way. Finally, he was directed to a member of the Chabad brotherhood of *shelichim* who was currently stationed in the wilds of Singapore and who would be delighted to help him.

"Hello. Is this Reb Ezriel Berger?"

"Yes."

"Hi, my name is Shaya Goldstein. I'm going to be in Singapore on business next week and I was wondering if you would know anything about minyanim for *Ma'ariv* in that neck of the woods?"

"Sure we have minyanim for *Ma'ariv*," Berger said, and Shaya's heart jumped for joy, "every *leil Yom Kippur*." Shaya's heart came back down with a thud. "Other than that, we really don't have much going in the way of minyanim."

Shaya was desperate. "Well, how about for five hundred dollars? Do you think you could swing me a minyan for five hundred smackaroos?"

There was a shocked silence on the other end of the transatlantic line. Finally, the *shaliach* spoke. "For five hundred dollars, I think we can come up with something," he said, and the die was cast. Shaya was going to Singapore and he would be davening *Ma'ariv* with a minyan. There would be no stopping him.

Signs went up all around Singapore on the day before Shaya arrived, with information about the party. The signs were written in the three main languages that Jewish tourists in the Far East are familiar with: *Ivrit*, Hebrew, and *Ivrit*. Chabad house was throwing an enormous party the following evening, the sign stated. It was free and the beer was on the house. From all over Singapore came hordes of Israeli teenagers, intent on a good shnitzel sandwich and some down-to-earth Israeli company. They arrived with their backpacks, they came with their friends, they brought their own drinks and cigarettes. And Bisli. But they came. Streams of them. All there to have a good time. To see some friends, to read an Israeli newspaper. To smoke a hooka.

By the time Shaya arrived at the Chabad house, it was packed. There must have been a good 300 people there. Some were lying on the floor. Others were availing themselves of the delicious Israeli cuisine. There were triple-decker felafel sandwiches, plates of humus and techinah. Platters of shnitzel and shwarma. The room reeked from the melange of aromas. The guitars were all over the place; the singing was hoarse, heartfelt, and off-key. Everyone was having a grand old time.

Shaya introduced himself to Berger, the proprietor, and told him that time was of the essence. Without further ado, Berger gave a *klop* on the table and informed the assembled that a minyan for *Ma'ariv* was forming in the shul right at that very moment. Some of the crowd decided to attend for the experience. What an exotic idea! Praying in the evening? *Ma'ariv*! How come they had never heard of that one back home in Hertzliah?

Meanwhile, the minyan got off to a successful start, with an entire cadre of Israeli Jews who were high on life. And Shaya sallied forth with *Ma'ariv* once again. After the davening was over, Berger took him over to the side and Shaya handed over the moola. The evening had been a success by anyone's standard, and Shaya was invited back anytime he should ever be in Singapore again. Next time around they would give it to him half-price.

◆　◆　◆

Shaya told me the whole story. What can I say? I was supremely proud of my *talmid*. He took the gauntlet and ran with it. He had grown up. And, sometimes, a *rebbi* can learn so much from a *talmid*. This was going to be one of those times.

It was on my return trip to Eretz Yisrael when the message sunk in. I was taking the afternoon flight from Newark airport and I was utterly exhausted. It had been a completely crazy few days. I had been constantly on the move, from city to city, and had barely slept. I had a book about Rav Shach with me and I was reading it as long as my eyes were open. They announced my flight and I boarded the plane, found my seat, and waited for takeoff. In my mind, I knew that I had to remain awake until I had davened *Ma'ariv* with a minyan. Then I would be able to go to sleep for a couple of hours.

I kept on falling asleep. I'd blinked for a second, and suddenly the plane was in the sky. I blinked again and the next thing I knew, I could hear the tail end of *Ma'ariv*. I had missed the minyan that I had been counting on. For a second I wondered if I was going to have to daven by myself, and then I began to laugh. Here I was, making my *talmid* absolutely *meshugah* to daven with a minyan for *Ma'ariv* — even when in the nethermost regions of the Far East — and when it comes to myself, all it takes is one small glitch and I'm ready to give up! Well, I was going to take a lesson from him.

I began making the rounds, asking the *bachurim* who hadn't davened yet whether they were interested in joining me for an uplifting experience at the back of the plane. The common consensus was a resounding "No."

"It's not my *minhag* to daven with a minyan on planes," I was informed by one *bachur*.

"I haven't davened *Ma'ariv* for twelve years," I was told by someone else. Things weren't looking good. And then I had a brilliant idea.

Someone in the States had given me a beautiful stack of twenties for *shaliach mitzvah* money, and the bills were sitting in my hand luggage doing absolutely nothing, just waiting for the giant mitzvah I was going to throw their way.

Removing the stack of twenties from my luggage, I returned to those who had previously spurned the chance at davening with me, and I offered them twenty dollars to join me for an uplifting experience. This time they looked sheepish and said yes. Some went to get their yarmulkes from their luggage, others had to borrow from their neighbors.

Ten minutes later, there were twenty people at the back of the plane and we were able to begin *Ma'ariv*. At the prayer's conclusion, I made the rounds with the money, which was turned down by everyone except for one guy. They all said that they were embarrassed by their previous refusal and told me to use the money however I saw fit. All in all, it was a tremendous *kiddush Hashem* — all because of my *talmid* and the inspiration that he had provided.

At the end of the day, *klal Yisrael* is a nation of holy people. Sometimes it takes a little nudge, but the spark that's inside always emerges, moving on to inspire others, in a never-ending chain.

As heard from Rebbi

Happy Birthday

My father always loved telling me about the night I was born. He would stroke his long, unkempt beard and look at me with eyes the color of steel, and then he'd smile. His slender fingers would drum on the seat of the chair he was sitting on, and he'd raise one eyebrow in my direction.

"You know," he'd begin, "that we waited for you to arrive for quite a few years. Of course," he'd continue, "once you arrived, the others weren't far behind." By "others" he was referring to my younger brother and two sisters who had followed me into the family at two-year intervals.

"Anyway," he'd go on, "there I was in shul on Yom Kippur night, knowing that I might have to run out to the hospital at any moment, when the *gabbai* sent me up to the *aron kodesh* to do *pesichah* for *Shema Koleinu* at the end of *Ma'ariv*. I went up to the ark and was about to open the door when there was a commotion at the back of the shul. Together with the rest of the congregants, I looked over to the doorway and saw our neighbor, Yisrael Wagner, charging into the shul looking for me. It took him a few seconds to locate me, since I wasn't at the back in my regular place, but by the time he'd turned around I was standing beside him. He whispered to me that Mommy was going into the hospital. Slipping off my tallis, I ran out into the darkened streets in the direction of home.

"Yisrael, however, told me not to bother going home. His wife had already called an ambulance, and Mommy was almost definitely at the hospital by now. So instead, I headed down to the hospital, where I was told by a nurse with faintly disapproving eyes that Mrs. Resnick had already been given a room and things were moving along." Here, my father always paused for a second to marshal his thoughts, before jumping to the end of his tale.

"I ran up the stairs to Mommy's room and then I came to room 701. As I rushed through the door, I heard the most beautiful sound in the whole world: the cry of my firstborn son upon his entrance to the universe. It was Yom Kippur night," he'd say, "and that's something special." There was a pride in his voice when he spoke of the night I'd been born, as if there really was something special about being born on such a holy day.

And, even though my father himself wasn't very religious, he was filled with the deepest respect for Hashem and the Torah, and I'm sure that my being born on Yom Kippur made his connection much stronger than it would have been otherwise. Be that as it may, Yom Kippur was always a day of introspection in our home, a day of poignancy, a day of remembrance and hope, a day of renewal and happiness. And most of all, a day of holiness. From when I was a very little boy, I could feel the atmosphere that seeped into our home with the onset of Elul and the approaching holy days. There was an awe, something plaintive, an intangible something that enhanced our lives without being too intrusive. And I, the Yom Kippur baby, felt this more than anyone.

◆ ◆ ◆

The closer we got to Yom Kippur, the more my father's eyes

would begin to sparkle. And then he would begin the deliberations. Where should we daven this year? For some reason he liked davening at a different shul every year. I think he wanted me exposed to as many different types of Jews as possible. One year we davened with the Moroccans in their shul near the impossibly crowded Tel Aviv *shuk*, and the next year we joined the Ashkenazim at the Beit Knesset HaGadol. We davened with Jews from Yemen, with Gerrer chassidim from Europe, and with many, many others. Iraqi Jews, and Jews from Kurdistan, and even with a Yerushalmi minyan on one memorable Yom Kippur spent in the Old City of Jerusalem. And all the while, father would be impressing on me how special it was to have been born on the holiest of days, and how lucky we were to daven *Kol Nidrei* with a minyan every single year.

Even today, if I concentrate just a little bit, I can hear the strains of those wonderfully solemn tunes reverberating through my very essence. If I close my eyes and stand still I can see them: the ghosts of my past converging on me like shipwrecked seafarers to a desert island. I feel their presence. I smell the perspiration, the tears on their faces. I see the whiteness of their garb, the serenity in their walk, the purpose in every movement, the knowledge deep within every one of them. I can see the feeling in their eyes: the caring, the warmth, the emotion of those Jews of not so long ago.

There was one shul we must have gone to more than once, since I remember it better than the others. There was a fragrance there, the air was redolent of *esrogim* and *tabak*. The *chazan* in this shul had a voice which reminded me of honey; warm and rich, flowing slowly but surely from one end of the davening to the other. It was a crowded room. Buried in talleisim, each man was free to express whatever he was feeling, as the chazan chanted and their voices rose and fell with the cadence of the day.

"*Ayei!*" the *chazan* sang, and the *kehillah* roared along with him, so that we were swept up along in the tide. Those were beautiful days of simplicity and joy, of tenderness and absolute belief in the truth. But the *yetzer hara* never stops; it is constantly at work, and I, too, had not been destined for an easy ride.

◆　◆　◆

The older I got, the more complicated life became. For some reason that I couldn't explain or even comprehend, I was not getting along with anyone. In class I fought with my fellow students and almost all of my teachers. At home I didn't get along with any of my siblings, and the same applied to almost everyone I came in contact with. Things came to a head in my last year of high school, and by then, I knew that I would have to leave my home and my neighborhood and go on a long search for myself. Things couldn't go on this way, with me fighting everyone. I needed to discover where it was that I truly belonged.

Being a voracious reader, I had spent many long hours in the library closest to my home. Every time I had an argument I'd run to the library, to immerse and lose myself in a world that never did me any wrong. A world where I could be myself, where nobody would judge me. Mark Twain never had a disparaging or discouraging word to say. Neither did Dickens or Kant. They were just happy that someone was reading and internalizing their works. I "grew" with Freud and other "experts of the spirit," and the more I read, the more I considered myself intellectually sophisticated, especially compared to the simpletons around me.

After all, I had devoured Tolstoy and Eliot, and what had they read? I had been all over the world (in my imagination at least), while they had been content to stay shackled up in Tel Aviv's old-fashioned obscurity. I had grandiose plans for the future, while they were content to spend their entire lives in the simplest of professions. And so, a week after finishing high school, I packed my bags, used my savings to purchase a ticket to Europe, and hit the road.

◆　◆　◆

I hitchhiked through the Continent, stopping anywhere that caught my eye. My heart beat quickly at the sight of all the paintings in the Louvre, and the view from the Eiffel tower made me gasp in delight. Venice was architecture and beauty, midnight on the canals. Florence was a walk in the sunlight, shadows dappling the ancient buildings, all adorned with stone carvings and the etchings of stonemason geniuses.

Rome was a bustling metropolis of Fiats, bad-tempered drivers, priests, nuns, and pizza shops. Spain meant drinking endless cups of cheap red wine and watching the bulls run while the gaily colored streamers swirled in the wind. London was Big Ben, red double-decker buses, and the wax museum. I worked the barest minimum that I needed to survive, then moved on to the next place, and all the while, the disquieting feelings threatened to engulf me like a ship in storm.

Eventually, I discovered that Europe, while being beautiful, colorful, and fun was not the place for me. I moved on to more exotic locations, searching for that ever-elusive person, the young man who was Yaakov Resnick and proud of it. I stood at six foot, with muscular shoulders and arms of strength, and I looked vaguely Mediterranean with light-olive color skin, curly black hair, and eyes a shade of steel. People mistook me for Greek or Italian, and that was fine with me.

I picked up many languages, and I learned a variety of trades. I signed onto a boat and worked as a sailor, and I volunteered for the fire brigade in Milan. In Lisbon, I studied furniture making, and in Frankfurt I was a waiter in one of the fanciest restaurants in town. I apprenticed as a chef in Zurich and discovered that the cuisine over there was nothing special — unlike France, where even the simplest bistro has something on the menu to remember. I was a garage mechanic and I taught myself to ride a motorcycle. And always, I wondered why it was that nothing I saw or did was sufficient to excite me, was enough to make me want to stay. Why did I have this endless urge to roam from country to country, from place to place?

And then I went to the Far East.

◆　◆　◆

The Far East is so very different from anything Western, it's scary. The things that people back home took for granted and considered important, were treated like nothing, and my eyes were opened to a new and amazing way of life. It was fascinating watching the cows meander up and down the streets, untouched by passersby, their "moos" a noisy part of life.

Mysticism was part and parcel of everyday life in this part of the world. It caught me unawares and spoke to me like nothing had before. I traveled from place to place, discovering new sects and religions, wanting to know what each one had to offer. I was constantly in contact with the most self-disciplined people I had ever encountered. Each sect I came into contact with impressed me more than the previous one, but still I traveled, wanting to see what lay beyond the next mountain, what nestled behind the rushing waterfall in the next village.

I witnessed elderly men performing bodily feats that men thirty years their junior wouldn't have been able to do. Monks who had spent their lives training their bodies to be subjugated to their souls. And I knew that these people had figured out what life is all about. And then, after searching for many a month I finally found the group of monks whose way of life spoke to me like none other, and I knew that this was the place for me.

I will not go into detail about the exact services they carried out or the philosophy behind their beliefs. Suffice it to say, they were in direct opposition to much of what is written clearly in the Torah.

But I liked what I saw and I wanted to join them. I remained with them for many months, studying under their expert tutelage, gaining expertise in their thought processes, learning from their masters, becoming proficient in many ancient rituals and ideas. And eventually, they told me I had gained their trust and that I was ready for the big leap into the deep water. I was to be accepted as a permanent member of the tribe.

◆　◆　◆

The actual acceptance procedure was something I remembered from long ago. It consisted of a number of simple things capped by what they considered to be a holy and intense experience: the offering of *ketores*, incense. There was a small altar and dim lights...and you get the picture: *avodah zarah* at its best.

The service was set for the following morning. The whole sect was invited, and there was to be a festive gathering afterward to celebrate what I had accomplished in so short a time. That evening, I walked to my simple room as if in a trance. Within my soul, emotions vied for center stage. Happiness at finally finding the right path for me mixed with the confusion of knowing that I would be violating one of the basic tenets of Judaism: Thou Shalt Not Worship Another G-d.

I prepared myself for sleep, but sleep would not come. On this most important of nights, when I needed every minute of rest for the work of tomorrow, I could not fall asleep. I twisted and turned, and almost succeeded in drifting off to sleep when a vision came unbidden into my mind. I saw a shul, a crowd of men, each hidden by a tallis. A sound rose through me like the sweetest of melodies: the sound of my childhood, the sound of *Kol Nidrei*. I could hear the *chazan*'s voice, strong and rich, soaring over the rest. My drowsiness evaporated, replaced by a feeling of dread.

I shrugged off the vision, attempting to sleep, and again the vision emerged before my eyes. The piercing sound cut through me like a celestial knife. Feverishly, I jumped out of bed and began throwing my belongings all over the room, looking for the pocket calendar that I had tossed haphazardly into my bag. I finally located it and I scrambled through the pages, searching, needing to know what day it was.

Yes! There it was. That evening's date. It was the night of Yom Kippur and it was Friday night. It was my birthday.

I didn't sleep for the rest of the night. How could I? Doubts assailed my being and gave me no rest. I told them that I needed to speak to the guru. They looked at me, sympathy in their eyes. I met the master, eyes of kindness, hair the purest white. When I told him I was a Jew he shook his head back and forth...no, no, no. After staring into himself for quite some time he turned back to me and said, "Go back to Israel. Whatever we have, you Jews definitely have."

I left the mountain top and went home. Goodbye flora and mountains, farewell land that was never mine, welcome back to the home of my youth.

I began studying in a yeshivah, learning the Torah which, until then, I had never thought relevant. I began keeping the mitzvos, and I finally found all that I had been searching for all that time.

I guess you could say that I was born twice on Yom Kippur.

Of Cars, Court Cases, and Collecting

I always thought that when I finally got to take that long-awaited trip to the United States, it would be something I would never forget. A moment in time that I'd be able to look back on with enjoyment and nostalgia. Well, the trip did create memories. It was an experience that I will never, ever be able to forget as long as I live.

I was a South African learning in Eretz Yisrael, and it was there that I became a Torah-true Jew. It was also there that I ran into Witco, as he liked to be known. Witco and I were studying in the same yeshivah, and he was absolutely huge. His fists were the size of grapefruits; he towered over me. I wish I had been able to know who he really was, to look past the jocular persona he presented to the world and see the sick person inside that immense shell.

The truth was, that I was still basically the same naïve person I had always been. So, when Witco came up with his brilliant idea I got very excited and decided to go for it. He knew how much I wanted to visit America, and he suggested that we become collectors for an Is-raeli-based institution, thereby getting to see America while making enough money to cover our trip plus a little more for ourselves at the same time. It sounded good to me. It was only when we were on the plane about to leave the country that Witco sprung the first of his many surprises.

"You know," he said, as we were settling into our not-so-comfortable seats at the beginning of the flight, "that I'm from Canada?"

I hadn't known and didn't really care that much, one way or the other. "Yep," he continued, "home of the Blue Jays, Tim Hortons, and Niagara Falls." I wanted to point out that the Falls spent some of their time in America as well, but hesitated when I saw the fierce look in his eye.

"The thing is," he went on, "I will never be able to go back to my hometown."

"Why is that?" I asked curiously.

"You see these hands?" he asked me, showing me his huge, sausage-sized paws. "These are classified weapons!"

"What do you mean?" I responded, a trifle nervous at this point.

"Well," he went on, "years ago I used to spend a lot of my time in the gym working out. I swam and played ball and lifted weights, but mostly I spent my time working on my boxing skills. There's no feeling that can compare with how I felt when I put on those gloves. The power..." I watched the glow in his eyes and I got very nervous. He was reliving his fighting days right before my eyes.

"Anyway," he went on, "it wasn't long before I had become a fighter. I was a boxer, and if anyone had the misfortune to get in my way, they quickly learnt that they had made a big mistake." I shuddered without him seeing and wondered what exactly I had gotten myself into.

"Sometimes," he said, "we held amateur fighting events. It was at one of those that I killed the boy." He delivered this last line with no emotion, with an astounding lack of feeling.

"I hadn't meant to do it, of course," he went on. "But in the heat of the fight anything can happen. Before I knew it, I had knocked him down, and the next thing I know everyone is yelling that I killed the guy." His eyes had a faraway look in them.

"The lights," he whispered. "The crowd screaming themselves hoarse, the frenetic energy of hundreds of people all battling alongside you, even if only in their minds! But the guy had died and the cops would say it was my fault. So I ran for my life, got into America, then took one of the earliest possible flights to Europe." I stared at the cold-blooded murderer sitting beside me and was as terrified as I had ever been in my life. And that was just the beginning.

◆　◆　◆

We reached the States, and to my horror, the previously happy-go-lucky Witco was a different person. He dominated me and put me under his complete control, making sure that I did every single thing that he told me to do. He didn't let me out of his sight. One morning he said to me, "I'm going out to meet my brothers and sisters at the mall. Why don't you come along?" It wasn't really a question. I went.

He led the way through the crowded mall, weaving a path among countless diners all sitting and enjoying their *treif*-as-*treif*-can-be food. And there, right in the center of the food court were his *mishpachah*, sitting and enjoying a couple of cheeseburgers together. Witco's brother was even bigger than him — if that was possible — and he was a real redneck. And his sister... I won't even get into it. Suffice it to say that at this point I was having some serious doubts as to whether Witco was even Jewish! And things were only getting worse.

Everything I did only served as a reason to get him upset. Wherever we went — and we went all over — he found something to threaten me about. We would enter a neighborhood and decide which block to collect on. Since the majority of our money went to tzedakah, we really needed some serious donations, otherwise our trip would become a financial strain. We would split up and go to separate houses, ring the bell, and present our credentials. And, time after time, I would be given more money than Witco. Either I was more soft-spoken and genuine looking, inspiring more trust in the people who opened the door, or he was just scary-looking and crimi-nal-like. The fact remained that I was making more, much more, and that really made him mad.

"How much did you make?" he'd ask me when we met at the car, after a few hours of trudging up and down the boiling hot streets.

"What's the difference?" I'd try to reason with him, but that got me nowhere.

My success made him so upset that he began to threaten me physically. He always wanted to know exactly what I was doing every second of the day and he'd blow up, always managing to hurt me in some way. I tried to ignore his requests but that got him even more upset. Things were looking really bad. And that was before the car is-sue.

As one who was reverting back to his *goyishe* origins, Witco had acquired the perfect vehicle for the transformation. He had rented (I don't know from where) a huge, gas-guzzling behemoth of a white car. It actually wasn't exactly white, but that was the closest it was to any color. It had big patches of rust, broken fenders, trailing bump-ers, almost no door handles, an opened glove compartment, no sun visors, a door which swung open if he hit anywhere above sixty-five miles an hour, too many antennae on its roof, about thirty bumper stickers stuck on every which way, a trunk which had to be held closed with a rope, a broken air conditioner, no radio, and the smell of every single person who had been lucky enough to use it before us. Needless to say, we stood out on the road.

Although no fun to ride around in, I was in no position to complain. The problem was that Witco wanted me to drive. Being as the car definitely attracted attention everywhere we went, it was only a matter of time until the cops would pull us over. Then they would get his I.D., and then they would check him out, and before you could sing "*Chad Gadya*," they would be arresting him for the murder back in Canada. So he wanted me to drive.

The thing was that my international license, although covering just about every single country in the civilized and not-so-civilized world, from Lower Cambodia to Singapore, did not cover the United States. Then, too, being from South Africa, I was used to driving on the wrong side of the road, and I did not relish the thought of being caught in six lane traffic during rush hour in a vehicle this size. But Witco wouldn't listen to anything I said. In desperation, I suggested that we visit a *rav*, any *rav* he wanted to go to, and present our dilemma.

So we found a *rav*, who listened to both sides of the story and then informed Witco unequivocally that he was to be the designated driver from then on. Surprisingly enough, Witco listened to the *rav*, but he hated me even more than before. And, after a few more days of me doing better than him in our collections, things came to a head.

It was a swelteringly hot day, and we were in the mountains traveling from colony to colony, collecting. I was wearing a simple cotton shirt and light-colored pants, perfect for the weather. Witco, on the other hand, was decked out in a black jacket a few sizes too small for his ample frame, a dirty white shirt, and huge sunglasses. In short, he looked like a crook, like a guy on the make. And that's exactly what almost everyone he came in contact took him as. He was in a fine temper when we met at the car, and he shoved me inside the steaming vehicle with his meaty paw.

I sat in the passenger seat, trying to present a brave front to the world. Witco settled himself into the driver's seat and delivered this little message from between clenched teeth.

"Listen to me," he said. "I am going to kill you very soon, or at least put you in the hospital for the foreseeable future! Do you understand?" His eyes were bloodshot and his breath stank of beer and mustard. I felt like my life was over. That was the day we moved to Woodbourne.

◆　◆　◆

Woodbourne, USA, though very small in size, more than makes up for it in activity. The whole shebang is about half a block long, with stores on both sides of the street, and in the wintertime the place has about as much life as a hibernating bear. But come summer, the place takes on the look of a county fair. Music blares out of the *sefarim* store, traffic is at a standstill, and tempers fray at the edges. There are half a dozen pizza stores, a bunch of restaurants, and a couple of game rooms all along that little street. There are bungalow colonies right around the corner and thousands of kids coming and going from all the surrounding camps in the mountains.

There is also an inn, where Witco decided we would stay. The inn is located about a block away from the main area and has a shul on premises. We kept our luggage in our room and traveled around during the daytime. I desperately wanted to shake him off at this point, but he kept me firmly in his control, never letting me out of his sight. Even when we were collecting he was always just a few houses away.

My bags were at the inn, out of my grasp and my days were spent accompanying this nutcase around the Catskills. The guys who ran the inn saw what was going on, but they were afraid to get involved for the same reasons I was afraid to run away: they were scared of those fists. I begged them to reason with him, to threaten him, to let me go my own way, but having caught a glimpse of his ferocious temper, they refused. His anger was constantly on his face, waiting for a chance to release itself.

And when he blew his fuse, they knew it over in Loch Sheldrake, they heard it in South Fallsberg, they could feel the vibrations over in Monticello. And people ran for cover. Objects flew around the room, people were physically terrorized. Nobody, nobody wanted anything to do with this person. And so, I lived in a state of constant terror, never knowing when the promised beating would materialize, when the moment of truth would arrive, when he would get so angry at me that even the threat of a police arrest wouldn't be enough to deter him. And then we went for a ride and Hashem heard my prayers.

◆　◆　◆

Looking at me today, you would never guess that I went through such an experience. With my medium-length neat beard and quiet ways, you would imagine that nothing interesting ever happened to me. But you would be wrong. Never judge a book...

We drove around the country in that eyesore, blaring Led Zeppelin because that was what Witco liked, although I had told him that I never listened to stuff like that anymore. We rode through Ferndale, passing Camp Agudah and collected at any bungalow colony that let us through their gates. And still I made more money than him. We stopped for pizza at Izzy's Knish Nosh, and Witco was hot and sweaty and angry with everything and everyone.

The next day he decided to take a break from the mountains for a day or so and go to Teaneck instead. He'd heard that there were a lot of well-off Jews living there, and he figured that he might as well cash in on the action. We were cruising through the well-tended streets, heading to the first address on our list, when off in the distance we caught a glimpse of a police car moving our way.

I saw him flinch. He blanched in horror and broke out in a cold sweat. He was scared. The police car approached rapidly, lights on, and blinked for us to move to the side of the road. Witco drove the car over to the curb, and before I knew what he was going to do, he physically lifted me up and performed some complicated maneuver which transported me from the passenger seat to the driver's seat, while at the same time moving himself over to what had been my seat.

Suffice it to say, when the officer finally approached to demand license and registration, Witco was comfortably ensconced in my seat, and I had to cough up my South African international license which didn't even cover the United States.

The cop was tall, about 6"2. He looked down at me and I could swear that he understood that I wasn't the bad guy here. "License, please," he said and I handed over my license. "You know that you're not covered in this country," he said to me. Not knowing what else to do, I pretended that I hadn't known. Giving me a sympathetic look, he gave me a court date and told me where to go and to make sure to be there or there would be trouble.

Things couldn't get much worse. Even Witco knew that he'd gone too far and was uncharacteristically quiet on the way back to the mountains. And I wondered what on earth I was going to do! Would they put me in jail? Would I have enough cash to pay a hefty fine? Would I ever get out of this nightmare?

It was only much later that evening that I finally understood the opportunity that had presented itself to me. I was going to have to present myself in court in about a week. I would ask Witco whether he would accompany me to Teaneck, making it appear that doing so would be a great favor. He would undoubtably refuse. And then I would escape. Even if I would be forced to leave all my luggage at the inn, it would be worth it just to escape the animal I had paired myself up with. Hashem had given me a way out and I would seize it with both hands.

◆　◆　◆

Sunday evening I mentioned to Witco that I would be heading down to Teaneck on the morrow, and I asked him if he would drive me there. He smiled at my discomfort and told me that he would stay in the mountains and collect money the next day and that he was sure I would be alright on the train. "Just make sure you leave your bags behind," he warned in a don't-mess-with-me voice. I assured him that I wouldn't dream of taking anything with me.

I had to make three connections: from the mountains to Brooklyn, stop there to daven *Shacharis*, then catch a train to New Jersey, and then get from the train station to the court house somehow or other. I set out early with just my money and tefillin, made it to Boro Park in record time and davened *Shacharis* with a lot of *kavanah*. Then I caught my New Jersey-bound train, arriving at the court house in the nick of time.

There was a huge backlog of cases, and the judge appeared to be very overworked. The cop who had pulled me over was there as well, and he smiled at me when he caught my eye.

"Listen to me," he said. "I see that you're here without that 'friend' of yours and I want to help you out. I'm going to tell the judge that you didn't know your license wasn't good for the United States and I'm sure he'll let you go."

And so it was. The cop told the judge that he had pulled me over, found my license to be invalid but was sure that I hadn't known that I wasn't covered. The judge listened to the cop, banged his gavel, and said "case dismissed." Just like that. I was free to walk out of the courtroom without even having to pay a fine.

"Sir," the cop said to me as I was leaving, "stay away from that evil-looking guy who was sitting next to you in the car. He's not a good friend." I agreed with him and told him that I was on my way to New York where I would fly back to Israel as soon as I could. I

57

thanked the cop for helping me out and, before I knew it, I found myself back in Brooklyn, wondering where to go next. I had almost nothing beside the clothes on my back — but I was free!

◆　◆　◆

The first thing I did as a free man was to walk into a travel agency and have myself booked onto the next flight to Israel, which was the following evening. I had almost a day and a half before my flight, no luggage, and nowhere to go until then. The nearest hotel was way too expensive for my meager budget, and it looked like I was going to have to spend the coming evening on the sweltering Boro Park streets.

People were rushing here and there, intent on their own business, and no one paid me any attention. In the meanwhile, though, doubts were assailing my self-confidence. Maybe I had been wrong to run off like that? After all, we had agreed to be business partners! Fresh *ba'alei teshuvah* are often unsure if what they're doing is right, and I was no exception. So I walked into the nearest yeshivah and asked to speak to the Rosh Yeshivah. I told him the whole story. He probably thought I was crazy, but he stroked his beard, looked at me seriously, and told me that I was asking a tough question and he knew just the person I should go ask.

"Rabbi Rottenberg is the best *rav* to go to for *she'eilos* like these," he said, and he gave me directions. I set off through the steaming streets towards the home of the *rav*, hoping he'd be home but fearing that the opposite would be true. I just wished the whole story was over and I was home, back in yeshivah, and far away from Witco and the United States. The truth is, what I really needed was for someone to give me a hug, reassure me, and tell me that I was a good person. After everything I had been through, I needed someone to show me that he cared. And I found him.

The *rav* opened the door with a giant smile that lit up his eyes. I felt instantly at home with him. He ushered me into his living room and asked how he could help me. I explained the whole story from the beginning, culminating with the Rosh Yeshivah having sent me to him. Then I waited for his answer.

"As to having done the right thing by running away," he began, "the answer is an unequivocal yes! The man you were with is dangerous, unstable, and had threatened to kill you. You are under zero obligation to him."

When he saw that I had relaxed, he invited me to stay at his home until the following day. "You know," he said reflectively, "I was in the mountains this morning, with no plans to come home, but the *rebbetzin, zol zein gezunt*, sent me home for something which we suddenly needed. So here I am, just in time to host you." What could I say? This man was just what I needed after the brutality of Witco, my run-in with the law, and everything else I had been through in the last few days.

◆　　◆　　◆

I davened *Shacharis* the next morning at Munkatch, which was right across the street from Rabbi Rottenberg's home. I davened with extra *kavanah*, thanking Hashem for sending me to the home of so special a man. As I was winding up my tefillin, I happened to glance towards the front of the shul, and I saw an old friend of mine from Aish HaTorah, standing off to the side and finishing up his morning prayers.

I ran over to him and practically embraced him in the middle of the *shteibel*. "Steve," I screamed, "what are you doing here?" Last I'd heard, he was in Cleveland, not in the middle of Boro Park.

"Nothing much," he replied. "I'm in town for a *shidduch* scheduled for tonight. What are you doing here?"

So I told him the whole tale, and before I knew it, we were back at the *rav's* home, where he invited Steve for breakfast. Then the *rav* started frying some eggs (yes this *chashuve* rabbi with his long beard had the time to do something like that), while I told Steve exactly what happened to me. His face grew darker and darker, and when I finished the story he said, "Your luggage is still there? You left your stuff with that maniac?!"

"What was I supposed to do?"

"Listen," he said. "You and I both have the day to ourselves. I am going to rent a car, and we are going to drive up to Woodbourne to at least mount an attempt to get your stuff back. At least you are going to try."

"But Steve," I protested, "by now Witco is no doubt frothing at the mouth in his desire to kill me. How can you expect me to put myself back in his clutches like this?"

Steve looked at me. "We'll go. We'll do our best, that's all. If Hashem wants you to get back your stuff then you will and everything will be okay."

So off we went.

◆　◆　◆

The ride up to the mountains was uneventful. The Maxima that Steve had rented drove smoothly, and we covered the miles up to Woodbourne quickly. As we drove into the town's main drag, I leaned my seat as far back as it would go and lay down, so that I could not be seen from the street. I directed Steve around the corner from the inn, and we pulled into someone's driveway and debated the best course of action. I could see the inn through the surrounding foliage, and I knew that Witco was in town by virtue of the big, white beast sitting outside the inn, covering two parking spots and bringing back horrible memories.

As we sat there in the driveway, I suddenly noticed three people who worked in the inn coming out and heading in our direction. As they approached, I told Steve to motion them over to our car.

"What are you doing here?!" they shouted at me. "Don't you know that Witco will kill you if he ever lays his hands on you again? Turn on the ignition and get out of here as quick as you can!"

"But what about his bags?" protested Steve. "C'mon guys, there must be a way for him to get his stuff." Everyone thought for a moment until one of the guys said, "I have an idea. I'll go into the inn and tell Witco that he has a phone call down at the *sefarim* store and that it's from you. Knowing Witco, he will race out of here, desperate as he is to rip you apart, and then you run inside, grab your stuff, and get out of here. How's that for a plan?" We all agreed that it was a good idea and he set off on his mission.

Not two minutes later, the door of the inn flew open and Witco came barreling out the door. He jumped into his white monster, turned on the ignition and, throwing gravel every which way, zoomed out of the parking lot in the direction of the *sefarim* store.

"Go!" they all screamed and I took off like an Olympic runner.

I flew into the inn and ran into the shul, where we had always kept a spare key to our room in the *bima*. It wasn't there!

Not willing to give up, I ran upstairs to my old prison cell and tried the door. In his haste to lay his paws on me, Witco had left the door unlocked!

I ran inside, grabbed my still-packed bags, and manhandled them out the door, down the stairs, and across the parking lot to Steve's car, with its trunk waiting open. The guys shoved my gear into the trunk, wished me all the best, and we took off out of the driveway, tires screeching in disbelief, taking the corner on two wheels and heading straight to Kennedy Airport and my return flight to Eretz Yisrael. We parted at the airport, handshakes on both sides, and it was only when the plane took off a few hours later that I felt my heartbeat return to normal.

◆   ◆   ◆

Many years have passed since those crazy days. I've seen Witco once or twice, but thankfully, I was on a bus while he was on the street, and he missed me. *Baruch Hashem.*

Oh, and by the way, Steve did end up getting married to the girl he went out with the night of my great escape. He still credits the mitzvah that he did for me that day with bringing him his *bashert,* since as he always says, "One good deed deserves another."

As heard from David Kentridge

Kiruv on Court

On a college campus, some days are good days, some days are bad. When they are good, they are very good, but when they are bad, everything goes bad all at once. As you might have guessed, I work in the *kiruv* world. I spend the majority of my waking hours either meeting with students, or trying to arrange meetings with students, or being told by students that they do not want to meet with me. To tell you the truth, if I were them — twenty-one, free for the first time, with plenty of money — I would probably work hard to avoid me, as well.

There are a number of ways to reach students, all of which work to a certain degree. If someone comes up with the perfect approach, I would really appreciate if he'd share it with me. As it is, some students I meet through mutual friends, some I meet on the college's web site, some I pick up by asking them ever so gently if they are Jewish.

Me: Excuse me, are you by any chance Jewish?

Student: Who, me?

Me: Yes.

Student: I'm kind of in a real rush right now. See, I have this previously unarranged engagement to arrange and if you'll excuse me...

But sometimes I meet a guy and we hit it off and I get his phone number and I call him up and I actually get through to him (a miracle in itself) and he remembers me and doesn't try to protest that he was drunk when he gave me his number. In such a case, I will invite the said fellow for the Friday night meal, and sometimes, sometimes, he actually comes. Then the action starts. In many of those cases when the student — either boy or girl — comes, they find themselves somehow drawn to the beauty of Shabbos. Then my work becomes much, much easier. In fact, once they see what Judaism is all about, I'm able to set up study time with them, and this can lead to bigger and better things.

Anyway, that's how I met Avi. See, one morning I'm standing on the main campus thoroughfare and I stop this guy on his way to class and we begin talking. I ask him where he's from and he tells me Israel.

"Wow," I say. "Whereabouts?"

"Ah," he says. "You're not going to know this place."

"Try me."

"Ra'anana," he says, and I turn to him and say on a whim, "Do you know my aunt and uncle, Josh and Karen?"

"Yes," he says, getting all excited. "Karen is my mother's best friend."

So, he gives me his cell phone number and I promise to be in touch. When I get home there's a e-mail from my aunt waiting for me. Karen writes that her best friend's son is studying on my campus and would I be so kind as to look him up and talk to him a little. Talk about *hashgachah*!

Anyway, he comes for Shabbos and he brings along a friend who is also from Israel, a guy named Avi. Over the course of Shabbos I'm told bits and pieces of their life stories as they gradually open up. Turns out that Avi comes from a family with a lot of money. They're originally from California, where they had a ranch, horseback riding, swimming pool, four cars...you name it, they had it. Totally secular. Except for one thing. They went to shul on Yom Kippur.

Anyway, one year, Avi's father is sitting in shul on Yom Kippur afternoon and suddenly it hits him how empty his life is! Here's a guy with everything in the world, and he feels completely and totally empty inside, as if life is just passing him by. And there, in the middle of the shul, this rich gentleman begins to cry. His shoulders heave. He just cries and cries. Then he decides to change his life around.

The family moves somewhere with more of a Jewish community. A few years later they move again, then again. Eventually, this fellow moves his family to Israel and decides to devote his life to learning. He goes on to complete two halachah courses for the Israeli Rabbanut and receives rabbinical ordination two times over. He lectures on the radio. A real bright light. Avi's crazy about him. Still is, even though Avi's not *frum* anymore.

"So what happened to you?" I ask him.

"Well," he replies, "I was inducted to the army and did my basic training. I did really well there. I served for about a year in my division, where I did even better. So much so, that the army decided I was officer quality. They sent me to the officer training academy, where I wowed them once again. I sailed through the courses with top marks in every subject. I was sent to command a unit. We went into battle and I led them firmly and showed courage on the battlefield. I led my men into war and stayed at the front the whole time. I was an exemplary officer. Before I knew it, I had been promoted once again. I now commanded a bigger unit. This, too, went well. I moved up the ladder very quickly. When I left the army last year, I was commanding a couple hundred soldiers and the army wanted me to stay on as a career officer. But I said no. I had had more than enough fighting for someone of my tender years and besides, I still wanted to see the world. So I handed in my gun and uniform, removed my medals, and left the country in the direction of LA.

"Somewhere along the line, in the service of home and country," he says, "I forgot about the service of G-d."

"I came to California," Avi goes on, "to the home of my aunt and uncle. He's the CEO of one of the leading insurance companies this side of America. She helps him. They want to groom me to take over the company. They love me, always have done, and they give me every single thing I want."

It was true. I mean, I had seen him drive up to my door *erev Shabbos* in a BMW convertible, the kind of car that would cost my whole year's salary to look at, never mind buy. Yes, I could see what he was saying.

"You know what," he goes on, "I was lonely living out there on their estate, so my uncle pays for some of my friends to live there as well. Pays all their expenses so I can have a little bit of company. Kind of wild if you think about it." I agree with him.

"But life is a little more than cars and top-of-the-range computer systems," I say.

"True," he admits, "but really, what would you do in my position? Would you give it all up, say that's it, I'm chucking it all and becoming religious again? What for — I never really appreciated it the first time around. It was always Dad's thing and we just went along with him. But it never sunk in. The truth is," he told me, leaning close across the coffee table, "the truth is, I never could see the point of all this religion thing anyway."

We had a good Shabbos, but it was far from being the blow-out experience that it can be when a kid is living it for the first time. These guys had been there, done that, and they weren't interested in going back to what they had thrown out so cavalierly just a few years before.

◆ ◆ ◆

It can be hard getting in touch with students on a college campus for a number of reasons. One, because they are partying during the night. Two, because they are studying (at least some of them) during the day and don't always leave their phones on. Three, because if they don't want to talk to you they won't take your call — and they definitely won't call you back. I don't think it was reason number three, but whatever it was, I had no luck in getting through to either of them after that Shabbos. I figured that that was that. Maybe I'd see them again, probably I wouldn't.

But then one afternoon, I meet Avi's friend and he's bouncing a basketball. He throws it to me and I pretend that I'm taking the shot and pass it back. He tells me that they all play ball together once a week and that I should come play with them. "Sure," I say, but there's no way I'm going to go play with them since I'm sure that he's saying this just to be nice.

The next week I met him again, and again he tells me to come down and play some ball. This time I say why not? I take down the time and place and tell him I'll be there. The following week I'm at the court decked out in my sweats, all set to show them a thing or two. They're really nice to me and pass me the ball, and we have a great time on the court together and I'm wheezing like no-one's business, realizing how out of shape I am. "I'll call it '*kiruv* on court,' " I think to myself, and resolve to do this from now on. Then Avi comes over to me and there's a worried look on his normally placid and handsome face.

"What's up, doc?" I say and toss him the ball, which he catches on his way over to me.

"Rabbi," he says, "do you know some *tehillim* for me to say for someone who's sick?"

"Who's sick?" I ask, and he tells me that his father is undergoing some tests. "Is it really bad?" I ask, and he kind of shrugs and walks away. His friends tell me that his father is in a really bad situation and that he has cancer and it's all over his body. He was going for surgery the following week and that's why Avi wanted to know what to say.

◆ ◆ ◆

We get together but Avi has had a change of heart. I sit with him in the coffee shop and he nurses his espresso and I try to get him to talk to me. Finally, he bursts out, "How could I start saying *tehillim* now? All these years I ignored G-d and pretended like I thought He didn't exist. Now, when things aren't going all groovy, now I get all *frum* and come crawling back to Him. Now I pray? I didn't pray when I was stranded on the battlefield! I didn't pray when the Arabs were shooting missiles at us! Now I pray. How can I turn to G-d now, when I ignored Him all this time?!"

It was a scream of agony, a guilty soul begging for absolution. "You know," I tell him, "that is the stupidest thing I've ever heard you say! So you didn't do what you should have done, you ran away from Hashem and pretended like you forgot that He created the world. That doesn't mean that now you don't say *tehillim*, that you don't beg Him to save your father's life! What's wrong with you? Come home now! Say the *tehillim*! This is your chance to save his life. Are you just going to let it slip away?"

We're both crying by this time, and I put my arm around his broad shoulders. Together, we go over the sequence of chapters for him to say, and he promises that he's going to say them first thing when he gets home.

The next morning I remembered something very important, something that couldn't be pushed off, not while Avi's father's life hung on the line. I called Avi up. He answered, a miracle in itself.

"Avi," I said. "There is something you have to get done, but like immediately!"

"What's that?" he replied, not sounding his usual cheerful self. Sounding like someone who was spending his time saying *tehillim*. "You're not going to understand why this is so important," I continued, "but trust me on this one. This is huge, crucial! This could make the difference for your father."

"What are you talking about?" he asked me.

"There is a holy man in Yerushalayim," I said, "by the name of Rav Don Segal. He is widely accepted as someone who can accomplish things other people have given up on. I want you to send someone to him, to his home, for a *berachah*."

There was a silence. Then, "If you're sure this is going to help..."

"Trust me here on this one, this is crucial!"

"Fine," he consented. "I'll give one of my army buddies a call and tell him to go take care of this right away." I gave him Rav Segal's address and he promised to get moving right away.

Avi's army buddy — a totally secular fellow by the name of Dror — was somewhat taken aback by the mission he was being sent on, but he agreed to go on the spot. The entire platoon had loved and respected Avi, and on the rare occasions they had met his father, they had seen where the apple had fallen from and had respected him as well. So, Dror was more than willing to do anything if it might conceivably help make the man better.

Dror took a bus to Yerushalayim and knocked on the Rav's door. The Rav wasn't home, he was told, but he'd be back in an hour. He waited and waited for the Rav's return, unwilling to jeopardize his chance to carry out his mission. Something, however, had come up and the Rav wasn't coming home anytime soon. Dror didn't care. He had committed himself to getting the *berachah*, and he wasn't leaving until he received what he had come for. Finally, the Rav returned home and Dror put forth his request for a *berachah*, which the Rav gave him. He was then able to report to Avi in America that he had fulfilled his mission and done all he could do. The rest lay in the hands of Hashem.

For Avi, the hours ticked by slower than a broken clock. He said *tehillim* with feelings he hadn't known he possessed. And then the operation was over and with trembling fingers, he put the call in to his mother at the hospital. She answered the phone but couldn't speak; she was too overcome. They put the doctor on the line and he tells Avi about his father, a man whose entire body had been riddled by disease, to the extent that it had really been incurable. He tells him that they had wheeled him in for tests earlier that afternoon and then they had done the tests again because, as it turned out, almost the entire disease had disappeared! They repeated those tests again and again, but it was true! The cancer was almost entirely gone. Then they operated and removed the part that had stubbornly insisted on remaining.

"Clearly a miracle!" said the doctor, and Avi was able to calm down for the first time in weeks.

◆　◆　◆

We met again a few days later and things had, for the most part, reverted back to normal. Avi looked the same as before, a little skinnier, a little bit more serious.

"Rabbi," he says, "I can't do it!"

"Can't do what?"

"Look, I know that I prayed and that G-d answered. I know that, really I do. But if I start becoming religious now, well, there goes my life! I won't be able to do anything anymore. I won't be able to live with my aunt and uncle any longer. That's it, my life is as good as over!"

I sympathized with him. This was a very hard decision, but I knew that he had to make it by himself. I could listen to him, I could be his sounding board, but when it came down to it, the final decision was his.

"Rabbi," he said to me, and the regret was right there in his face. "I think that I'm slipping away."

An amazing thing happened just a few weeks later. We threw a party for all the kids on campus who were interested in what it means to be Jewish. It was at that party that Avi met Anna, the girl who would become his wife. She was an incredibly hard worker, who had made the very hard decision to become *shomer Shabbos* while still in college and still on campus. She was a person with tremendous convictions. I was unhappy that they had met and I told him so.

"Avi," I said, "it's simply not fair for you to get to know her better. You are not holding in the same place religion-wise, and it would be criminal if she ended up throwing away everything she worked for. I don't want that to happen."

"Me neither, Rabbi," he replied. "After meeting Anna, I know exactly what I want out of life. Don't worry, Rabbi, it's only going up from here, I promise."

And so it was.

As heard from Rabbi Dave Markowitz, kiruv man of the year

From Jo'burg to Jerusalem

"What is life, after all, other than a string of experiences designed by G-d to give you every chance to recognize and appreciate His greatness." My thoughts on many an occasion, especially after moving to Eretz Yisrael and rediscovering something that had long lain dormant inside the heart and soul of my family.

South Africa. A world of its own. A world where everything was possible if one was only willing to try hard enough. Most of my parents' generation was willing to do just that, and they were rewarded by material wealth beyond their wildest dreams. A world of pristine beauty. Vast sand beaches stretched as far as the eye could see, with room enough for everyone who arrived from the cities and the Cape. Palm trees swung gently in the evening breeze, while guests glided from resort to resort holding iced drinks. All that and more was South Africa.

The thing is, that G-d sends each person down a highway built especially for him, equipped with as many bridges, tunnels, and overpasses as He deems necessary. If only my Daddy hadn't left it all behind, he might have reached the point where he could have come to terms with the bends and turns of his particular stretch of road. But alas, his father died when he was twelve, freeing him of all obligation, and the years had weakened religion's tenuous hold.

On marrying Mommy, the last links with his past rusted and snapped, completely eclipsed by her atheistic upbringing. So you see, nothing in the way of religious resources was left by the time he needed them most. Only doubts sitting restlessly on doubts, accompanied by an elusive search for peace.

Above all, I think that I can safely call myself a Zeidy. Moving to Eretz Yisrael has given me the ability to spend much more time with my grandchildren than most people are able to. We are a Bubby-Zeidy team of epic proportions, and many are the times a neighbor will knock on our children's door only to find my daughter and son-in-law temporarily replaced by us. The other night, while giving one of the babies a bath, our eyes met, hers mischievous and uncomprehending, mine loving and tender. My mind takes me back in time, my hand unconsciously patting my left arm, memories of the terrible pain converging all at once.

I clearly remember finding out about the fatal illness that was beginning to ravage my younger brother's body. It shocked the family, Daddy most of all. Yet, shocked and distressed as he was to see his son withering away, Daddy was there to the end. He sat beside him, holding his hand, soothing his spirit, murmuring sweet nothings to his ravished soul. And then he died.

Daddy went to shul. Never missed a day. Saying Kaddish for his son was something that took precedence over every facet of his life. It was ironic really, to see the old *apikores* in shul, swaying over a *shtender*, eating a piece of herring or a kichel after davening, together with the crowd of old men by the coffee urn. I imagine that he received some sort of comfort from all of this, but it wasn't enough to ward off the second blow. Only a few short months after Daddy had finished reciting Kaddish for his youngest son, my second brother was diagnosed with leukemia, a prognosis which, once again, sent shock waves up and down the family spine.

This time Daddy couldn't deal. His mind refused to understand, to acknowledge, to come to terms with something he felt to be a betrayal of such magnitude. The One Above had let him down, and he was never the same again. When the issue of saying Kaddish for my second brother arose, he locked himself into a room and refused to even contemplate such a scenario. Daddy could be stubborn at times, and this was one of those times. There was nothing to talk about. No Kaddish, and that was that.

Except that that was not that. I approached the rabbi and asked if I could recite Kaddish in my father's place, a request which the rabbi agreed to. And so, yours truly, the eldest of three, having had very limited experience with the concept of davening in general and Kaddish in particular, took over what should have been my father's job, to give my brother what I felt he deserved. It was a beginning, although at the time I had no clue where it would lead to.

My having a heart attack soon afterwards changed everything, of course. It didn't shock my father, since he had nothing to do with the whole religion thing anymore. Lying in the hospital bed for hours on end, there was nothing for me to do but contemplate what had brought me to my present situation. I didn't understand why this had happened. After all, wasn't it me who was reciting Kaddish for my brother, refusing to ignore his death and providing him with what each Jew was owed by his family? Why had my reward been a heart attack? Why had this occurred? What did the One above want from me?

As I went through the rigors of open heart surgery and continued on into recovery, this question occupied my mind, never giving me a moment's peace. Step One took place right then.

Akiva and I are spending some quality time together on the couch. I'm reading him a story and he's listening with his mouth wide open. I look down at the small head, bobbing up and down, eagerly assimilating every detail of the story. He turns his head up in my direction and we share a Zeidy-grandson moment of eye-twinkling intensity. Something he says triggers my memory suddenly and my mind takes me back in time.

I was the owner of Man-O-Mens, supplier of top-of-the-line clothing in Johannesburg. We carried a full supply of brand names, such as Dior and Pierre Cardin, as well as many of the best South African brands available. We were the number one stop for hats, as well as sweaters and blazers.

It was a quiet morning, possibly the beginning of vacation, and I, together with the rest of the staff, was tidying up the shop for the start of the workday. I straightened a pile of blue shirts, making sure the creases were precise, and then moved on to check my hat inventory. Then I put in a memo to remember to get in touch with my supplier at London Fog. There was a tinkle at the front of the store, informing us of a customer's entrance, and a group of black workers came in together, searching for the perfect hat.

I replaced a number of ties which had fallen in a heap on the floor and, when I turned around, I felt the sharp end of a knife sticking into my side through my sweater and shirt, and beginning to tickle my skin with its point.

"Turn around slowly," drawled a voice, and I see the leader of the group of Blacks standing at my side, eyes like smoldering coal in his smoky face. For the first time in as long as I can remember, I felt fear. Real, genuine fear. It rose up like a fountain within my chest and I felt like I was going to faint. These things happened to other people, not to me! But it was happening and, as I watched, the group of Blacks fanned out through my store and began shoving my merchandise into their sacks.

I watched impassively as they cleaned out my store, the knife's point digging deeper any time I moved an inch in any direction. I could hear breathing. I could hear everything around me: sharp, clear. Finally, they had collected enough stuff. They shoved me and my staff to the floor and raced out of the store, carrying tons and tons of my top-level clothing. But we were alive! And that was something totally out of the ordinary. Which brought me to Step Two on the path of discovery.

Elisheva came for Shabbos just by herself, and her grandmother and I are having a grand old time listening to her opinions on life. She is bright eyed and sharp tongued without even meaning to be, and her vibrancy brings a luster to our home. I stare at my oldest granddaughter, basking in her cheer and personality, and I can't help but remember that I almost missed all of it...

It was early in the morning and I was on my way to work. The weather was glorious as usual, and I breathed in the wonder of the universe. What a country! Easily one of the most beautiful places on earth. As I walked, I let my mind run wild through the country, spending a little time in every place. Cape Town came to mind first, a marvel beyond description. Table Mountain: a natural paradise, brimming with animals of all sizes. Monkeys roam free, undisturbed by modern man, and the view of two oceans meeting off the coast is worth gold. South African gold, of course.

Suddenly, I was brought back to reality by the shouting that was beginning to penetrate my consciousness. Suddenly alarmed, I looked to my right and a sea of black appeared. Between 800 and 1000 angry Zulus were heading straight in my direction. They were holding many weapons. Some of the home-made variety — such as bicycle tire treads and fire extinguishers, while others had a more professional look to them. By the minute, the noise was changing from "far-off wave hitting shore," to "avalanche," to "earthquake."

The men were heading towards the building on my left, which, besides being my place of work, happened to house the political headquarters of a competing tribe. The competition was waiting for them: a couple hundred Blacks from the opposite side, armed with the best in modern weaponry (which they were no doubt planning to use).

In the space of five seconds, I took all this in, and I dove for the closest shelter, which happened to be the driveway leading to the office building's underground parking lot. Gunfire began to resound on all sides and, as I flung myself on the ground, taking shelter on a friendly oil patch, war broke out above me. The exchange of fire was incredibly strong: sounds of revolvers, hunting guns, and machine guns merged together in one colossal death whirl. Chips of concrete flew in every direction as the bullets struck the building's walls and rocketed off in every which way. The cries of the wounded and the groans of the dying could be heard down in my hiding place, and I tasted the asphalt for what seemed to be forever.

Security guards were suddenly tapping us and telling us to remain where we were — as if we had been planning to go somewhere else! And as I lay there on the cold earth, I knew that G-d must have something in mind for me, after all.

Outside, what had been a pristine street just half an hour before, was now flowing with blood, dead littering the sidewalk. Carnage. And I was left wondering what message I was meant to take from it all. Step Three had been incredibly traumatic, but I had still not learnt my lesson.

Avigail has the sweetest disposition and we consider ourselves fortunate to count her among our grandchildren. She is sensitive and caring, and the combination makes for a very special little person whom we love to have around. The feeling is mutual. As we feed her pet hamster, she gives me an update on the events in his life. It hurts me to realize how close we came to missing out on all this quality time together...

It was becoming more and more dangerous to run a successful business in Johannesburg. At any time, one could be held up, and that could easily lead to violence and sometimes much more.

The morning began uneventfully, but quickly changed gears, and once again I found myself in a life-and-death situation.

The doorbell tinkled and the door was pushed open by a tall, muscular black man, wearing expensive clothing, who began to browse through our large selection of raincoats. He was soon joined by another few men, who seemed content to look around, flipping through ties, trying on shirts and modeling a blazer or two. Since many of our customers were black, this development wasn't unduly suspicious.

As I turned around on my way to the cash register, I bumped into the tall one (or he bumped into me), and his jacket happened to shift to the side revealing a revolver! He looked down at me and smiled.

"Don't mind that," he said. "I work for the C.I.D., the South African detective force." There wasn't anything I could do at this point, even if he didn't work for C.I.D., since with his eyes taking in my every move, I couldn't very well press the emergency button connecting me to the police station. I began to walk away and, in one fluid movement he had removed the gun from its holster and was pointing it at my head. The rest of the men were brandishing guns at the other employees. The situation looked pretty bleak.

He stuck the end of his gun into my head and, looking up at him, I could tell that my end was imminent.

"Listen, Whitey," he said, using the slang nickname for white people that was so popular with the underclass, "I'm going to kill you! You're dead. Either by gun or by knife." Here, he moved aside his jacket, revealing a couple of knives wedged comfortably in his waistband. I knew that the end was near. I could only hope that it would be quick and relatively painless. Suddenly, he whirled the gun up in the air and brought it down with all the force of his arm on my head. I collapsed in a bloody heap on the floor, knocked unconscious by the sheer force of his blow.

The next thing I knew, I was being prodded by his gun butt, and a belligerent voice was demanding that I wake up this instant and take him over to my safe. Through the thickness of the fog, my brain recognized the voice of the intruder and conveyed the earnestness of the situation to my broken body.

I slid back into myself. Head throbbing fire, I wearily got up and led the way to the safe, which I opened for him. He removed all the money, along with about half the merchandise in my store, leaving me with empty shelves and a much emptier heart.

That was Step Four, and it inspired me to say to my wife when I finally got home after a lengthy stay at the nearest hospital, that maybe, just maybe, the time had come to consider moving to Eretz Yisrael. It wasn't like we didn't have anyone there already. Our children were residing in the Old City and would have liked nothing more than for us to join them. It was ironic, really, that my father the atheist had a grandson as well as grandson-in-law learning Torah in the Holy City. I could see how happy and fulfilled they were — perhaps there was something in Israel for us, as well. Maybe Torah was the answer to all the questions. We were closer and closer to finding out.

Rochel and I share many common interests. We both love ice cream, we adore playgrounds, and we can't sit still for a second (she, because she's three and has the energy level of a basketball player, and me since I'm chasing after her). When I look at that impish little face I can't even imagine not having had the chance to get to know her...

When I turned fifty, I felt an inexplicable urge to get myself checked out by a doctor. Officially, I was in the best of health, but for some reason, something told me to go and get myself a thorough examination. Having confirmed that I appeared to be a healthy specimen, the doctor nevertheless went ahead and put me through a round of tests, which culminated in him inviting me back for round two.

Round two showed something strange on the X-rays. Before I knew what was happening, I had an appointment with a urology consultant, who called me into his office for a little chat. They had been able to find localized kernels of sickness, which would spread given a little more time.

A few months later, the growth having been successfully removed, the consultant asked me what I intended to do next. What did I intend to do next? It was very simple. We was going to move to Eretz Yisrael, where we would get closer to G-d and to our family.

And, that's exactly what we did. We joined our children in a town not too far from Jerusalem, allowing us to see them all very often. This was also the time for renewing our connection with Hashem, for allowing ourselves to see Him everywhere.

Step Five brought us to the land of our heritage, where we celebrate a *se'udas hoda'ah* every year, commemorating the many miracles that brought us to where we are — especially miracle number six: a full connection with the One Above and the observance of His holy Torah.

Tzipora Friedman

Ever since I was a little child, I needed to be put back together. I was like Humpty Dumpty. Forever in the hospital for this operation and that treatment, I became very at home in the place. The result: I made friends with many of the people I came in contact with. Some were sick, others were sicker, but every one of them had a story, and somehow I came to know and hear many of them.

Each trip was an adventure in its own right, but there was one particular hospital stay that hit me hard between the eyes. I was seventeen years old, unbearably friendly and insatiably curious. While recuperating from the latest attempt to piece me back together, I found myself sandwiched between a man recovering from the removal of an abscessed tooth and a recovering alcoholic. The truth is, the alcoholic was very impressive, having fought a terrific battle and emerged victorious. So there I was, lying in bed, and the alcoholic strikes up a conversation.

"You know something," he says as he begins his little speech, "it's because of people like you that I'm off the bottle today."

"Really?" I ask.

"Yup," he continues. "You guys in the black hats and jackets, got me to return to reality." I'm all ears to hear exactly how the *frum* community influenced this guy to give up his drinking problem, and I tell him so.

"Well, it's like this," he says and proceeds to relate the preface of what would become a fascinating story.

"It was one cold day in the middle of the winter," he began, "just freezing! Snow was coming down all over the place, the wind was blowing like one hundred miles an hour, and I ran out of cornflakes! In my state of mind at that time, not having any cornflakes seemed like a terrible thing, and I decided to brave the storm and take a train down to the supermarket to get myself some cornflakes.

"There I was," he went on, "lying on the floor of the car that I'm in, as carsick as I've ever been, when I hear the sounds of a scuffle from the other side of the railway car. Not feeling very brave, but wanting to know what was going on, I inched around the seat that was blocking my view and saw two of those black hat dudes sitting by a window and pretending not to exist. At the same time, four of the car's inner-city occupants had made a decision to teach those young fellows a lesson they'd remember for life.

"Next thing I knew, the four guys were standing screaming all sorts of things at the young men sitting there, who were trying their best to be brave and ignore the tough guys. Well, that approach didn't work. It only served to aggravate the situation, though I don't know if there was anything those boys could have done that would have made a difference. They were doomed from the start." My roommate scratched his balding head and took a drink from the can of warm Coke that was sitting on the table next to his bed. I waited to hear where this was going.

"So, the whole time this is happening," he went on, "I'm pretending to be looking into my brown paper bag, while in reality I'm checking out the gang, trying to decide whether I should make a run for it while I still have half a chance. Then the train stops by a station and one of the Jewboys tries to get through the doors, but they throw him back into his seat. Then they start to beat him up."

His rheumy eyes look sideways at me from beneath a pair of the longest eyelashes I have ever seen and he nods to himself, remembering the scene.

"Those guys beat the Jews up like I never saw anyone beat someone up. Ever. They destroyed them and left them for just about dead, their broken bodies propped up on their seats. And that was when I knew that I had to get off the bottle and go back to a normal life."

"Wow," I said, "you mean if you wouldn't have been drunk, you would have fought those guys off?"

"No," he replied, "I would have joined in with the other four guys and beat up those Jews. But good. So the next day I joined a program which really helped me out and here I am, as good as new. Almost."

I looked over at my roommate and I realized that for the first time in my seventeen years of life, I was talking to an anti-Semite. This guy really meant what he was saying, and I was completely revolted.

"You know something," I burst out at him, "I think that you're really sick in the head if that was the reason you overcame your addiction! Just so you could beat up Jews? What's the matter with you? Did a Jewish person ever cause you pain, ever hurt you? So why would you want to do something like that to them?! You know what," I said to him, "you are one of the most horrific people I have ever met." With that, I turned over to my other side and blocked him out.

The next morning he called out to me and, having had a good night's sleep, I was in a more charitable mood than I had been the previous evening.

"Listen," he said. "I like you and your attitude. I admire your frankness and I see how I must have disturbed you with my comments yesterday evening. Today, I'm going to be transferred to another part the hospital, but I want you to know that I'm going to come and visit you in a short while. You impressed me more than you can imagine."

"Wonderful," I told him and waved goodbye, hoping that he would change his mind, get over his favorable impression of my impetuous and fiery nature, and decide that he never wanted to see me again. That, however, was not to be. He came over a few days later, clearly in the mood for a good shmooze. Sitting himself down at the side of my bed, he began telling me all about himself, where he had been born, grown up, about his family. At some point I must have dozed off, but then something he said brought me up sharp.

"So my mother, the nun, came to see me," he said, "and I..."

"What did you say?" I demanded.

"Nothing special," he answered. "I was simply telling you something that my mother, who is a nun, told me on her last visit to me here in the hospital."

I couldn't believe my ears. "You got to be kidding," I said. "Your mother is a nun? What in the world is going on here?!"

"Nothing that crazy," he says. "At some point she had gotten married and she had me, but then she decided that the whole thing wasn't for her and she gave up everything to become a nun. That's it, just gave it all up to devote her life to her religion."

"That's really interesting," I said and I still don't know why I did this, but I asked him what his mother's name was.

"Tzipora Friedman," he replied, and that was when I knew that I had stumbled into the twilight zone and would have to find my way back home with my flashlight.

"I don't know, man," I said. "That's a very Jewish name. Are you sure that you yourself aren't Jewish?"

"I don't know," he said, "but, like I said to you before, my mother comes to visit me from time to time and I'm sure she would love to me you."

"Great," I said. "I am truly looking forward to this meeting." And I wasn't disappointed.

◆   ◆   ◆

A few days later my ward was graced by the presence of the "holy" nun, Tzipora Friedman. She came bustling into the angular room decked out in full nun gear. Long black robe, white headpiece and, most incongruous of all, a chunky wooden cross that hung beneath her elderly face. Behind her thick glasses, her eyes stared at the world with a look of benevolence. She was the very picture of nunhood. She had the nauseating "I've seen the light" look, as well.

"So, you're the boy that my son was telling me about," she said to me with a big smile.

"That's me," I agreed.

"My son told me the whole story and he mentioned that there was some confusion as regarding my Jewish name. Don't be so confused. I'm a Jewish woman and I became a nun many years ago."

"One second," I interjected. "I don't understand. You sound so Jewish, you look so Jewish. In fact, you could pass for a Jewish *bubbe*! You must have found something really profound in Christianity if you decided to devote your entire life to it like this."

Tzipora Friedman stared me in the eye and, without answering my question, declared, "There is absolutely nothing in Christianity. Truth belongs to the Jewish people."

This was getting more and more bizarre!

"So how did you, of all people, decide to become a nun?" I asked her.

"Now that's a long story," she said and she smiled, but it was a smile that didn't reach her eyes.

"I have plenty of time," I said.

So she told me her story.

◆　　◆　　◆

"As you can see, I'm not exactly young anymore," she began. "But many years ago, I was young and very beautiful. As a child, people used to comment on the brilliance of my blue eyes and the cornflower color of my golden hair. But pretty as I was, I was still a Jew. And, being a Jew meant that I was taken away to be killed along with my entire family and every single Jewish person from our town.

"Although I was very young," she said, "I will never be able to forget. Who can forget the brutal shouts, the snap of the whips, and the terrible barking of those horrible animals, those satanic creatures in the guise of dogs. I will never forget the sounds of the trains filling up with our brothers and sisters; filling up and filling up, stuffed in a way that those cattle cars had never been stuffed before.

"I can recall the scratch of pen on paper as the guards wrote down the exact tally in their notebooks. I remember the clang of the doors shutting; the very final clang as the bar swung into place, and the motor began to roar. I can hear the *chug, chug, a-chug* of the wheels on the tracks, bringing us closer and closer to the largest cemetery ever created in the history of the world. But we were powerless.

"Sure, there were a few brave and resourceful people who were able to saw through the walls of the train with a file, who threw themselves off the speeding train as it rounded those curves, who lost themselves in the European forests and joined the partisans. But, the majority of the Jewish population were ill-equipped, both mentally and physically, for such action. Thus they ended up at the gates of Auschwitz, and I was among them.

"There was a grayness unique to the concentration camps. It

was the grayness of despair, of the kingdom of death, of the knowledge that we had just entered the kingdom of death and could expect to remain as permanent guests. The smell of death emanated from the smokestacks and crematoria, the hellish sizzle of lightning from the electric fence. The crowds of faceless Yidden were going straight to their deaths.

"And then there was me. I stood out from the crowd. I was a little girl: vivacious and chattering, flitting around like a little butterfly even in the face of our destruction. My blond hair stood out like a ray of sunshine in the gloom. My eyes took it all in, smiling at the guards, smiling at everyone I saw and, somehow, they all found themselves smiling back at me.

"Our line stretched forward, eventually reaching Dr. Mengele (may he roast for all eternity), who sent us to the left — to the house of death. And there I stood, still fresh-faced, still innocent and lovely, still four years old. The line to the "showers" moved slowly, letting in more and more people, and it was almost our turn. But then, just as we were about to enter the shower room, one of the tough SS guards approached us and motioned me to come to him.

"Nobody said a word. My mother knew that protest meant death and so she was quiet. No one else cared. And so, I walked to his side and he bade me to follow him. Together we strolled across the grounds of the most infamous slaughterhouse ever to exist. Together we walked, side by side, past the gas chambers and ovens, past row after row of barracks, past the miles of barbed-wire fences and tall watch towers. We went past the infirmary and the kitchen, the soldiers' dining room and row after row of train tracks, and together we left the camp and entered another world. A world of cottages and oak trees, where mothers sat in the sunlight with their children and little dogs lay sprawled on the grass. This was to become my home for the next four years.

"As I passed into the peaceful, idyllic world that had been created for the soldiers of Auschwitz and their families, I let go of everything I had known. Somehow, I knew that life as I had known it was over — I had entered a brand new existence. I was introduced to the soldier's wife, a homey woman with thick, honey-colored hair and the sweetest smile, and they showed me round their cottage and into a room perfectly suited for the newest member of their family. There were frilly curtains hanging by the windows, and a little rocking chair sat in the corner of the carpeted room. There was a tiny desk, the sweetest lamp, and a row of dolls propped up over the bed. I clapped my hands in childish delight and began my new life, thinking that later I would meet my parents again.

"Later never arrived, and the little girl with the golden hair became part of that Nazi family. They treated me like their daughter and I, in turn, completely forgot my previous life, considering myself their little girl. The war years passed and I was treated as a little princess. I called the SS beast 'Pater' and his wife 'Mutter,' and I never wanted to go anywhere else.

"But the war came to its eventual end, and the soldier and his wife had to return to Germany. They took me back to their village, where they introduced me as one of their family. And it was only years later that my 'father' told me the truth: that I was not their daughter, that he had seen me in the camps waiting in line for the gas chambers, that I had won his heart and he had decided then and there to adopt me.

"When I learned the truth about who I was, understandably, I was more than a little confused. For almost my entire lifetime, I had been an integral part of a Nazi family. Their only daughter. Their precious, beloved princess. But I had grown up not only with their love, but with their hatred, as well. I had imbibed daily doses of Jew hatred and Nazi love. I hated myself for being a Jew. But, deep inside my heart, I vaguely remembered a place where my life had been different. I could dimly recall the love of other people, of a man with a long and tangled beard, a woman with an apron and kerchief, brothers and sisters who spoiled me and carried me around. And with some part of me, I wanted to go back to all of those people. So I wandered from place to place, not knowing who I was, always searching for my lost identity.

"Eventually, I married someone whom I felt was right for me, but with a past like mine, it was a miracle that the marriage lasted as long as it did. And when it was over, I became a nun. I devoted the best years of my life to a religion that I know is untrue, ignoring my heritage. This gives me no rest, for the past has come back to me with a vengeance, and I recall everything that happened as if it was yesterday.

"Now listen to me, young man," she said, her face serious. "I have a mission for you, a job that you can't refuse! You've met my son and you know what a miserable kind of person he is. Make him Jewish! Give him a life, give him purpose!"

I looked at the nun in astonishment, "Lady, there is no way I can do this! I'm just a seventeen-year-old boy! I'm not an outreach professional — I'm still in school. I'm really sorry, but you're going to have to find somebody else to do this job."

She looked at me and spoke chillingly. "I am someone who has gone through the Holocaust," she said. "Spiritually, I died long, long ago, and I'm going to die physically in a few more years at best. There is no way you can deny me my request!"

"Okay," I told her, "this is what I can do. I will give your son the number of a rabbi, a man who can do a good job of directing your son where you want him to go. Calling him, though, is up to your son. That's the best I can do."

It was strange saying goodbye to the lady. I felt like I had come to know her a lot better in one hour than many people I had known for most of my life. I gave her son the number and wished him well.

A few days later I left the hospital, eager to move on with my life. Slowly, I forgot all about my roommate, his anti-Semitism, and my strange connection with his mother. I went back to yeshivah and threw myself back into learning, the encounter fading ever so gently from my mind.

◆ ◆ ◆

Three years flew by. I was now twenty. I had arrived home from yeshivah for *bein hazemanim* a few days before, and I was on my way to shul for *Minchah*, when my mother handed me an envelope that had come for me in the mail. I glanced at the wedding invitation and slipped it into my jacket pocket to peruse after davening. On the way home from shul I took a good look at it. As I studied the names, my breath suddenly caught in my throat. I had to sit down. The invitation was from my anti-Semitic hospital roommate. He was now *frum* and he hoped that I would grace his wedding with my presence. Would I attend?

I thought it over and smiled to myself. Of course I would go. After all, I hadn't seen the mother of the *chassan* for quite some time and we would have a great conversation. Here was one candidate who was way overdue for some good *Yiddishe nachas!*

As heard from Yehuda in Shalmei Simcha

Nothing's Perfect

Chaim Boruch heard the sound of the doorbell and ran to let the painter into his home. He flung open the door and ushered the tall man through the beautiful entranceway. Chaim Boruch saw a sturdily built man in his mid-forties, with a weatherbeaten face and intelligent eyes. The man introduced himself as Ralph and asked Chaim Boruch where he wanted him to start and where he could put his equipment.

Ralph had come highly recommended by a friend from work, and Chaim Boruch could see that the recommendation was more than deserving. He watched as the man gave his hands a thorough wash, and asked him with a wry smile whether the house was ready for the onslaught.

Before Ralph started working, Chaim Boruch asked him whether he wanted a cup of coffee. Ralph accepted gratefully, and they went into the kitchen where he boiled up some water and added the coffee, sugar, and milk. Laying some cookies on a plate, Chaim Baruch carried the whole ensemble over to the coffee table in the living room and, over the man's protests, waved him onto the leather couch.

The living room, in his opinion at least, was the nicest room in the house, furnished in an elegant yet understated manner. Silk drapes were pulled back from the windows letting in the sun, and a vase of fresh flowers perched proudly on the piano. There was thick pile carpeting on the floor, and the walls were covered with quality artwork: a lithograph of a wedding scene in the forest and a couple of oil paints. And, occupying a place of honor were five pictures of various *rabbanim* with whom the family had a connection.

They were terrific shots, and they were arranged to catch the light from the window, showing them off to their best advantage. The painter took a sip of coffee from his mug and, picking up one of the cookies, was about to take a bite when his attention was caught by one of the portraits. His hand stopped in mid-air, and he admired the beautiful picture of the Bobover Rebbe lighting the Chanukah menorah, his face suffused with the brilliant light of the mitzvah.

Chaim Boruch watched in surprise as the painter's face took on a nostalgic look and his eyes seemed to stare off into the distance. Eventually, the man came back to earth and, turning to Chaim Boruch, he asked, "That your rabbi?"

Chaim Boruch replied in the affirmative. The man seemed happy to hear that and said, "That rabbi? He's my rabbi, too. That's right — that holy man is my man!" He pulled out his wallet from his pocket and, flipping it open, showed an astonished Chaim Boruch a picture of the Bobover Rebbe. "That's right," he went on. "That man has been my rabbi for a good fifteen years already. In fact, he taught me one of the most important lessons of my life!" At this point Chaim Boruch's interest was piqued, and he eagerly waited for Ralph to continue.

◆　◆　◆

"This story happened quite a way back," the man began, "at a time when I wasn't doing as well as I am today, you know what I'm saying?" His host nodded to show that he understood. "Anyway," the man went on, "one day I got a call from my boss, telling me that we have a job to do in Boro Park, smack bang in the middle of all the hasidim.

"Now, I have nothing against any of you but, like I said, back then I hadn't been around that much. This was pretty much a first for me, coming in contact with the black hats and sidelocks." Ralph took another sip from his mug and looked Chaim Boruch in the eye. "Well, there I was, kind of wet behind the ears, looking anxiously over my shoulder at the people on the street, who were staring at me as if they thought I was going to rob them or something. I was carrying my toolbox and wearing my old paint clothes. I wasn't the cleanest sight around, if you know what I mean.

"Well, I finally reach the right block and I'm looking for the house number, and there are just so many big men around dressed like you that I almost lose my nerve totally and run the other way back. But I keep telling myself not to be such a wimp. I finally see the house and I walk through the gate, headin' for the front door, when this big guy stops me and asks me what I be wanting from the Grand Rabbi.

"I look back at him and tell him that the Grand Rabbi needs his house painted just like everybody else and I happen to be the man they sent to do the job. He steps aside, and I walk over to the front door and ring the bell. I can hear some footsteps, and then the door swings open and this really holy-looking man is standing there in the doorway. All I can think of is the fact that I haven't shaved in three days and what's this holy man going to think.

"But, he invites me into his home as if it was the most natural thing in the world for the Grand Rabbi of Boro Park to be hosting someone like me." Chaim Boruch could see how much the story meant to Ralph, and as he watched the painter's facial expressions, it was as if the man was actually reliving the story right then and there.

"So, we walk into the kitchen," Ralph says, "and the holy man asks me whether I had any breakfast yet! That really shook my book! I mean, this guy must have about a million things on his mind and he finds the time to ask some little nobody like me whether I had my Wheaties yet?! Shocked as I was, I mumbled that no, I had not had any breakfast yet that morning.

"Well, the Grand Rabbi gets busy preparing me a special breakfast like nothing I had had in a very long time, and then he sits down with me at the table. While I devour my food, he sits and talks to me and tells me something that I never forgot.

"He looks at me with his wise and very beautiful eyes, and he says something so very deep that I was humbled for a very long time afterwards. 'You're a good painter, right?' he asks. I answer that I tried to be. 'Then let me tell you something,' he says. 'Let me tell you what I am not going to tell you to do.' I look at him curiously, waiting to hear what he's going to tell me. 'What I won't tell you,' the Grand Rabbi goes on, 'is to do a perfect job.'

"I stare at him like I don't have any clue what he's talking about. He smiles at me and continues talking. 'It's very simple,' he says. 'We Jews were once very lucky, and we had a Temple in the holy city of Jerusalem. Unfortunately, it was destroyed, and our nation was exiled and scattered all over the world. Since that time, so long ago, there is no such thing as perfection in our world. Perfection can only return when we are living with G-d's presence in our lives, serving Him the way we are meant to serve Him according to His laws. When that happens, there will be perfection in our lives once again.

" 'Therefore,' he goes on, 'I will not ask you to do a perfect job. All I request of you is for you to do your very best. Okay?' I promise him that I will, his gentle smile and warm words touching me in a way I've never been touched before. I get to work and indeed, it was one of my best jobs ever."

Chaim Boruch found himself staring at the man, experiencing for a moment what it must have felt like for him. He was about to say something when the man went on. "Wait," he said, holding up his hand, "that isn't the end of the story.

"After the job I did for the Grand Rabbi, I began getting lots of calls in this neighborhood, and I've made quite a few friendships here over the years. One morning, I got a call from someone booking me for the next few days. I took his address and told him what he should do so I can begin work right away. Early the next morning I knocked on his door and he showed me into the house. Right away, I could see he was in an impatient sort of mood so I lay low, trying my best not to get in the way. He didn't offer me a drink, not a cup of coffee, not a cup of water, nothing.

"Then, taking me by the hand, he pulled me into the first room that he wanted me to paint and said, 'Listen up. I'm paying you a lot of money to do this job. Therefore, I want this job to be absolutely perfect. You hear me: PERFECT!'

"But, somewhere in my mind's eye, I heard a little voice step out of its hiding place and say, *No! That's not right!* And before I knew what's what and who's who, I told that guy a thing or two.

" 'Listen to me for a second,' I told him. 'Once upon a time the Jewish people had a Temple in Jerusalem and that was where they served G-d to the best of their abilities. And you know something, maybe life was perfect then. But since the Temple was destroyed, there is no such thing as perfection in this world. I will do my best and that's it. Any questions you have on the subject, you can bring them up with the Grand Rabbi of Bobov and that's it.'

"Well," finished Ralph, "the man didn't really have that much more to say after that. But that's my story with the Grand Rabbi and how I became his hassid." He then replaced the wallet in his pocket and finished his coffee. And, as he was taking out his paintbrushes from their wrappings, he said, "Now, I'll just do the very best job that I can, so don't worry about a thing. After all, he's your Rabbi, too!"

As heard from Eliyahu Dolinsky

Miraculous Moments

Sweet Dreams

Now, I'm just a simple person, so don't you be going and quoting me on this one. The fact is, that I've been told by some really important people, people I truly respect, that one mustn't put too much importance on dreams and that to rely on something as flimsy as a dream is sheer gullibility. Maybe they're right. It wouldn't be the first time I was wrong about something. But, maybe they're wrong.

The thing is, I was there at the time and I saw the whole thing. Maybe if someone had told me about it afterwards, maybe then I'd have shrugged my shoulders and just moved on, but when you are personal witness to such an event, well, then it can be just a little difficult to disregard. In fact, I dare say that those very same people would have looked at the story a little differently had they been there while it was happening.

These days I'm quite an old man. I still put in a day's labor (more than many younger men half my age, I'll wager) but I feel my age more and more. Back when this story happened, though, I was still young and in full possession of a tremendous youthful strength. I had served in the IDF for a number of years, and this story took place when I was still being called up once a year for the army reserves. My greatest satisfaction came from being out, protecting my fellow Jews, and I looked forward to my reserve service the whole year. My friends used to ask me why I hadn't become a career officer...but that's a story for a different time. Suffice it to say, I was a feisty individual.

◆　◆　◆

One of the happiest times for my family was the day known as Lag B'Omer, the thirty-third day of the *omer* calender. It is a day for rejoicing, for singing and dancing, for eating large and delicious meals, and for praying at the graves of the holy men. On Lag B'Omer my family travels from all over the country and converges at one spot; all of us, year after year. Some of the younger members of the family even bring along a tent and camp out in the wilderness, either before or after the special day.

Obviously, I speak about the grave of Rabbi Shimon bar Yochai in Meron. We love to visit this particular grave and we go there more than once a year, but Lag B'Omer is the one occasion that nobody in the family — and I mean absolutely no one — would miss. Old Saba tells us some Torah thoughts based on the holy writings of the *Zohar* and Savta makes sure that all of the family, as well as the dozens of guests who happen to walk by, are well fed and happy.

The children chase each other around the rocks and the hills, and the adults talk and sing together like they did when they were young. Voices are raised in bubbling laughter, petty arguments, and in tears of sadness when we speak of those who are no longer with us. There is a wonderful feeling of merriment and *achdut*.

Traveling to Meron for Lag B'Omer became our family's *minhag*, our tradition, and it was done despite every weather condition conceivable. Except for one year, the year this story took place, the year of the Six-Day War.

◆　◆　◆

The war began with unceasing military buildup on the part of both Israel and Egypt. Gamal Abdel Nasser had one of the biggest mouths I'd ever heard — and it seemed like it was constantly being used in speeches against us. The tension at the border grew by the day, and the two sides studied each other carefully, waiting for the order to attack. Then Nasser closed off the Suez Canal to foreign shipping, and that was the beginning of the end.

From morning to night, all that was broadcast on Arab radio was nationalistic military music, along with crazy speeches that stirred up the entire Arab world into one big, churning mass of anti-Israel animals. The threat to Israel's existence was very real: feelings of hopelessness began surfacing, especially among those individuals who had survived the Holocaust. These broken people had somehow made it to Israel and rebuilt, and now they were finding their lives threatened yet again, by another madman.

And then the war broke out and the miracles began, but we would only learn all that occurred much later. How the Egyptian air force had been almost totally demolished in the first few hours of the war. How our air force had swept in like a destructive cloud, while the Egyptian pilots were still brushing their teeth. How the Egyptian infantry had run from the advancing Israeli troops as if pursued by the devil himself, abandoning their army boots in the middle of the desert and continuing on bare foot, since the boots were slowing them down. How Abba Eben, Israel's ambassador to the United Nations, had enjoyed himself at the expense of his rival, the Egyptian ambassador, El Koni, otherwise known as "The Sphinx."

The miracles continued for five days and, with the obvious help of the *Ribono shel olam*, the enemy was completely routed. The nations of the world watched openmouthed as, with poise and confidence, a tiny country moved straight over the borders, conquering all, until the Arab hordes were defeated. The UN, having pulled out of their role as "keepers of the peace," leaving the Israelis unprotected and vulnerable, was suddenly back in full force to ensure that the cease-fire was put into effect. But we would only find out about all of this much later on. In the meanwhile, the people of Israel sat in their homes and said *tehillim*.

In our family there was an added troubling factor: we wouldn't be going anywhere this Lag B'Omer. In fact, this would be the first Lag B'Omer in a very long time that there wouldn't be a minyan at the grave of Rabbi Shimon bar Yochai. Two days before Lag B'Omer, however, I received a call from the commanding officer of my unit, ordering me to report for active service up in the Galil. I had been anxiously awaiting such a call from the start of the war, offended that my country felt I was too old to take an active part in the ongoing hostilities. So I went.

This is not the time or place to go into what went on over the next few days. Suffice it to say, my unit was kept very busy with all sorts of military things. But then, wonder of wonders, it was Lag B'Omer evening and somehow we had ended up right in the vicinity of Meron. I knew that Heaven had destined that I would still be a part of the solitary celebration taking place at Rashbi's grave.

I asked the unit's commanding officer for a few hours off, and as it was a quiet night he gave me the go-ahead. He told me to make sure I had returned by three in the morning. I agreed without hesitation, and taking one of the unit's vehicles, I drove off in the direction of Meron and the grave of one of our nation's holiest men. The closer I came, the more excited I was, as I remembered all the Lag B'Omers spent together with the entire family.

The memories just came marching on by themselves. How Uncle Yacov had been sleeping in the tent and had awoken when it collapsed on his head... How the family had hired a *shochet* to slaughter a lamb and some wild fox had walked off with half the lamb in the middle of the night... Before I knew it, I had reached the entrance of Meron and was guiding the jeep off the paved street and onto the dirt road leading to the Moshav Meron of those days.

The road was bumpy and full of potholes. I danced up the dusty path in the general direction of the top, my teeth chattering each time I hit another bone-jarring rut. It was pitch black outside, but from the weak light shining from the slits on the sides of the covered windows, I could just make out the *kever*. I was hoping that there would be a few people there to keep me company. It was a day of rejoicing, most definitely not a time for being by yourself. The closer I came, the more it appeared that I would have some company, for I could see a few people standing in the shadows of the gates. They looked alarmed at the sight of the army jeep barreling up the hill in their direction.

I braked to a stop next to the building's gate, turned off the ignition, and prepared to enter the building. There was a stillness all around me, and I could smell the damp in the nighttime air. The faint sound of prayer drifted through the doors out to where I was standing, and I followed the sound to it's source. *Abba, here I am,* was the thought going through my mind.

The inner chamber was almost completely deserted. There were one or two people sitting in different corners, davening from a siddur, saying *tehillim,* or learning the *Zohar.* I let the atmosphere wash over me like a wave from the depths, and I sank into its embrace. The men's side held four people, and the women's side held a grand total of one: this year's representatives of the Jewish people. The sole occupant of the *ezrat nashim* was an elderly Sefardic woman, wrinkled beyond repair, diminutive in stature — but with enough fire to power a rocket, if you know what I mean.

She was saying *tehillim* with little sobs and muted cries, pausing every few moments to let loose one of those pure grandmother sighs. They were deep sighs, emanating from the depths of her heart, and they were sensitive and beautiful and they made me shed a tear. Three of the men appeared to be what looked like common laborers, but the fourth man had an angelic look to him, enhanced by his sparkling eyes and long white beard.

He sat in the farthest corner, learning *Zohar* with a gentle sing-song tune, and I studied him for a while before taking another *Zohar* off the shelf so I'd be able to join him. And there we sat companionably, as the hours moved on and the hands of the clock became more and more blurred. I guess I must have dozed off, because the next thing I knew, there I was in the middle of the loudest commotion.

The elderly woman had emerged from behind the *mechitzah* and approached the holy-looking man, clearly wanting to relate something to him. She was speaking in a high-pitched voice, one that everyone in the room was able to hear loud and clear. The rabbi calmly finished the paragraph he had been in the middle of reading and gave her his full attention. His smile was encouraging and she began to speak, to tell how she came to be here at the grave of the tzaddik on this night when almost no one else had merited to arrive.

◆　◆　◆

"My name is Mazal," she began, "and I live on a little *moshav* not too far away from here." She was speaking in a loud voice and I could hear exactly what she was saying. She didn't seem to mind that she held us all as captive audience.

"My son," she continued, "is a captain in the Israeli army. He is now chasing the Syrians in the Golan. He drives a tank and we are all very proud of him."

"As well you should be," interjected the rabbi.

"But because my Chanan is in the army," she said, "I spend my days in fear. I am afraid of the knock on the door. I am afraid of the officers with the letter and the sad looks on their faces. Chanan has good *mazal*, but still I am afraid. So, I travel to Meron for Lag B'Omer, even though it is dangerous. I must.

"Here I am, an old, tired woman, davening for my Chanan,

when my eyes start to close. I am not quite sleeping but not quite awake, when I see a big man, a tzaddik. He comes from the back of the cave. He stands beside me and then he speaks.

" 'What's the matter?' he shouts. 'Why are you disturbing our sleep?!'

"I was scared by the man. There was something about him, like he was here but not here...

" 'What are you talking about?' I whispered.

" 'Your crying,' he replied. 'You were crying since you arrived. It's enough!'

" 'But I'm crying for a reason,' I said to the man. 'I'm crying because my son Chanan is sitting in a tank with thin metal walls! I have dreams — I hear the sound of the mortars and the rockets flying straight at Chanan's tank. That is why I'm crying!'

" 'Don't worry,' the man said. 'Everything will be good. My father is very angry at the Arabs for creating a war over Lag B'Omer and scaring the people from coming to celebrate Lag B'Omer with him. So don't worry, everything will be good.'

"And then," said Mazal, "then he disappeared and everything was a haze. But this happened to me just now and I wanted to tell you right away before I forget all that he said."

So there you have it. I know it was a dream. But the war did end right after that, so, who knows? I'd like to think that it's all part of the puzzle. We each get a chance to give our piece, and at the end, we have the most amazing puzzle anyone ever saw. And as I look around the crowded room each year on Lag B'Omer, I know one thing: that was one Lag B'Omer I will never forget!

As heard from Rabbi Levi Yitzchak Bender, zt"l, the rabbi in the story and one of the leaders of Breslover chassidim in the previous generation

Voices in the Night

I want him... I need to get him... I have a mission to fulfill!"

"No! Get away from there, I don't let you stay there! Leave the area...leave the area! Leave the area... Do you hear me? Leave right now!"

"They sent me, they sent me, what should I do?"

"I don't care. Leave right now!"

"No! I won't! I have a mission and I won't leave until it is fulfilled!"

The voices came to him, night after night. Tzion lay in bed, dreading the moment sleep would hit. He, who worked hard all day and slept the "sleep of the just," couldn't get a few decent hours without The Dream — a recurring dream that hit him almost every time he closed his eyes. Voices...weird voices, strange sounds...hissing sounds, answered by a commanding voice telling whatever was making the sounds not to do something.

All he knew was that this situation of zero sleep was making his life miserable. He needed a good seven hours every night and he was barely getting four. Tzion was at his wits' end when the solution presented itself to him.

◆　◆　◆

It was a boiling hot day, and Tzion was driving his old Fiat through the sweltering streets of downtown Teveria, searching without much success for a parking spot. He inched passed Supersol and sat, stalled in traffic, breathing in the fumes of the Egged bus idling in front of him. The radio was on and he tapped his fingers on the hot dashboard to the rhythm of Benny Elbaz singing one of his old favorites. The song was followed by an ad sponsored by the religious council of Teveria, urging people to attend the *yahrtzeit* celebrations for one of the sages buried in the Galil area.

He made a mental note to take the day off and attend the ceremonies at the grave, and as he did so, an idea popped into his mind. Why should he shoulder his burden alone, when there were so many people out there who could help him understand what was happening to him each night?

It took Tzion a couple of days of serious sleuthing to find the right person. His neighbor suggested one rabbi in Tzfas; his wife's grandmother, a long time devotee of Rav Ovadia Yosef, put in her two cents; and his co-workers all gave him different names, each in a different section of the country. But then someone told Tzion's wife about Rav Abuchatzeira. When Tzion arrived home that night, he was treated to an hour's worth of stories about the miracles this holy man had wrought. He was almost convinced, but there was so much going on at work that he kept pushing it off.

Then one night, the dream came back and stayed for what felt like forever. Tzion tossed and turned, screaming out in terror and sweating up a storm. Those voices!

"Get away from there!" The commanding voice was back, yelling — at what? A sinister sound, low and raspy, scaring him more than ever before. "No," it replied, "I will not obey... I will not obey... I WILL NOT OBEY! I have no right to listen to you. I have a mission!

How dare you prevent me from carrying out my job?"

"You must!"

"I will not, never..." The voices drowned out Tzion's scream. At that moment, he made the decision to go.

He stayed up the rest of the night and, as the darkness turned into a silky dawn, Tzion witnessed the sun, glorious in its awakening, murderous in its strength, rising above the endless beauty of the Kinneret. At five in the morning, he was already on the road. Destination: Netivot, home of the holy presence of Rabbi Abuchatzeira.

◆ ◆ ◆

The roads were more or less deserted at this hour, Tzion's only companions being an occasional milk and bread truck or workers heading home from the night shift. He flicked to the classical station on the radio and tried to soothe himself. He had been more scared by last night's dream than he cared to admit. Even now, the sounds of the argument, the voices, reverberated in his mind with ever-increasing force. His head pounded.

Tzion rolled down the window and breathed the fresh morning air deeply. He could smell the grass growing on the side of the road and he could still feel the dampness of the early-morning dew. As he drove on, Tzion gradually became calmer. The sun grew bright and he was forced to close his window against the ever-increasing heat. And suddenly he was approaching the city of Netivot and the home of the tzaddik Rabbi Abuchatzeira.

Shacharis was over by the time he arrived, and many people were milling about outside the *beis medrash*. He ignored them all and followed the crowd heading in the direction of the rabbi's private rooms, where he received the many people who came to see him. Tzion sat in the waiting room: part of the eclectic mélange but uncomfortable with the people around him.

Workmen shared benches with rabbis in long black coats. Wrinkled old women in colorful garments told stories and gave blessings to anyone who'd listen, while soldiers and chassidim made themselves coffee and fresh *ba'alei teshuvah* mumbled *tehillim* to themselves. Apparently, this was where the action was.

Placing his head in his hands, Tzion tried to keep his mind off the night's terrifying experience, but to no avail. The voices echoed through his mind. His lack of sleep, combined with the long drive, had given Tzion a rousing headache, and he longed for a comfortable bed to rest his weary body. He was just nodding off when the *gabbai* walked out of the Rabbi's study and asked if there was anyone from Teveria present.

Not even bothering to wonder why the rabbi would ask such a question, he jumped to his feet and bellowed, *"Ken*, yes, I'm from Teveria."

The *gabbai* beckoned him to approach, and Tzion followed the man into the study. The holy Rabbi was sitting at his desk, hood low over his forehead. Without having heard a single word from the Rabbi's mouth, Tzion understood that he was in the presence of true greatness.

"You came all the way from Teveria," Rav Abuchatzeira began.

"Yes," mumbled Tzion, his voice having somewhat disappeared.

"You must go back to your home," the Rabbi commanded. "All the way back to Teveria. The first thing you must do when you walk into your home is to go into your bedroom and look under your bed."

Head spinning, Tzion was completely confused.

"But Rabbi, can't I just tell you what happened to me? I've really driven a long way."

"No," the Rabbi replied. "Go home right now and look under your bed. Then I will be more than happy to discuss anything you want."

Not knowing what to think, Tzion left the Rabbi's house, got back into his car, and began the long return journey. He drove straight home, stopping only to pick up breakfast on the way and, five hours later, he pulled into the outskirts of Teveria.

He entered his home abruptly, flinging the door open. Ignoring the questioning looks his wife was throwing at him, Tzion rushed through the small apartment, straight into his bedroom. Dropping onto his stomach, he turned his neck to peer under his bed. The sight that greeted him took his breath away. Lying under his bed, spread out full length, was a huge poisonous snake — dead! Tzion could only whisper thanks to Heaven that he hadn't encountered it alive.

But now, everything made even less sense than it did before. What on earth was going on? Why had there been a dead snake lying under his bed? And how did the Rabbi, hundreds of kilometers away in Netivot, know about it?

◆　◆　◆

The drive back to Netivot took less time than it had the day before. Tzion was burning with questions and his wheels burned rubber. He reached Netivot in time for sunrise and joined the prayers along with everyone else. He made sure to be the first one in the waiting room, and he sat there, biting his nails, until the *gabbai* let him into the Rabbi's office.

The tableau was eerily similar to the day before. The Rabbi sat, hood over his eyes and waited patiently as, shuddering, Tzion told him of his discovery.

"Yes," the Rabbi said. "I know all about the snake." He said it simply, as if it were the most natural thing in the world for a rabbi in Netivot to know about a snake crawling under a bed on the other side of the country. "Not only did I know about the snake," he continued, "I communicated with him, as well."

Tzion leaned forward, entreating the Rabbi with his eyes to go on with his explanation.

"For almost a month," said the Rabbi, "I argued with the snake night after night. He had been sent on a mission; one he was most anxious to carry out and one which I was almost equally against. His mission? To kill you and your wife! The reason: your failure to fulfill the mitzvah that has kept our nation pure and unsullied all these generations. Every single night, the snake tried his best to leave his hiding place and put an end to your life, and every single night I argued with him, using all my powers of persuasion to save you and your family.

"I've done my part," said the Rabbi. "The snake is dead. Now you must do your part. Live your life in the purity and sanctity of the Torah. Ensure that my efforts are not in vain."

Heaven Sent

Well, our first few years as a family passed by pretty much uneventfully. We lived in a two-bedroom apartment in a neighborhood not too far away from both sets of parents, and we spent most of our Shabbosos with either set. As the family grew larger, *baruch Hashem*, we began to feel that our once-spacious apartment was roomy no longer. And when we arrived home from the hospital with child number five and couldn't decide where to put her, we knew the time had come. We would have to move.

Obviously, we weren't happy about it. We didn't want to move, especially since moving meant we wouldn't be able to see the family as much as we were used to. We consoled ourselves, however, with dreams of airy kitchens, living rooms big enough to hold more than one couch, and enough bedrooms for all the kids. And so, we began to search in earnest. I went through numerous classified sections in the newspaper and kept my ears tuned anytime I heard the word "house." Together, my wife and I must have seen at least fifteen apartments until things finally began to fall into place.

Someone happened to mention to me in shul one day that a contractor had just finished putting up a few buildings in a newer section of the city and the price sounded pretty good. I called the contractor later that day, and by the evening we were in our car heading over to the area.

What can I say? It was everything we had always dreamed of. The buildings were brand new and sparkling clean. There were kiddie parks all over the place. The streets were wide and quiet with plenty of parking spaces, and the price was doable. Yes, we would have to take a slightly higher mortgage than what we had been paying up till then, but it was well worth it for the palace we would receive in return. And so we waited impatiently for the day we could finally move into our brand new home — the home of our dreams.

◆　◆　◆

The big day finally arrived and we left our old neighborhood, the place where we had grown from a young, freshly married couple into a mature family. Our friends threw us a goodbye party and there were presents and good wishes. Then the moving truck came and swallowed up our entire home, and we followed the monster over to our new place of residence and set up shop.

There was the whole settling-in period, you know — getting to know the neighborhood stores, finding a shul where I felt comfortable, and making sure the kids were happy in their new schools. But eventually everything seemed to be working out for the good. I discovered a shul whose *rav* had gone to yeshivah with my father and was someone I could talk to, the kids made new friends, and we found the stores we liked and became their steady customers.

That was when things became complicated.

◆　◆　◆

The days were growing longer and, as I drove home from work, I whistled to myself. I was in a good mood. The *daf* hadn't been too hard that day, I had solved a problem that had been baffling the whole office, and here it was, the end of the day, and still light outside. As I approached my house, I saw a sight that ruined my mood instantaneously. There was a truck idling outside the building, and workers were busy unloading furniture of all kinds and shlepping it into the building. There were couches and beds, *sefarim shranks* and *shtenders*, breakfronts and coffee tables. And they were all being brought into my building, whose ground floor was obviously being turned into a furniture business. I couldn't believe my eyes!

The ground floor of the building had not been occupied up until then. I had always assumed that the contractor was holding out for the best price possible. Just as I got out of my car to head into the house and give the contractor a call, I was given a friendly "*Shalom Aleichem*" from someone whom I presumed was the owner of the store.

He was sweet and jolly, and he said he hoped that we would become friends and that he was looking forward to seeing me around — and all the time he was talking, all I can think about was how I was going to go upstairs and give that contractor a call. Finally, he released my hand. I waved goodbye, ran up the stairs, burst into the house, grabbed the phone, and dialed the number for the contractor's office. I must have caught the guy as he was about to leave, because he wasn't in the most receptive mood.

"Hello," I said, "this is Binyamin Kaufman."

"Ah, Binyamin," he replied. "What's happening?"

So I told him what was happening and how I didn't understand why he never told us that the ground floor of our building was destined to become a furniture warehouse.

"One second," he said. "What exactly did you think the ground floor was going to be? It is very clearly designed for a business or two! I never hid that from you!"

"But," I interjected, "a very big part of why we decided to move here was because this street is quiet and peaceful. Now it will be anything but that!"

"I'm sorry you feel that way," he cut in, "but this is how it's going to be. I wasn't trying to con you into anything and I'm sorry that you aren't satisfied. I'm sorry." And then he hung up.

◆　◆　◆

The furniture warehouse had a gala opening that attracted many customers to what had been a quiet street. Advertisements kept going up all over the place, and Mr. Silberger, the new owner, a jovial fellow with a never-ending flow of jokes, was all over the place.

"Hey, Binyamin," he called out as I approached the house after *Minchah* one afternoon, "did you hear the one about the elephant and the mouse?" Before he could get to the punch line, however, my eyes noticed something they hadn't seen before.

"Wait a second," I said. "What's all this?"

By "all this," I meant the three couches, the bed, and the bookcase that were spread out all over the sidewalk in front of the building.

"Oh, that," Mr. Silberger replied, frowning a little. "Well, the contractor refused to allow me to install a big picture window which would let passersby see into the store. So to compensate, I'm simply moving some of the furniture onto the street and using that for my display area."

"Wait a minute," I protested, "that's very dangerous! Any kid who passes by on his bike or tricycle, or any mother who's trying to push her carriage down the sidewalk will have to walk into the street because all this furniture is in the way. That's very dangerous!"

"Well, what should I do?" he said to me, throwing his hands up into the air. I didn't know what to say, but I did know that something inside me was rebelling strongly.

A few days later, while on my way to the grocery store, I happened to notice one of the kids on the block walking down the street. When he came to the area where all the furniture was, he stepped off the sidewalk onto the street and was almost hit by a car. Thank G-d, the kid was okay, just shaken up, and the irate driver honked at him and sped off in a cloud of unfriendly smoke.

I had had enough.

I marched into the furniture warehouse run by our friendly neighbor, and I informed him, quietly but insistently, that this whole story was growing too big for me and that I wanted to take this to a *din Torah*. We would abide by whatever the *rabbanim* decided. Silberger agreed, more bothered by the fact that I was upset than by the upcoming *din Torah*. He was such a nice man that I wished I had met him under different circumstances. In the meantime, though, we would never be able to get along.

◆ ◆ ◆

Silberger was in the anteroom making himself a coffee when I arrived at the *beis din* for the *din Torah*. "Two sugars," he was telling himself as I walked in, "now for the milk..." He looked up and saw me and his face broke into a smile.

"Binyamin," he said. "How are you?" It was funny, but it looked like he really meant it.

"Listen," he said to me as we were filing into the room, "whatever the *beis din* decides I would really like to stay friends, okay?"

"Of course," I agreed. Why not? The *beis din* was going to hear my point of view, so why shouldn't I want to stay friends?

The *din Torah* began promptly. We, the neighbors, presented our side of the situation, explaining that we looked at this as a matter of *pikuach nefesh*.

Mr. Silberger was very apologetic, and he explained that had he known that the contractor hadn't been up-front about the whole thing he most certainly would not have gotten involved at all. But the fact remained that this was his place of business and there was no window to the street. This was his way of getting customers. The *beis din* informed us that they needed a few days before they could present their verdict.

I felt like we had done a good job presenting our side of the situation and I was sure that the *beis din* would see it the same way. Silberger clapped me on the back as we left the building and said, "Binyamin, whatever happens, we'll stay on good terms, right?" And I replied that of course we would.

A few days later, the *beis din* gave their *psak* — in favor of Mr. Silberger. They gave Silberger permission to keep his furniture in the street since it was for the good for his business. They told us that we should stress the danger of the street to our children. But, since they could still walk — albeit with difficulty — on the sidewalk, it was not a good enough reason to take away another Jew's livelihood.

"Well, what do you say now?" Silberger asked as we left the room. "I won't make any trouble for you," I replied through clenched teeth. "A *psak* is a *psak*. But I don't feel that it's right! Not at all!"

Two months later I had occasion to change my mind about the whole thing.

◆　◆　◆

It was a Tuesday evening, and I was on my way home from work. The shadows were lengthening on the asphalt as I drove into my block. As I pulled into a parking spot, I caught a glimpse of the furniture store and its contents strewn all over the sidewalk and I felt a familiar surge of anger. I had just gotten out of the car and walked across the street toward my apartment building, when I saw Silberger standing at the entrance of his store. He walked out towards me and said, "*Nu*, are you still angry about all this?"

I didn't know what he was talking about and looked at him blankly. Then, nodding to him, I walked into the building and took the elevator to my apartment.

I reached the door to my home and, after knocking lightly, pushed it open. The living room was packed with people. Both grandmothers were there. All my sisters-in-laws, some aunts and uncles, a bunch of cousins. Many of the people in the room appeared to have been crying a short while before.

My insides turned to jelly. What on earth had occurred (who had passed away?) to have caused almost the entire immediate family to have gathered in my home?

My mother turned towards me as I walked into the room and, with tears in her eyes, she asked, "Binyamin, why don't you have your cell phone with you?"

"What happened?" I demanded in exasperation and fear.

My wife spoke up. "It was a miracle, Binyamin," she said. "A true miracle." And then I noticed that she was holding on to Chezky, our two year old. Tightly.

"What happened?" I asked again, nervousness making my voice rough and impatient. This time she finally began to tell me.

"I was in the kitchen making supper and the kids were all playing in the boys' room. Chezky must have shlepped a big chair over to the window, and he stood looking out at the street. Duvi told me that while the kids were all playing Monopoly, Chezky climbed up on the windowsill and stood there, looking out. And then, all of a sudden, he was hanging over the edge of the window. They heard an ear-piercing shriek as Chezky went flying head first out of the window and down all those floors to the ground!

"When I heard the scream," my wife continued, "I ran to the room. I saw the chair standing beside the window and I realized what had happened." Tears were running down her cheeks as she related the nightmare she had lived through.

"So what happened?" I demanded.

"So I stood there in the room and I felt that I couldn't go to the window to look out. How could I? I just stood there and cried and cried. But then I heard Chezky screaming from down below. I raced down the stairs, taking them three at a time until I reached the ground floor. I ran out the door expecting the worst...but there was Chezky, lying on one of Silberger's beds — and he was one hundred percent fine!" I felt the tears in my eyes as I watched my wife reliving the whole thing, crying with happiness at the way things had turned out.

"Mr. Silberger called an ambulance, but Chezky was totally fine. Binyamin," she said, "there was no other way to look at it. It was a miracle, *mamesh* a miracle!"

All the relatives were whispering, "A miracle, you guys had an honest-to-goodness miracle. Thank G-d there's a furniture store underneath your home!"

◆　◆　◆

I went down a little later. Down to Silberger and his furniture store. And I walked into his store and, with an embarrassed look on my face, I told him that I finally agreed with the *psak*, oh, how I agreed with the *psak*...

And then Silberger took out a bottle of Johnny Walker Blue that he kept in the store for big sales, and we made a *l'chaim*, together with the rest of the customers in the store. I thanked Hashem for the miracle He had done for us. I thanked Him for the furniture store that He had put right under my house which had been so, so, against my wishes, and for the furniture that He made sure was parked right outside, strewn all over the pavement. And for the bed that was made in heaven.

Bamba Baby

The smell was the yummiest part of it all. The sheer pleasure of that tantalizing fragrance overcame the kids time after time. They only wished that there was more than one bag. By the time each of the kids had had their handful, there was barely any left and, rather than fighting over it, they enjoyed feeding the last of the crumbs to the baby, who loved playing with the little plastic figure that came in the Bamba bags: a figure known in Israel as the "Bamba baby."

The Bamba baby was a fixture in the Shapiro home. Symbol of Israel's most popular children's snack, he was everywhere, irresistible, toothy grin smiling at people wherever they went: from the Bamba dispensers in the stores to the Bamba advertisements on every bag that was bought. Who didn't identify with the Bamba baby? And then the manufacturers decided to take the Bamba campaign to the next level. Suddenly, every family-size bag of Bamba contained a miniature guest, complete with toothy smile and cowlick.

You could see armies of the little fellows roaming the schoolyards during recess, being traded for apricot pits, marbles and *rebbe* cards. But they only arrived in the family-size Bamba bags — and that came with a price. That didn't bother the kids from the more affluent families — they could afford to buy a couple of bags a week. But the children from the less affluent homes found themselves in a predicament where there was seemingly no solution. That's the way it was in the Shapiro family, at least.

◆　◆　◆

Friday afternoon would find Mr. Shapiro pushing a wagon through the neighborhood supermarket, laden with everything a family his size needed to sustain itself. He would be whistling to himself as if he had not a care in the world, as if he could walk right up to the counter, pull out his leather wallet, whip out his Visa card and say "Swipe it through and make it one payment. When? you ask. Whenever you want, it makes no difference to me!" The reality was just a little bit different.

As he neared the checkout counter, his shoulders began to slump lower and lower, until by the time he was almost there he was the picture of failure: the failure to support his family. The truth was, he had no way to pay for all the groceries that his family consumed on a weekly basis. In fact, he had an outstanding bill in almost every store that the family patronized. He owed the shoe store a couple thousand shekel, the vegetable store another few thousand, and he was backed up in his tuition payments. But all those debts were nothing in comparison to what he owed the supermarket.

Every time he even thought of the colossal bill awaiting payment in the manager's office, he broke out into a cold sweat, knowing as he did that one of these days the manager would ask him to come into his office and inform him rather regretfully that he would not be able to shop in the store any longer until he settled the outstanding amount of money he owed. And so, week in, week out, he steeled himself for the confrontation that was sure to come. He did his best to pull himself into his shell, like a turtle attempting to defend himself against the harshness of an uncaring world, a world he can never even hope to comprehend.

And, week after week, as the summons didn't come and the showdown was pushed off for another time, Mr. Shapiro would give a sigh of relief, bag his huge stack of groceries and, with as much dignity as he could muster, tell the checkout girl to "put it on the bill. Just put it on the bill!" As if it was just a matter of time until he got around to paying the tremendous amount, like he had just forgotten his wallet at home or something.

The girl behind the counter would shake her head and commiserate with his predicament, and dutifully write another week's worth of groceries down alongside the long line of figures on the Shapiro page. She, too, knew it was only a matter of time until he was exposed for the pauper that he was, not even able to pay for the food that his family needed.

Mr. Shapiro made sure to stock the cart with what he considered to be the necessities, the things the family couldn't do without, and he did his utmost to remain at that level. Except for one thing. As he pushed his loaded wagon towards the checkout, he'd unfailingly pass by a certain tall, clear, plastic container, covered from head to toe with pictures of a certain Bamba baby, and he'd picture how much joy the bag of Bamba brought his family. Sighing under his breath, he'd reach over to the plastic container, grab one of the large, family-size bags, and slip it into the wagon. What could he do? he asked himself, he was a father over all! The shrieks of joy with which the bag of Bamba was greeted was reward enough for him and yet...he did wonder how it was all going to end.

◆   ◆   ◆

Shuey Shapiro was an all-around kind of boy. Kind to his classmates, pleasant to his elders, and helpful to all, he was all parents could hope for in a child. Growing up as he had in a large family, Shuey was even-tempered and undemanding. The rest of the family was more or less the same way, leading them to hours of uncomplicated family fun. They hardly fought with one another — except when it came to one thing: the Bamba baby. The atmosphere had begun to spoil until the family reached a compromise: a rotation system would be introduced. Each week another member of the family would receive the Bamba baby.

The rotation system worked well, and every week another sibling received their prize. For a kid from a regular family, where a bag of Bamba wasn't such a major deal, what happened that Shabbos wouldn't have merited the uproar it created. But Shuey didn't have the privilege of a constant influx of Bamba, and for him, becoming the owner of a brand new Bamba baby was a huge deal. That was what made it all the worse.

That Shabbos it was Shuey's turn to get the baby, and he watched as the Bamba poured out of the bag in a tantalizing flow, straight into the hands of his brothers and sisters. But the flow came to an end and no baby was in sight. A catastrophe of epic proportion! The last time Shuey had gotten one of the babies was about six weeks before, and his dashed hopes was just too much for a ten-year-old heart to bear.

When he had ascertained that the baby was well and truly not there, a hysterical Shuey went running off to the corner of the room that he shared with five of his brothers, kicking anything that had the misfortune to be in the direct or not-so-direct path to his bed. Screaming in frustration at the unfairness, he retreated to his bed, and there he stayed with the blanket over his head, moaning and crying as afternoon turned to evening and the nighttime shadows began taking over outside. It was not the happiest *shalosh seudos* the Shapiro family had ever eaten.

◆　◆　◆

The electric doors slid opened in front of him, ushering him inside with a jet of air-conditioned air. He wiped his sweating brow with the back of his hand and fished in his pocket for a five-shekel piece which he stuck into the wagon. Then, pulling the wagon towards him, he released it from the rack, and Mr. Shapiro began his rounds.

It was *erev Shabbos* and *erev Sukkos* as well, and Mr. Shapiro had a feeling that today would be the day. Today the manager would call him in for the showdown. Deep in his heart he knew that *parnassah* is decreed on Rosh HaShanah, that it is Hashem who decides how much money everyone receives, and he accepted his lot in life. He just wished that it wouldn't be so hard!

Like a man fulfilling a death wish, Mr. Shapiro shopped like he hadn't done in five years. If he was going down, he might as well make the most of it and go down in style. He assumed that the manager would allow him one last spree, and he intended to make the most of it. With wild abandon, he began flinging food into the wagon. Bags of *parve* hot dogs and packages of meat, cans of corn and pickles, bottles of soda, and jars of jelly all made their way into the overflowing cart, as well as two big bags of Bamba to make up for the previous week's mishap.

Then, pushing the mountain-like cart in the direction of the counter, he willed himself to become invisible, hoping beyond hope that the manager wouldn't choose that moment to walk out of his office and survey the store. But, with what could only be heavenly irony, the manager put down the phone with a decisive snap and, stretching his arms, stood up and headed in his direction. Shapiro could see him coming his way and he knew that this was it. It was only a matter of time before the manager saw him and motioned him over.

Quickly, he maneuvered the cart to one of the counters and began piling the items all over each other. From the corner of his eye, he happened to notice a big yellow truck pull up outside the store,

"Osem" painted on its side. He stared as the delivery man entered the store, clipboard in hand, ready to take his weekly orders from the manager. But the manager was busy. He was headed straight in Mr. Shapiro's direction and hadn't even noticed the Osem representative.

Like two magnets from opposite ends, they began homing in on him, the manager from one side and the Osem guy, intent on catching the manager's attention, from the other. The manager reached Shapiro first and, placing a calming hand on Shapiro's arm, was about to begin speaking when Shapiro started talking first — to the Osem driver of all people!

"You'll never even believe what happened to us last Shabbos," he began, forestalling the manager and catching the delivery man's attention. "You know, we buy one of those big bags of Bamba for the kids every Shabbos since they love the Bamba babies so much. But, wonder upon wonders," he continued, "last week we opened the bag, poured out all the Bamba, and there was nothing there! No Bamba baby, no nothing! You cannot even believe what our house looked like for the rest of the day. It was just horrible! My son had been waiting for that baby for so long and he was so disappointed, you can't even imagine!"

Shapiro went on and on, while the Osem man whipped out a cell phone from his pocket and began dialing a number.

"Yeah, shalom Yossi," he began. "I'm here at the Zol V'Zol supermarket and this guy told me something you would never believe." He then proceeded to tell the man on the other end the entire tale. He listened in silence for a while and then said, "Okay, I'll tell him what you said. Bye." The man hung up the phone and turned to his audience.

"I just spoke to my supervisor over at Osem," he said. "He told me to tell you that Osem will be covering your entire bill at the market to compensate you for the inconvenience we caused you with the missing baby. How's that?" The manager released Shapiro's arm and extended his hand to the delivery man, while Shapiro, face white from the amazing experience, replied, "That will be just fine. Just fine."

As heard from "Shapiro" himself

Just a Normal Guy

I'm just a normal guy. When you look at me, you see a *bachur* who learns in yeshivah, gets along with his friends, and who tries to do what Hashem wants us to do. I'm into my learning and *avodas Hashem*, but when you look at me, you see a regular guy, just one of the boys. I'm not one of those guys who have huge *peyos*, or who always walk around with a *sefer* in their hands. But this story happened to me, regardless of the fact that I'm not a *gadol*.

My sister was expecting her second child, and things weren't going smoothly. It was not the first time, either. Her first child had been born with complications and had been in and out of the hospital for months after the birth. We, her family, were hoping that the second time around would be a less traumatic experience for all concerned. I was learning in Eretz Yisrael during the crucial months leading up to her second birth, and so I was on the phone to America all the time, doing my best to stay abreast of the situation which, in the final months of the pregnancy had gone from stable to critical.

Being the family representative in Eretz Yisrael and also feeling very close to my sister, I wanted to do my utmost for her. And so, I began davening for her at every special venue that I could think of. It was towards the end of her pregnancy that things really began heading in the wrong direction. She had been admitted into the hospital and there was talk of emergency procedures. The situation was critical. Sunday morning I was at the Kosel, pouring out my heart to the *Ribono shel olam*, begging Him to grant good health and *mazal* to my sister and her unborn child. As I mentioned previously, I'm just a normal guy, but the urgency of the situation hit me strongly, and my davening was anything but normal. I spent part of my morning at the Kosel and then decided that I would return there later for *Nishmas*, which is recited at the Kosel every evening at midnight.

That day was an emotional roller coaster. I was constantly connected to Hashem, asking Him like a son to his father that He send my sister the help that she needed. Later that night I returned to the Kosel. It was a warm night and the scent of spring was in the air. I entered the Kosel plaza and made my way over to the crowd standing in a group in front of the last remnant of our Beis HaMikdash. If there was one place in the world that it made sense to be in, to daven for a *yeshuah*, it was here at the Western Wall, and *Nishmas* was just the right prayer for the moment.

I opened my siddur and began to daven. My davening had undergone a revolution in the last few days, and my siddur was a familiar friend. I held the pages with a love that I had almost never before experienced. Every word took on a new meaning, a vibrancy, a life pulse. It was an exhilarating session. I was surrounded by people who were there for so many reasons, all davening to Hashem, all confident that He would send them what they so desperately needed.

But, the time of the *yeshuah* had not yet arrived and in America the situation was serious. The doctors spoke in solemn tones and the family was in turmoil, waiting anxiously to see what the future would bring. That was Sunday. The next day was Monday and we were going to Meron for Lag B'Omer. If there was a chance that things would change for the better, I believed that this was the thing that could bring it about.

◆　◆　◆

Meron. The mere mention of the word conjures up visions of bottles of *Chai Rotel* wine being handed out with abandon. Swirling circles of dancing chassidim, interspersed with men in suede *kippot* and knitted ones and no *kippah*s at all. It's a tent city, and a convention of all the buses in the country. It's a musical festival of love for Hashem and belief that His answer will come through the davening that takes place at the *kever* of Rabbi Shimon Bar Yochai each year. There are so many stories, so many tales of miracles that happen at this very place every year.

People stream to the site from all over the country. The highways are one gigantic traffic jam from beginning to end. People's nerves are frayed and they arrive exhausted and they fall asleep on top of a *shtender*, or in a corner somewhere in the *hachnasas orchim* area. You follow the crowds as they converge on the building with all those domes and sense the excitement of the day. A day when no prayer will go unanswered.

The vendors are doing a brisk business of all kinds. People are eating, drinking, talking, taking pictures; it's a giant kaleidoscope of Jewish humanity, a veritable rainbow, a feast of the senses, a high for the soul. It's Lag B'Omer at the *kever* of the Tanna, and it's a day like no other.

We arrived in Meron, thirty *bachurim* in a group together with the Rosh Yeshivah. And, as I was being hooked into the spirit of the place, in another country, my sister's fate was being decided. I could feel the urgency, the fear flying across from the other side of the ocean all the way to me up in the beautiful hills of the Galil. Some strange kind of telepathy was coursing through me, and I knew what she was going through right then. I could feel it in my heart and with every fiber of my being. I needed to find the key that would unlock the door to the gates of mercy.

We in Meron had a choice. We could begin pushing our way into the *kever* right then, at seven o'clock, or we could attend the candle-lighting ceremony up on the roof and then attempt to enter. Attending the lighting would push off our entry to the *kever* by a good hour and a half, and by that time it would be much harder to get inside. But my Rosh Yeshivah wanted us all to go to the candle-lighting, which was being hosted by a famous chassidic Rebbe, and I elected to follow him up to the roof. We watched as they lit the candles, but the only thing I could think of was that my sister was lying right then in the hospital, not knowing what the future held. I felt that I had to get down to the *kever* and push my *tefillos* up through the mass of prayers emanating from this particular spot, straight through to the *Kisei HaKavod*, where they would be received by Hashem.

I struggled against the mass of humanity coming up at me from the opposite direction. Throngs of people held me back, but I was like a salmon fighting against the current, swimming upstream with all its strength. The odds were against me, but I persevered. I had no choice.

Somehow, I forced my way down the steep and narrow flight of stairs that led from the roof to the *kever*, and I found myself standing near the entrance. It seemed like every single person in the Holy Land was crammed into the entrance leading to the courtyard and the inner rooms where the *kever* was located. Taking a deep breath, I plunged into the crowd, parting them with my arms, swimming in the sea of people. The waves moved me, the current pushed me from side to side, a bottle of wine spilled on my head, but I began to make progress. There were swirls of dancing that I had to wade through. I didn't stop for a moment. In my mind's eye, I could see the terror on my sister's face and the solemn look in the doctor's eyes.

Against all the odds, I made it to the end of the courtyard and was almost in the first room. People's beards were in my face. I couldn't care less. Nothing was important right then. The only thing that made any difference to me was getting through this wall of Yidden with my *Tehillim* intact, to the place where everyone came to every year on exactly the same day to daven. Slowly but surely, I pushed my way through until I had passed through the first and second room and was entering the actual room of the *kever*. It was 9:05 p.m., and the place was more jammed than any place I have ever seen in my entire life.

I inched up to the *kever*. All around me were people crying, waving their arms, and letting out ear-piercing shrieks. I ignored them all and opened my *Tehillim*. I began to daven and something came over me. I felt like Hashem had picked me up in His arms, that He was holding me, that I had the closest connection that a person could experience. It was the most amazing *tefillah* that I ever had. I started to cry. My chest heaved with silent screams and the tears just rolled down my cheeks as I begged Hashem to grant my sister a *yeshuah*. More tears poured down as I recited *Esa einai el heharim* with every bit of concentration that I possessed. The page was soaking wet, it had begun to tear, to rip from its place in the *Tehillim*!

I knew that this was it. The crucial moment. The time that could change the *gezeirah* from bad to good. I was going to accomplish what I had come here for. I soared upwards with the angels and, somewhere deep inside, I knew that my prayers had gone to the right place, that they had flung open the Gates of Mercy. I davened like that for about twenty minutes, until I had exhausted myself. It was about nine thirty when I decided to try to get out.

◆　◆　◆

It was easier getting out than it had been getting in. Most of the traffic was traveling in the opposite direction and the going was good. Still, it took me almost twenty minutes to push my way through the people. As I emerged into the fresh air outside the gates, I gulped down huge breaths of fresh air. I could feel the teardrops on my cheek where they had dried and left their smudges. Then my cell phone rang. It was my mother on the line.

"Hello," I said. My voice was scratchy from the davening and the tears. My mother didn't seem to notice.

"*Mazel tov*," she shouted. "Esti had a boy and the baby is healthy and Esti is fine and everything is okay, *baruch Hashem*." And I knew that it was my prayers that had pulled them through. I don't know how I knew, but I did. Maybe it was the ripped page in my *Tehillim*.

My mother had no time to talk to me then, but she called back later and then I heard the entire story from beginning to end.

◆　◆　◆

"The situation was very bad," she said to me. "The doctors had begun doing different procedures, but nothing was working. At one o'clock, they decided that they would wait just one more hour. At 2:05 American time, they wheeled her into the operating room.

"Suddenly, the baby began to show signs of movement. But it was touch and go. The baby hadn't moved at all for so many hours and suddenly, the baby was moving and the end was in sight.

"At 2:20 the baby was born. I was so happy! The baby looked normal, everything was going to be okay! But he wasn't breathing well! There was something horribly wrong. What would be? People were rushing all over the place. The sounds of panic filled the air. The baby's lungs hadn't developed properly. Just when we had thought that the worst was over, the nightmare was beginning.

"But just as things reached a crescendo and our worst fears seemed to be coming true, the baby began breathing well. Big breaths, open mouth. A miracle. It happened at 2:25."

"Mommy," I said, "at 2:05 I had just entered the *kever*. At 2:25, I was davening my heart out, crying to Hashem for a *yeshuah*. Right then, right at that moment! Right at that exact moment! I had fought with all my might to get into the *kever* and had experienced the greatest prayers of my life! And right then, at the climax of my *tefillos*, the baby began breathing! The doctors waited an hour so that I would be inside, davening, when they began!" There was nothing more to say. The Gates of Heaven had been opened.

◆ ◆ ◆

Sometimes I think that just like there are highways down on the earth where cars drive, and shipping routes across the ocean for all the boats, and we know that even planes have their pathways clearly marked, so, too, there are other types of highways. There are heavenly highways. One can rise above this world, to a place where the road signs are clearly marked, and connect with the spiritual highways, just as I did a short time ago. And then the prayers, those precious prayers, will be answered with love, so clear and strong, from the merciful King in *Shamayim*.

As I said, I'm just a normal kind of guy, but when normal people connect our *tefillos* with the One Above, nothing can stop us. The future lies in our hands.

As heard from the bachur himself, a few days after
Lag B'Omer of the year that the story took place

Traffic Jam

It happened on one of the busiest days of the year. The phone started ringing from the moment Suri entered the office, and it hadn't stopped for breath, filling the air with its incessant, shrill trilling. By the time half the day had gone by, Suri was already mentally planning her next vacation. Then it was back to the accounts, back to the bills, back to the hundred and two things she still had to do before she could officially call it a day.

Eventually, through a calculated effort to stay undistracted for the next hour and a half, Suri was able to get through a substantial amount of work. Then she had to make sure that the secretary was on top of her projects. Thirty minutes later, she was able to close up shop with a clear conscience, knowing that all was ready for tomorrow. Suri left the office and walked a little way down the street to where she had parked her car, breathing deeply of the late afternoon air.

Her car had been waiting for her all day with a somewhat reproachful look, as if asking why she had abandoned it for so long. She gave the hood an absentminded pat before unlocking the door and getting inside. It was nothing fancy, just a run-of-the-mill car, but it ran smoothly — an undemanding and uncomplicated friend.

Gently, Suri eased the car away from the curb, waiting for the traffic to let up for a second so she could swing into the road with space to spare. Then she stepped down on the gas and hit the road.

Thankfully, the traffic was moving smoothly, and Suri kept the car at a rapid clip, skimming along the sea-hugging highway that ran along the Tel Aviv coastline. All was fine. The traffic was moving, the day had been busy but productive, and her favorite CD kept up a steady stream of hits. She tried to imagine how the day had gone at home.

Batsheva had probably heated up supper, and Tzipora had definitely been the one to set the table. Eli was either out playing ball in the nearby park or busy with some school activity that involved lots of planning and many meetings with friends — and neglect of any domestic duties. By the time she arrived home a delicious smell would fill the house. Five minutes later, Tatty would come in from work and they would all sit down for supper... But that was when Suri hit the traffic jam.

It wasn't that it never happened. Suri got stuck in traffic jams on average twice a week, due to all sorts of complications: roadworks, accidents, and plain old bad driving. But today was not a good day. Instead of hitting the couch or the kitchen for a cold drink and a good shmooze with one of the girls, she was idling away on the highway, directly under the dozing sun and moving about an inch every ten minutes or so. It just wasn't fair!

It took Suri about ten minutes to admit defeat. She was prisoner on the road, and she wasn't going anywhere for a while. That being the case, she decided that she might as well make the best use of her time and say some *tehillim*. She clicked open the glove compartment and removed a well-worn, almost-falling-apart *sefer*. Most probably there had been a serious accident somewhere along the way, and the people could use all the help they could get from her davening. Wasting no more time, she flipped open the *sefer* and began.

The interesting thing was that after davening for about five minutes, Suri really got into it. She forgot about the annoyance and inconvenience, the fact that the car would probably begin overheating any moment, and the fact that she was tired, hungry, and dying to relax. It was just her and the *Tehillim* and, as she was alone in the car, she really gave it her all, intoning the words with fervor and pathos, reliving the ancient words, their sweetness and flavor, savoring every nuance and hidden meaning.

All of a sudden she heard a cacophony of beeping horns from behind. With a start, Suri realized that the line of cars in front of her had already cleared and it was her turn to move. Suri closed the *Tehillim* and released the hand brake and, with a sigh of relief, rejoined the racing cars. Sure enough, the traffic slowed soon after for a few moments as they passed a couple of police cars and an ambulance. Suri looked over at the scene for a second and saw the paramedics wheeling a gurney into the ambulance. For a second, she even thought that she recognized the woman lying there under the sheet...but she told herself that she was mistaken.

Having passed the scene of the accident it was smooth sailing all the way home, and a mere half hour later Suri was parking her car and walking up the stairs to her house. Her daughters, used to their mother's incessant energy, were a little taken aback at her silence. Suri told them what she had seen, omitting the fact that she thought she had recognized the woman involved. But she did tell them of the *tehillim* she had said and what it had done for her, of the otherworldly tranquility she had experienced. Suri's daughters listened, entranced, and it was a magical moment in a family not known for its reflective nature.

And that, Suri thought, was that. Except that it really wasn't that at all.

◆ ◆ ◆

A few months later, Suri was attending some *tzedakah* event, and she happened to bump into Chana — Chana from her cousin's shul, from the P.T.A. — and from the highway where she had lain unconscious as thousands of cars had passed her by. And Chana wanted to tell her something, that much was clear. Suri looked back, waiting for whatever it was that was coming.

"What?" Chana asked, not knowing how to interpret the look Suri was throwing at her.

"Nothing," Suri replied. "What did you want to tell me?" She wasn't about to go into the whole story. Maybe it hadn't even been Chana in the accident, maybe her imagination was running away with her. Just when she had made the firm decision not to tell Chana that she had recognized her lying there on the stretcher, Chana completely surprised her by saying, "I don't know if you heard, but I was in an accident a few months ago."

She couldn't help it, she nodded in that "I know exactly what you're talking about because I was there" look, which Chana wasn't sure how to relate to. "Yes," Chana continued. "And I died."

Suri gulped and almost spilled her drink all over the place. *Oh, you died, did you?* she thought to herself. *And here I was, thinking you were alive and talking to me the whole time.* The questioning look must have been pretty obvious, because Chana continued telling her what happened.

"Yes, I died," she went on, "and it's due to one thing and one thing only that I'm standing here today and telling you this. And the reason that I'm sharing this with you is because I want you to understand exactly what you did for me there in your car."

Suri looked at Chana. Beside her daughters, nobody in the world knew what she had been doing in the car — certainly not the woman who had been in the accident. In fact, how did Chana know that she had even been there in the first place?

"Allow me to take you back in time, to a faraway place not too far from here," Chana said, as she maneuvered Suri in the direction of some leather couches off to the side. They sat side by side on the couch and Chana told her...

◆　◆　◆

It had been a crazy day for Chana, as well. She had been working long hours and the job was demanding. It was too much, really, but they needed the money and there was no way for her to back down from her responsibilities. When she had left the office that day, she wasn't exactly herself. She was so tired, so bone tired...and her concentration was shot. "And, as everyone knows," Chana went on, "all it takes is one moment, one perilous second of dozing off."

One minute Chana was cruising along, taking in the glory of the setting sun, and the next there was a tremendous crash. That was it. Life was over, she knew that instinctively. It was clear to her that she would never be returning to this world. She was unhappy because she had a family and so many of her kids were still young, but a light was glimmering, beckoning her from a distance. She headed straight in the direction of that intense, sweet light, with a pull all its own.

She rose effortlessly, lighter than air, like the string at the end of a balloon heading to the far-off sky. It was all over. There were no second chances and, for some strange reason, she was reveling in the knowledge that her earthly quest had come to an end. She was frightened, yet deliriously happy at the same time. She was coming home!

As she rose, it was like she could see from one end of the country to the other, no, from one side of the world to the other. She saw the ocean, the waves gently lapping on the shore, boats skimming the surface. She saw people in the buildings lining the coast and the myriad drivers confined to their cars in the heat, all waiting for the ambulance, all waiting for her. She could see them all, row after row of vehicles, just sitting, while she rose higher and higher. So many people.

"It was by far the most amazing experience of my entire life," Chana told Suri, who was listening intently.

Chana smiled at Suri and continued telling the story. "I moved upwards towards heaven, and then I realized that there was something holding me back. I tried to figure out what it was, and eventually I understood. There were letters, holy letters, flying towards me. A cloud of letters and words — such holy words, the words of *tehillim*. Like tiny, precious diamonds, one more beautiful than the next. I could see that they were emanating from one particular car way down below, just one of hundreds of cars idling on the highway. In this one car, *tehillim* was being recited with utter devotion, and chains and chains of holy words were lifting upwards and coming towards me, halting me. Yes! Your *tehillim* was stopping me in my place and not letting me go!

"I was fighting against the words," Chana said, "for at the time I thought that going to heaven was the best thing that could happen. But those words held on, and then they began pushing me downwards, down...down... Down in the direction of my body, my shell. Gently, ever so gently, the words moved me down until my *neshamah* was situated directly over my body, and then maneuvered me right back into the body which had been lying on the stretcher, dead, just a few minutes before!"

And Suri remembered her annoyance at having been stranded in that traffic jam. She remembered every detail of what Chana was telling her. And, for the first time in her life, she really understood that there are so many things going on that are way above us. But sometimes, just sometimes, heaven allows us to catch a little glimpse of the tremendous force that we are all a part of.

As heard from "Suri"

Hiding behind My Shtender

I was one of those "here for the year" kind of guys, I'm sure you know the type. There's a good-sized crop of us at the beginning of each new Elul, here for the Israel experience. We're different from the regular yeshivah guys, in more ways than one. While they fly into the country knowing that they will be spending a good couple of years here before going on to Lakewood and the *chuppah*, we come for the break after high school and before college that the year affords us.

For the most part we want to have a good time, not study too hard. There are so many parties to go to, so many places to explore. The majority of our crowd comes, stays the year, and then heads back to the West to continue on the course charted for them by their parents. Coming to college or joining the family business are both acceptable options. Sometimes, though, funny things happen and, before you know it, your old buddy Josh is changing before your eyes. Suddenly, Josh is sporting a bigger *kippah*, has a nice woolen pair of *tzitzis*, and is taking life more seriously than the rest of the group. In other words, Josh is now "flippin' out."

Our parents send us for the experience and hope we come back the same nice, well-mannered kids we were on the way in. But some of the kids just don't come back home. They adjust to the "foreign" country, decide they like it, and one year stretches into two...and on and on. The whole thing really is a fascinating process. Someone should really do a study on this year thing..

Bottom line is, I was one of those guys' came to the country to do the "year." One of those excitable, fun-loving guys who cruised from party to party, drinking more than I should and using my time to the fullest.

Anyway, I had an enjoyable first year in Israel, and for some reason even decided to return for a second year of "learning." Over the course of my second year I began settling down just a little bit. I even began to try my hand at learning, and I was startled to discover that it wasn't as bad as I'd thought it was. In what was a major source of *siyatta diShmaya*, the majority of my old gang decided to transfer to a different yeshivah, where they were planning on giving up their old ways. They were going to turn over a new leaf; they would begin to crack the books. They were getting serious. Knowing these guys, I'd believe it when I saw it.

This was a great development for me. Their absence allowed me to devote myself to learning without the constant distraction they had posed. And so, my second Elul *zeman* was noticeably more *shtark* than anything I'd ever experienced up till then. I won't say that I didn't miss my friends, but the fact that they weren't there did make things a lot easier. I counted my blessings.

About the time I gave up my friendship with my old gang, I made friends with one of the more serious guys in the yeshivah, a boy named Meir. He was older than the rest of us, more mature, and he was willing to put in the effort for what he considered was important. He was also much more sensitive to doing the right thing than I was, and he would never dream of going to the kind of places my old gang used to frequent. Fact is, I was spending the majority of my time in the *beis midrash* and the remainder with him. I was slowly turning into a *ben Torah*. Even I was able to recognize the change in me, and it felt kind of cool in a good way.

But all this change didn't mean that I wasn't looking forward to *bein hazemanim*. After a *zeman* more intense than I'd ever had before, I was really waiting for the break. I was hoping to get together with my group of friends, do some touring, see the land and, above all, have some fun. I deserved it, after all the time I had put in, and I was preparing to take major advantage of the month-long break. That was when the Rosh Yeshivah chose to throw in the monkey wrench that threatened to destroy my fragile truce with the world of learning.

He requested (actually, it was more of an order) that the entire student body remain in yeshivah for the first three days of vacation. We were not to go anywhere out of the neighborhood. I couldn't believe what I was hearing! Was he crazy? What kind of rabbi was this? Didn't he know that after the learning we had put in, we were entitled to an unsupervised break without the rabbis breathing down our necks? What kind of jail was I in, anyway?! And on and on. There was no way that I was staying in the yeshivah for the first three days of vacation and that was that. If he wanted to throw me out, by all means!

Then, to make matters oh-so-much worse, I received a phone call from my old gang. They told me that they were leaving to Netanya the morning after Yom Kippur and did I want to come?

What kind of a stupid question was that? Of course I wanted to come! After all, I hadn't seen them for so long and I had learnt so well and I needed a break and the sun was shining and the beach was cold and there were football games on the sand and how could I not go with them? All right, it was the day after Yom Kippur and being with them would bring me down a couple of notches on the *yiras Shamayim* barometer, but it didn't matter to me in the least. Let my people go!

I was ready and willing to defy the Rosh Yeshivah, not caring at all about the consequences, but Meir my buddy wasn't leaving me alone. All day long he worked on me, convincing me that I had to remain in the yeshivah and how much better I had become *davka* because of the yeshivah's influence. He spoke with the utmost seriousness about what I had gleaned in my time spent here, and how it would be an absolute shame to just let it slip away. He didn't give up. He pushed me, challenged me, yelled at me, and made deals. He tried everything he could think of to convince me to stay for those extra three days. Finally when I couldn't deal with him any longer and just wanted him to be quiet, I gave in and agreed to stay.

◆　◆　◆

Netanya beach is quite a charming place in its own way. It's not pretentious like Ceasarea or Hertzliya; it's rather more down to earth, fronting an area mostly occupied by senior citizens and Russian immigrants. Many of the beachfront shops are restaurants, although very few of them have the kashrus certification that would allow religious people to patronize them. Despite all this, the boardwalk is long, the people are friendly, and the view out to the ocean would make any photographer more than satisfied.

That is, during the daytime. At night, however, the clientele shifts to other less desirable types. There are "business" transactions of all sorts going on throughout the night, and if you really have to be there, then keep a low profile.

My friends, unfortunately, were not of the low-profile variation. In fact, they enjoyed nothing more than making a *kumzits* smack bang in the middle of some really crowded spot (like the lobby of the Sheraton Plaza during *chol hamo'ed* Sukkos). They do sing nicely, I will give them that, but they most definitely like to attract attention. On the beach in Netanya they messed up. They attracted too much attention — attention of the wrong kind.

From what I understand, the spot they staked out was fairly close to another group of teenagers, who were most definitely not having a *kumzits*. Their singing, beautiful though it was, must have been disturbing the other group, for they requested that it stop in no uncertain terms. My friends, however, weren't used to giving in to anybody. To our *rebbe's* chagrin, disagreements had always been settled with their fists, and since they were big and strong they usually walked away the winner.

This time, however, would prove to be different. This wasn't a group of yeshivah guys they were facing. These guys were street thugs totally at home in a fight, and they knew how to handle themselves a lot better than my friends. And they didn't stop at fists. When the fight began to escalate, the guys pulled out knives. To my friends, a knife-fight was uncharted territory. They had no clue how to protect themselves, and before they knew what had happened, they were in a war and coming out much the worse for it.

Yossi was stabbed in the leg, and Binyomin received a deep cut in his hand. The guys gave almost as good as they got, but they were just no match for the Netanya crime syndicate's younger members. Besides, they were outnumbered about five to one. When the sirens of the approaching police made them put a quick stop to the action, the thugs disappeared, leaving my friends beaten and wounded and lying in the sand.

They were carried up the stairs from the beach to the waiting ambulance and whisked off to the nearest hospital, where they were left traumatized and badly hurt.

I received the news the following day, and I took the next bus to Netanya, anxious to see that they were okay. But deep inside, a little voice was telling me something. This was one time I wasn't about to ignore its truthful tones.

"Boruch," it said, "you know what would have happened if you would have gone with your friends. You were always the wildest of the group. You would've jumped right into that fight and would've been the first to be injured. Who knows what could have happened to you? You would be with them in the hospital right now, wounded and messed up! It was only the *zechus* of staying behind and learning for those extra few days that saved you. Come on, be honest this time!"

This time, I listened to that little voice which I had ignored so many times in the past. I listened, and I changed. And, as I walk to my *kollel* every morning, I thank Hashem for sending me friends like Meir and for giving me the chance to change for the better.

As heard from "Boruch"

Just in Time

I used to see him walking home from school, day in, day out. It went like clockwork, I could have set my watch by him. He was out of school by three thirty; by three forty-five he was passing across the street from my window. He would straggle along, his clothing either a few sizes too big or too small, or maybe it was really the right size and it was the way he stood that made it seem all wrong. All I knew, when I looked out that window and saw him shlepping down the street, was that he was a *nebich* and needed help.

I used to see him and wonder what on earth was going on in his life that had made him such a mess. I never thought that I would find out. I mean, he wasn't a religious kid or anything. I wasn't even sure that he was Jewish. And there was really no chance of our paths crossing — or at least, that was what I thought.

It was a winter's day when all that changed. As was my way, I had gotten hungry during the middle of my secular studies classes. As was also my way, I peered into my knapsack to see if there were any snacks inside that I had forgotten about. Perhaps there would be a long-missing granola bar or bag of chips. To my dismay, there was nothing. I knew that I wouldn't be able to hold out until the end of the day, I just wasn't built that way. So, I decided to make a trip to the grocery store the next block over, buy some stuff, and go back to school.

I left the building without telling anyone. I figured that I'd be out and back again in a matter of minutes and there was no need to make a big deal over the whole thing. It was drizzling when I went outside and I pulled my windbreaker closer around my shoulders, huddling into its warmth. My glasses were a little foggy from the sudden change from warmth to the cold outside, and I couldn't see that far ahead of me. The shouts, though, I could hear.

Wiping my glasses with my sleeve, I looked for the cause of the shouting. In the distance, I could see about five rough-looking kids surrounding one kid. It didn't look good at all. Now, I'm a New Yorker, and I've been in my share of fights. Most of the time, the kids involved are full of bluster, they want to intimidate without really fighting. Sometimes, though, they are confident enough to beat someone up. It seemed that this was one of those times.

As I approached the scene I could see that the kid in the middle was the *nebich* who always walked past my classroom window. He was weighed down by a schoolbag that looked like it was holding twenty books. He couldn't move fast enough, he couldn't defend himself. He was a goner. The group of kids had formed into a pack. They were a gang now, and they changed gear into mob mentality. That is to say, whatever their leader would tell them to do is what they would do. I knew that there was no time to lose. Already the kids were pushing him around, shoving him from one to the other. He was crying, while trying hard not to.

One of the gang reached down into a nearby garden and scooped up some of the wet dirt from inside. He threw the fistful of dirt into the kid's face, splattering his glasses, streaking his face and clothing with wet mud. The kid could barely see. The gang kept on pushing him until he tripped and fell on the floor. The boy couldn't hold back his sobs any longer and he began screaming, while the bullies laughed.

By this point I had neared the group and pushed my way inside. They were a few years younger than I, but there were many of them and just one of me. I shouldered some of them aside and turned to look at them. You can tell a lot about bullies from the way they look at you, whether they look down or look you in the eye. I wasn't about to fight them all, but I stood in front of the *nebich*, protecting him, and I stared them down. Some of them backed off right away, but three others stood their ground and I picked out one of them, the one who appeared to be the leader, and I put my hands down in front of me, palms up, and stared at him until his eyes dropped.

"Guys," I said. "My school is right nearby with about fifty of my friends. If you guys want to fight with somebody, we would be happy to provide a challenge. But five against one is just wrong. Now, get out of here!"

Amazingly enough, they turned and left.

◆　◆　◆

I looked at the kid lying on the wet floor. I reached down, grabbed his hand, and helped him up. He was fat; heavy and water-logged, and it was still hard for him to see. The rain had become a blessing, washing the dirt off his face and clothing. I hadn't felt so bad for someone since my next-door neighbor had killed his pet salamander by mistake when he was six years old. School was way out of my mind as I gathered his bedraggled books together and crammed them into his backpack. Then I asked him where he lived.

"Pine and Eighth," he replied, and I told him that I would walk him home. He protested feebly, but he needed someone and that someone was me. We made slow progress, and about twenty minutes later we reached his home. It was a stately house of red brick and Andersen windows, two columns holding up a mock porch. Five steps led up to the entrance: a polished wooden door, complete with gold knocker.

"The Donner Family" it said on the mailbox, and I stood under the porch and watched as the door swung open and a woman stood framed in the doorway, dressed in a severely tailored suit. Her mouth opened wide in dismay at the sight of her son, and she rushed over to him. "Benny, what did they do to you this time?"

He didn't answer her, and she herded him into the house, giving me a nod while doing so. I could just see a long, carpeted hallway with a mirror at its end before the door was shut in my face. Then I turned around, walked down the five steps and out through the garden. It was still raining when I reached the street, and I ran back to yeshivah, knowing that I had been gone a very long time and that the teacher would need an explanation.

◆　◆　◆

The teacher, a man in his mid-fifties by the name of Guant, was a charming individual to those who had the good fortune of knowing him on the surface alone. For those who knew him just a little deeper, he was as charming as a jellyfish, but with a lot more sting. He had a head of frizzy hair that popped up when he least expected it to and I could picture him at the mirror each morning, stapling the mass of frizz down to his scalp.

He was waiting for me with a malicious smile on his pallid face. "Ah, Mr. Singer," he addressed me in that blend that was uniquely his, a mixture of politeness and sarcasm. "I notice the water on your jacket, your windblown hair, and your waterlogged shoes, and I cannot help but wonder where you disappeared to for the last forty-five minutes." I glanced at my watch in surprise. It certainly hadn't seemed to have taken that long.

"Well, young feller-me-lad, what do you have to say for yourself?"

I'm not one to toot my own horn, but I didn't really have that much choice in the matter. His face turned thoughtful as I told him the story, and he had some admiring words to say when he heard that I had stood up to a crowd of Brooklyn tough guys and emerged unscathed. He even sent me back to class with a pat on the back. I guess he had inner depths that he'd been hiding from the class all this time.

◆ ◆ ◆

A few days later we met again.

I was outside my yeshivah at the end of the day, waiting for a few of my friends to come outside so we could go home together. It was a cloudy Sunday afternoon and we had finished early that day. The streets were muddy — the aftermath of a rain storm — and there was a grayness all around. Clouds the size of monsters rumbled by overhead, the sunlight filtering downwards through the sullen mass.

All of a sudden, there he was coming towards me. He was dressed in a button-down shirt and a pair of jeans. His glasses were foggy. His hair was tangled up. He was a mess. He studied me as he approached, trying to decide if I was the guy who had saved him not long before. I smiled at him, waved my hand, and he stopped next to me.

He was excruciatingly shy, and he looked anywhere but at my face.

"Hi," he said. "I'm Benny."

"I'm Yossi," I replied.

"Thank you for saving me last week," he went on, hesitantly.

"Happy to be of assistance."

"Maybe we could walk home together," he suggested shyly, and I graciously accepted his invitation, although wondering what we were going to talk about and where on earth we were going to find any common ground. We began walking home side by side, and I guess he had been searching for somebody to talk to for a long time, cause he just opened up his heart and began telling me about his life. About the pain and misery of being fat. How he was constantly teased because he was so clumsy. How his clothing never sat right, how every time he went to buy a suit, they never had the proper size.

It was like a dam had broken open and the water gushed out of him in torrents. For the most part, I just listened. We parted outside his home and he thanked me for walking him and I told him that it was my pleasure. Then I continued walking to my house, thinking the whole time how some of us have such hard lives and wondering why it had to be that way.

That was the first of many such walks. We became close in a fashion. He was a few years younger, I was *frum* and he was not, I was popular and he was the opposite. But, somehow, we connected and even became friends. We began learning together — it was his idea and he was thirsting for knowledge. Because he was so studious and quiet, and because he was not into sports, he had plenty of time to devote to intellectual study, and studying Judaism was right up his alley. Many times, I had to go home and ask my father the answers to the questions that he asked me. He was very bright and he impressed me with his sheer brain power.

Time, it is said, is the great healer and so it was in this case. I watched Benny change in front of my eyes. The changes were barely perceptible — but they were there. Slowly, slowly they became more noticeable. Benny was finding himself. The big pair of glasses that had blocked up half his face had been replaced by a stylish, more diminutive rectangular pair by Silhouette. As he matured, his face lost its roundness and baby fat, and his cheekbones started becoming visible. The weight began coming off as well and, by the middle of eleventh grade, he was no longer fat, clumsy Benny, but rather, Benny the boy who was rapidly developing into the leader of his class.

Because Benny had been treated like dirt, he knew how to understand people. He knew how to feel their pain, how to empathize with them. In short, Benny had become a people person who was well liked by everyone he met. He was still in public school, and he told me that he was debating whether or not to run for G.O. president. I convinced him to go for it. He ran. His team of supporters put together a great campaign for him, plastering the school with slogans in his favor. His opponents didn't stand a chance, and Benny won by a landslide.

The final year Benny spent at his high school was a great year for him. He was president of the student body and the editor of the school newspaper. Then he was chosen to be the valedictorian. I wasn't surprised. He told me about this great honor while we were sitting and learning in his room one afternoon, and he invited me to the ceremony. It would be taking place in his high school auditorium in a few weeks' time.

I told him that I wouldn't miss it for the world. I mean, it was more than just a party for Benny. It was a celebration of the person he'd become. Wild horses would not have been able to drag me away.

◆　◆　◆

The great event took place on a beautiful sunny day at the end of spring. Summer was quickly approaching, but the sun was benevolent that day. I joined the crowd streaming to the school and sat down near the back of the packed hall. There were parents with their cameras and grandparents with their presents, and everyone was just as jolly as could be. The ceremony began and the speeches were delivered and then, about three-quarters into the whole shebang, the principal introduced Benny as the valedictorian of the senior year. There was a roar of applause and approval from the crowd, and Benny made his way up to the podium.

Everybody sat up in their seats: no one was sleeping through this speech. Benny stood at the microphone, tall, slim, confident, and handsome; just what a valedictorian should be. He cleared his throat and began speaking in an almost-whisper. It was hard to hear what he was saying and all the people sitting there were kind of leaning forward and listening intently.

"There are a few people sitting here today whom I have to thank," he began. "These people looked at me and saw the potential inside the outer shell. To them, I owe everything." He paused for a moment, and that moment kind of hung in the air as if it had taken on a life of its own. I think that everyone sitting there in the auditorium thought back a few years, and suddenly they were remembering the fat, awkward kid whom everyone had made fun of.

"My parents stood beside me," he went on, "and for that I owe them more than I can say. But there was one day in my life that changed everything, all my perceptions." The hall was still and, I know that it's a cliché, but you could have heard the proverbial pin drop.

"It was a rainy day," he went on, "and I was walking home alone once again. I was carrying a very heavy schoolbag. In fact, all my books were in that bag, since I didn't want my mother to have to go back to school to get them. This way, I figured, everything would be much easier for all concerned. You see," Benny swallowed before continuing, "I was on my way home to commit suicide." There was a collective gasp all around the cavernous room as he said those words and the implications set in.

"Yes," he repeated. "I had had enough of life. I couldn't deal with one more day of being beaten up, one more day of the jokes, the shoves, of being pushed around all because I wasn't as cool as everyone else. It looked like life was always going to be that way — and I wanted no part in it. And then they came at me." He proceeded to tell his stunned audience how he had been surrounded by five neighborhood bullies, how they had begun pushing him from side to side. The entire audience was reliving that moment together. And as the memories hit him with strength, Benny was crying.

"And then," he said. "Then, my savior appeared." He raised his arm and pointed at me; the audience turned around in their seats to stare. "He broke into the fight and saved me. He walked me home. He gave me a shoulder when nobody else was there for me. For that, I owe him my life. Because it was after I met Yossi that I realized that the sun might be hiding behind a cloud after all. That, my friends, is my story. So Yossi, my friend, I want to tell you thank you!" The applause was like nothing I'd ever heard before.

This story really happened, and I just want you to understand what a little gesture means to a person, how that "hello," which was no big deal to you, might have changed the life of the person you said it to. How they might have gone home and decided to give life a chance — all because of you. And maybe — who knows, just maybe — they'll tell you about it someday.

In Other Words

The Teardrop

This is one of those stories that takes place in installments, continuing from year to year. The truth is, it really began with Grandpa. Grandpa was one of those men who belonged to the previous generation. He wasn't one of those grandparents who grow old as you grow up, if you know what I mean. No, Grandpa was completely from "then." In fact, to my sister Betty and I, there didn't seem to be anyone older than Grandpa.

We didn't get to see him that often. He lived in Boston, where he used to daven in a chassidishe *shteibel* a few minutes away from his house. I'll never forget walking into the *shteibel* on a Friday night before davening began: into the long, narrow room full of rectangular wooden tables, their scratched surfaces covered in spotless white tablecloths, the refrigerator at the back of the room full of glass bottles of soda awaiting the Shabbos morning kiddush. Grandpa sat at the table closest to the back wall, directly in front of the metal board displaying the light bulbs that commemorated the *yahrtzeit*s of the members who weren't around anymore.

Now Betty and I, we only got to see Grandpa twice a year, once around Pesach time and once around Yom Kippur. The rest of the year we were busy with our lives in Florida, where my father worked for the state electric company. But twice a year, our parents went on vacation and sent me and Betty to stay with Grandpa for a week or two. Those were days of simplicity, a far cry from the luxurious Florida lifestyle we were used to.

Staying with Grandpa meant eating the simple food that he cooked for himself, and sitting and reading for hours on the old, brown, cracked leather sofa in his den, where the musty smell of ancient books permeated the air in a strangely satisfying way. And then there was the pleasure of Grandpa's company. He wouldn't talk that often, but when he did, he blew us away with his humor, his insights into life, and the spice of his personality.

But I digress. The real highlight of my trip to Grandpa's was going the *shteibel* with him on Yom Kippur day. We'd arrive early, before the other men, and Grandpa would straighten up the room. He'd shuffle around, making sure old man Levy's big *shaliach tzibbur* siddur (which he used because he had bad eyesight) was exactly where it was supposed to be, and that the Rebbe's *gartel* was hidden behind the frayed velvet curtain covering the inside of his *shtender*.

How I loved the old man, as I watched him in the early morning sunshine that sent beams of light into the center of the otherwise dark shul, surrounding Grandpa with an entire company of dancing dust particles. I didn't know how to read Hebrew — Dad always said he ought to teach me but he never got around to it. But there, in that shul, it didn't matter in the least. When Old Fishel used to chant *Hineni* the way his *zeide* used to do it in Vilna, it sent shivers up my spine. And Grandpa would look into his worn-out *machzor*, its yellowed pages coming apart a little more each year, and he'd daven like nothing you ever saw in your life. He *shuckled* and *krechtzed*, and said each word slowly and clearly, beseeching the *Ribono shel olam* as only a son can do.

But he'd barely cry. Only once during each service would he shed a tear. It would be at the same spot every time. I'd watch as a teardrop slipped out of the corner of his eye and landed on the stained page. So it was, that the teardrop fell the same place in the prayers every year. I waited for it from year to year, not knowing in the least why it was shed. One year — I must have been twelve already — I looked at Grandpa as we left the *shteibel* after *Ne'ilah* and I asked him, "Why do you cry every year at the same spot?" He looked at me for a very long moment and his eyes filled with tears. I felt a rush of love for this frail, hunched-over man whose depths were hidden from me.

◆　◆　◆

The years passed, times changed, and me along with them. Our biannual visits dwindled and then ceased altogether, thanks to our parents having discovered the joys of "family vacations." And, I suspect, also due to their fear of our becoming just a little too close to our heritage. Our relationship was reduced to a phone call once or twice a year and, since Grandpa wasn't a big talker, you can imagine how those conversations went. And so we drifted apart.

As the years went by, I developed a love for math, and I got top marks on almost every test. My grades in almost all the other subjects were nothing to be ashamed of, either. They were so good, in fact, that at the end of my high school years I was awarded a scholarship to Harvard University. Accepting the honor wasn't even a question: of course I went.

Grandpa was still alive back in my freshman year, just hanging in there, so I attended Yom Kippur services at his *shteibel* with him, just like old times. It wasn't like I was religious or anything, but it made him happy and that made me happy in turn.

Harvard was an entirely new world for me. A place where connections were made and where they mattered. The network of friends made here could and would affect one's entire future. I made it my business to make the right friends, got invited to the best fraternity a Jewish boy could aspire to get invited to, and in general became the best example of what a Harvard student should be. What can I say? Almost every trace of religion that had returned to me by seeing Grandpa again, was steadily slipping right out the window.

◆　◆　◆

Grandpa died the next winter. I took care of all the funeral arrangements, spoke to the lawyers, and did everything that needed to be done. His will was mostly as expected. Most of his money went to assorted charities, except for his stocks, which he left to my mother, and bonds and things that he left for Betty and me. And he also left me a box of books. One of them caught my eye. It was the *machzor* he'd used forever and ever, and it called to me not to discard it. So I didn't. I installed it on a shelf over my bed, right next to a copy of *War and Peace*, and I promptly forgot about it. Life went on as usual. Parties to attend, campus politics to get involved in and, above all, I had to study.

Many things conspired to get me to shul that Yom Kippur. Firstly, my roommate slammed the door of my room hard enough to cause my calendar to fall off the wall and onto my bed. It clearly showed that today was Yom Kippur. It hit me hard. So hard, in fact, that I sat up quickly, banging my head on the shelf above my bed and knocked down some of my books, Grandpa's *machzor* among them. There was no way to ignore all of this. So I went to the shul at the campus's Hillel House. In my hand I carried my Grandpa's shredding *machzor*.

I entered the crowded Hillel House and took a seat near the door, intent on staying for a few minutes and then getting back to my room to study. But the memories of Grandpa just ganged up against me. Before I knew it, I was davening from his *machzor* and humming along with the rest of the crowd. And then we hit *Avinu Malkeinu* and I noticed something that made my heart jump. There was a huge smudge on the page, as if the teardrop Grandpa shed each year would join the one from the year before and the year before that. It was on one particular line in *Avinu Malkeinu* and, suddenly, I desperately needed to know what the line meant.

I noticed that the guy in front of me had a *machzor* with an English translation, so I asked him if I could borrow it for a minute. He handed it to me without a word. I went from line to line, until I found the line corresponding to the one that I was looking for:

"Our Father, our King, take pity upon us, and upon our children and our infants." And in the margins, Grandpa had penned in my name and Betty's name. It hit me like a ton of bricks. Those teardrops, year after year, were for one purpose only: *Father in heaven, have mercy on my grandchildren, who if not for You will be lost forever from their holy heritage.* Grandpa knew the chances of our surviving the spiritual holocaust were slight, and he was determined to give his all to the battle. "Please, G-d," he'd cry, "don't let us lose the children and the infants." And the power of a teardrop should not be underestimated.

So, I never gradjimacated Harvard, and there'll be one less mathematician in the world — *nu*, that's life. And every year as I take my place at the back table nearest the wall in that little Boston *shteibel*, I cry for our children and our infants who have no Grandpa to cry for them, my tears carrying Grandpa's smudge to places on the page that he'd never dreamed he'd reach.

This particular story first appeared in Horizons magazine. It is fiction: the concept was conceived on Yom Kippur and written that evening, when the inspiration was still present. I have since transformed it into a song called "Teardrop Revisited," on my album of all-English music, entitled "Visions."

To Die as a Jew

My first contact with the Zuckermans came on a frosty winter's night in Montreal. The snowdrifts in our area reach remarkable heights, and the temperature drops well below zero. It's the time of year when normal people can be found curled up in their toasty warm homes, drinking hot cocoa and playing Monopoly. I, however, was outside yet again, trekking through the snow and sleet on yet another episode of "track down the lost Jew," a game I always seem to find myself playing. The night, as I recall, was a brilliant one; the heavens clear of clouds, the stars bright. Long icicles hung down from the porch roofs, sending drops of water onto the wooden floorboards below.

I came equipped with my list of names and addresses, clutching it tightly in my hand and peering at it from time to time to decide where to go visit next. This was the third night of Chanukah, and instead of spending the evening with my family at home, I was busy trying to kindle the missing sparks of the Jewish neighbors around me. You see, I had come to Montreal from Israel just a short while before, my job description being to bring back as many Jews as possible to *Yiddishkeit*. To cut a long story short, I was not finding it very easy. But instead of giving up, I was outside again, about to visit another Jewish family whose name was on the list of the shul I worked for, to do my very best to interest them in the genuine light of *Yiddishkeit.*

Driving through the deserted streets, I saw menorahs in many of the windows. Some had candles and a few were giving forth the purity of oil light. Most were electric. Driving at thirty miles an hour, I finally found the block I was looking for, impressed despite myself at the immense homes and elegant cars. I parked close to the Zuckerman house and got out of the car, closing the door with a satisfying *bang!* which echoed through the residential stillness.

The melodious sound of wind chimes came in response to my ring and I could hear barking growing louder and louder as the Zuckerman's dog came running to protect them from the stranger at all costs. Now, I'm not any more chicken than the next guy, but that dog sounded like he was going to eat me alive, laugh, and then ask for another. But I stood my ground and waited as a man's voice asked who it was and I answered, "Rabbi Neumann."

Unlocking the door, he swung it open and ushered me inside towards the living room. He invited me to sit down on the spotlessly white leather couch which curled around the sides of the room. "Rabbi Neumann," he said, "I do believe your name sounds familiar." Indeed, I tell him that was probably from Rosh HaShanah when the couple had attended services at the shul where I served as assistant rabbi.

"Right," he said, "it's coming back to me. Yeah, you were the rabbi who was welcoming everyone into the davening. Wait a second, Rabbi, I want to tell my wife that you came to visit." This was going even better than I had hoped. Most people were not even close to welcoming, and this guy Zuckerman was being positively friendly! I relaxed on the couch, noticing the large electric menorah in the window and thinking to myself how nice it would be if it was replaced by a real one by the following year.

Five minutes later he returned with his wife, and I introduced myself formally this time, telling them that I like to visit all the couples who attend our services as a follow up, finding out how they enjoyed themselves, if there was something they felt could be done better, and so on. And of course, I also wanted to know if they'd like to get together maybe once a week for some Jewish studies. Nothing too serious, just the few of us y'know, and maybe my wife once in a while. Not too heavy — just so we could all together understand what G-d wanted from us.

This caught them by surprise. I think they had been expecting to be hit for a donation. Funny enough, they seemed to be seriously considering my offer, the wife even more than her husband. We then settled down, discussing the services and how inspiring they had been, and then the husband had a question about one of the prayers, and then his wife had something she wanted to know about Sabbath observance, and before I knew it I looked at my watch and it was eleven o'clock. No wonder I was feeling tired.

It had been a beautiful visit all around, and we made up to do it again the following week, this time with my wife as well. When they asked what we'd learn about, I replied, "What do you mean? We've been learning the entire evening! Why don't we just continue where we left off?" And so we did.

That was the first visit of many. The dog — Joshua of the very loud bark — was really a giant pussy cat and we became friends of sorts, meaning that he greeted me loudly and I arrived equipped with a bag of doggie biscuits for him to refocus his attention elsewhere. We began making progress. We moved along from discussions on whether the Torah is true to the understanding of the commandments, and then we split up, with my wife teaching Mrs. Zuckerman, and me and Danny learning stuff on our own.

◆　◆　◆

One evening, about three months after my initial visit, I arrived at the Zuckerman home to find both of them sitting and waiting for me in the living room with serious looks on their faces. Since they were normally pretty unflappable, I knew something was wrong. "What's up guys?" I asked them. They hemmed and hawed, and finally Danny told me that Lisa had been reading one of the books I had lent them and she had come to the belated realization that her conversion was probably unacceptable to the mainstream Orthodox community.

"That wouldn't have been so bad a few months ago," he continued, "but since Lisa's gotten to know the shul and your family, she's come to realize that this is the only way of life that is real and true. Lisa wanted to convert again, only this time, Orthodox." I was as shocked as could be. I never even dreamed that such an *aidel kneidel* like Lisa Zuckerman wasn't Jewish, and I knew that the process of conversion is a long and complicated one, taking time and requiring real willingness to understand the *beis din*.

The Zuckermans waited for my verdict. I explained to Mrs. Zuckerman that the Jewish religion really doesn't look for converts, that proselytizing just isn't our thing.

"But you aren't looking for me," she burst out. "It's me who's coming to you! I know now that I was totally misled."

"Wait a second," I said. "Why did you convert in the first place?"

"Because Danny is Jewish and he wouldn't have married me if I hadn't converted. So I went to the first conservative synagogue that I saw and asked them to help me convert. But now I want to convert because I feel that this is the real thing! And you, Rabbi Neumann, you have to help! You know that I don't have to convert, that Danny would stay married to me regardless, that the only reason I would go to such lengths is because I know there is only one G-d and this is the way He wants us to serve Him!" Her face had was flushed with emotion and I couldn't doubt her sincerity for even a moment.

"So what will it be, Rabbi?" Danny asked. "You going to help us?"

"Yes," I replied, "But I'm warning you now, this will take a lot longer than you think."

◆　◆　◆

The conversion process takes quite a long time. For an impatient person it feels like it's taking forever. First the *beis din* meets with the prospective convert to assess his or her sincerity and desire to really make the quantum leap to full Torah observance. Then they try to talk the potential convert out of undergoing this monumental change.

Lisa Zuckerman was as determined a person as I've ever seen, and I've known many determined people: from my roommates in yeshivah who were so determined to raid the kitchen that they devised numerous methods of besting a succession of high quality locks, to any of the many two year olds I'm acquainted with. But no one held a candle to Lisa Zuckerman. Sitting in front of the *beis din*, she responded carefully and truthfully to every question posed to her, and she was subjected to a barrage of speeches aimed at persuading her that she was making a mistake.

"Mrs. Zuckerman," began the head of the *beis din*, "have you ever heard of the Holocaust?" Indeed she had. "Well, then," he continued. "I'm sure you know of the cattle cars stuffed to the gills with hundreds upon hundreds of Jews, all suffering terribly for the sole reason that they were Jewish. You know that we were gassed, burned alive in ovens, and shot to death in huge mass graves. You know of the dogs trained by the Nazis to tear apart our brethren when given an order to do so.

"All this," the rabbi continued, "is nothing new, however. The Jewish people have been subjected to persecution and inhuman suffering for thousands of years. We were slaves in Egypt long ago and attacked on our way to the holy land. We were sent into exile from Israel by the Babylonians and the Romans, and we lived in captivity for almost as long as the world exists.

"We were burned at the stake during the Inquisition, and we were hounded and slaughtered by the Cossacks. We were subjected to blood libels every year at Passover time, and then we were killed by mobs made murderous by beer and rage. We were never accepted by the nations, and we never will be. And, as good as it is for us in America, who knows how much longer it will continue this way? Mrs. Zuckerman," he said again, "why put yourself through all of this if you don't have to? You can be a perfect non-Jew keeping all the commandments that G-d expects of you."

Lisa Zuckerman sat straight up in her chair and answered in the words of Ruth: "Your people will be my people, your G-d will be my G-d. Where you will go, I will go." One tear trickled out of her eye and she said, "This is the right path for me; there is no other way." With those words the die was cast. The *beis din* would help her become a Jew.

◆　◆　◆

Spring turned into summer and I was getting almost as impatient as the Zuckermans. It seemed as if she would never be good enough for them, never know enough halachah, never show enough piety. And then, one Shabbos morning when they were walking home from shul, Danny Zuckerman stepped off the curb without looking and was hit by a car trying to make the light before it changed. From one second to the next, their entire world turned upside down. Someone called an ambulance and I watched as they loaded Danny inside, good old Danny, who just wanted to do what Hashem wanted. Lisa climbed in with him and I watched them speed off, sirens wailing, to the nearest hospital.

We went to visit *motza'ei Shabbos*. I found Lisa sitting next to his bed her face buried in an ArtScroll *Tehillim*. My wife offered her comfort and *melaveh malkah*, and she told us what the doctors had said, how Danny was in stable condition, how he looked like he'd pull through. We were overjoyed by the prognosis and left her with some books and enough food for a while.

Days passed and Danny grew stronger. Lisa was pulled into the community's embrace, and barely an hour went by without someone else arriving to visit her and find out the latest update. Eventually, Danny grew well enough to begin physical therapy. Lisa was there with him every step of the way, encouraging and pushing him to give it his all, slipping away when she saw that he needed a break.

It was almost Rosh HaShanah when the Zuckermans came home from the hospital. Along with half the shul, we were there to welcome them as Danny Zuckerman climbed up the three stairs to the porch on his crutches. I'd even remembered to bring some biscuits for Joshua, who was overjoyed to have his master home again at last. Eventually, the crowd left to go home and we stayed just a little longer, helping Lisa tidy up the kitchen before going home to take care of the last-minute arrangements for Rosh HaShanah.

◆　◆　◆

The phone rang at eight in the morning on *erev Rosh HaShanah*, its shrill voice shattering any hopes for a peaceful morning. Lisa was on the other end and she wanted us to come over right that moment. "Can't it wait, dear?" my wife asked her.

"No, it can't," she replied. Knowing that Lisa wouldn't demand this if she really didn't need it, we acquiesced rather gracefully, considering that the *simanim* had yet to be prepared and the seating arrangements still needed some tweaking before the service later that day.

We got to the Zuckerman home in record time, and we were escorted inside. My mind took me back to my very first visit to their home and the warm welcome I had received then. That welcome had given me the needed confidence to move ahead and continue being successful with so many people who had come after the Zuckermans. Their acceptance had given me what I needed to succeed, and I was grateful. Lisa welcomed us inside, and Danny, still davening at the table, waved a cheerful hello.

Lisa took a deep breath and began to speak. "Rabbi Neumann," she said. "You cannot leave this house until you make all the arrangements ensuring that I become Jewish by this evening — in time for Rosh HaShanah." I looked at her open-mouthed. "Lisa," I said. "What brought this on?"

"I'll explain," she said, her voice trembling just a touch. "You see, that Shabbos morning, when Danny stepped off the curb and into the street, I realized something very important." We all waited.

"I realized," said Lisa, "that it could've just as easily been me who stepped off the street and ended up in the hospital. And I understood that I could have been fatally wounded or even, *chas v'shalom*, have been..." She couldn't finish the sentence.

"And," she went on, her voice breaking and the tears beginning to flow, "and if that would have occurred I would have died a *goy*! And I want you to know there is no way that I'm prepared to do that! Therefore, Rabbi Neumann, you must call up the *beis din* this very moment and make the arrangements for the conversion this very morning, just in case, because I need to know that I'm going to die a Jew!"

Needless to say, the proper arrangements were made and the conversion was carried out. And, as I trudge up yet another flight of stairs leading up to yet another upper-class home full of potential, I almost always remember a certain couple and the knowledge of what it means to die a Jew.

As heard from Rabbi Neumann

To Drink from Thy Waters

The Island

The island stretched out endlessly, or that was how it seemed to those who lived there, who thought it the most beautiful place on earth. And indeed, they weren't far-off the mark. Pristine sand stretched as far as the eye could see, ringing the coastline, whose waters were the color of cobalt and aquiline. At night when the sun turned a fiery crimson, the ocean took on a shade of golden red and the palm trees stood like a shadowy posse of guards on the beautiful shores.

Fields of flowers, their colors every shade of the rainbow, bobbed and waved at passersby. Blues, oranges, mauves, and purples dazzled the eye and filled the air with a heavenly fragrance. Orchards burst with delectable fruits. Banana bushes, orange groves, and grape vines perfumed the island with a heady aroma of fruity richness. Fields of golden wheat and barley, patches filled with every vegetable imaginable, provided the islanders with produce. Tomatoes were red and juicy, squash thick and flavorful, pumpkins heavy and round.

The islanders were tall and healthy, full of vigor and life. They led busy, worthwhile lives, toiling the fertile soil. Others operated the commerce for which the island was famous. They produced jewelry, combining precious metals and stones in intricate designs that had been handed down from their grandparents. Their bracelets, earrings, and necklaces were shipped all over, snapped up by an appreciative public in the most far-reaching places.

There were original thinkers and philosophers, employing their ingenuity and creativity in every subject and field, from classic literature and science to physics and metaphysics. They composed glorious poetry extolling the wonders of creation and the power of G-d, and they originated thought processes that gave the rest of the world a code to emulate. They were deep thinkers, full of mercy and compassion, eager to share their abilities with the rest of mankind.

But there was one rule of the island that displeased everyone, world over. You see, many ships came and went alongside the islands' quayside, huge supertankers transporting gasoline and crude oil, and commercial sea liners carrying people and merchandise, toys and spices, and all sorts of goods which the islanders needed or desired.

The sailors aboard the ships and the many people who had the opportunity to dock at the island's shores, all desired to visit the island to spend time there. But the island had one iron-clad rule. The only people to disembark at the port were the islands inhabitants. Everyone else stayed on their ships. Period.

Merchandise was unloaded at the dock, expertly carted off by the islanders, and the goods were paid for, with handshakes being exchanged all around. Plenty of food and drink were brought aboard for the hungry men. But they could not come ashore.

The Lake

At the center of the island, surrounded by exquisite shrubbery, lay the island's most prized possession: the lake. Shaped like a harp, calm waters forever lapping at its banks, the lake provided the island with cool, refreshing, drinking water. There was never a drought, never a lack. The water sparkled brightly during the day, warmed by the sun's rays, and it shone at night, when the moon's countenance could be clearly seen in its silvery depths.

The lakes water had the most satisfying taste. It quenched parched throats and all who drank from it walked away inspired and uplifted. The water invigorated them, infused them with joy and hope, ambition and clarity, comfort and goodwill

The lives of the islanders revolved around their beautiful lake, the jewel in the crown that was their island. Its waters could have been marketed worldwide, but all agreed that not one drop would be exported to the far-off public. Even the ships that docked there were never treated to a glass of the soothing elixir. For, the water made them special, granting them an intelligence and understanding that set them apart from everyone else. And so, the islanders frolicked in the shallow waters and reveled in the depths, all the while acknowledging the heavenly difference that the lake made in their lives.

Over time, people started to take on some of the characteristics of the lake. Some developed fluidity of movement, others seemed filled with novel and brilliant ideas, while others would water their friends' minds with depths of thought that kept them young and fresh.

Throughout the year there were many celebrations acknowledging the contribution and benefits of the lake. The islanders realized that without it they could never have come as far as they had. They appreciated the lake's uniqueness and never ceased praising its beautiful qualities.

The Brothers

Now, the king of the island was a wise and beloved man, filled with the wisdom of old age and the qualities of a successful leader.

He ruled benevolently for many, many years and was revered by young and old, scholar and simpleton. But he remained a modest man to the end, never ceasing to exhort his people to remain simple at heart, regardless of the wisdom they now possessed.

Alas, all things must eventually come to an end. The day arrived when the elderly monarch lay deathly ill. And then, then came the broken, anguished sounds of his loyal subjects' distress. And then, for the first time in many a year, the island's peace was replaced by discord.

For, the king had two sons. The older prince was considered by many to be a fool, although many of the islanders extolled his abilities and ambition.

"He will lead us into the future!" his supporters said.

"He will bring ruin to us all, " his detractors lamented.

The younger son was in many ways a copy of his father. He had the appearance of a saint: striking looks, penetrating and probing eyes. He was a thinker: an originator of brilliant ideas and lofty approaches. But, while these never ceased to impress the masses, very few of the islands' inhabitants were willing to live up to the standards of self-discipline he set, or able to sacrifice the many pleasures that his lifestyle demanded.

Gradually, a core of intense young men surrounded the second prince, intent on learning his ways and claiming his golden personality as their own. They would have been overjoyed to crown him as their king, but the majority of the tiny island kingdom was content with the cunning ambition of the older son. And so, the older prince was soon comfortably ensconced in the throne room where his father had meticulously dispensed justice for so many years.

The Project

The new king was dissatisfied with the island's development. His ambitions ranged further. He saw no reason why his beautiful is-

173

land should not become a haven to the world, drawing visitors from all corners of all the earth to their tiny paradise.

And so, together with a team of the finest planners, architects, and builders, the new king put together an international cultural center the likes of which the world had never seen. The breadth and scope of this undertaking dwarfed anything the team had ever done before; they were thrilled to be part of such an historic enterprise. Word soon got out to the street, and the public's reaction was mixed.

Some islanders rejoiced at their king's attempt to put their little island on par with the large, aggressive civilizations that existed all around them. The previous policy — of prohibiting visitors to step foot on their soil — was needlessly harsh, they felt. This gigantic project would be their bridge to the world, their link to the next century. And so, every bit of progress, every royal announcement, was greeted with wild jubilation.

The second group, led by the younger prince, wholeheartedly opposed the plan. There was no need to bridge the gap, they explained, since that gap had been created with a specific purpose. That gap had done tremendous good for the island all the time it had been in effect. Yes, they were separate: but look how much they had accomplished through their self-imposed segregation. Yes, they were aloof: but look at how much originality that had been generated. For every criticism of the island's separateness, they responded with many reasons why those traits were beneficial — no, critical — in a world that had increasingly fewer and fewer barriers. They argued the point to anyone who would listen, but earned contempt and dislike from the majority of the islanders.

The Opening

Oh, the joy and celebration, the sheer, unbridled revelry on the opening day of the international cultural center. Full orchestras assembled, filling the air with majestic symphonies. Historic displays revealed unknown secrets of yesteryear. Scientists dazzled the crowd with their discoveries, and engineers threw open the doors of tomorrow with their inventions and plans. And yet, for some strange and inexplicable reason, it wasn't the superb displays which caught the visitors' attention, nor was it the first-class entertainment that caught their eyes. Instead, as if with a life of their own, they were drawn to the lake that lay at the center of the island.

Even as the islanders forbade them entry and banished almost anyone who tried to get to the water, there were some who managed to get past the gates and the guards, and drink from and swim in the island's most revered site. They defiled the island's most precious resource, and they enjoyed the defilement more than any pleasure.

The more the visitors overcame the guards' defenses, the more those defenses relaxed. After all, what was the point? The gate had long been breached and there was no turning back. And so, eventually, together with the islanders, the visitors were allowed to take part in the water festivities. Not only that, they even created a special machine to filter the lake's water and ship it elsewhere, while integrating water from other places into the previously untouched lake.

Far from benefitting the lake, the foreign waters created havoc, introducing impurity into what had been crystal clear and pure. By now, though, the people of the island were far removed from where they had once been. From time to time it struck them that their civilization had ceased being the bedrock of morality that the world revered. But, they just shrugged it off and moved on to "more important things."

The Only Recourse

Of course, the students of the younger prince felt this loss, this horrific invasion of impurity. Their precious lake was open and defiled, and an endless number of tears were shed by this group of sincere and holy young men. But crying in itself is not productive — they needed to accomplished.

Long before this catastrophe struck, they had predicted what would happen. And so, they had stealthily gone down to the lake and stored away the precious water in every available bottle, jug, and canteen they owned. They, who understood the water's unique properties, knew that it could not be mingled with foreign waters, that the most sophisticated filters could not make it compatible with the sparkling liquid that filled their lake. It was imperative to save as much purity as possible.

They sheltered in some isolated caves that overlooked the waves crashing constantly over the boulders, and there they transported their special cargo. In secrecy and simplicity they carried it to a place where they could be safe to drink it, in peace and holiness.

And so, there they stayed, drinking the still, pure, untainted waters, continuing to unlock the secrets of the universe. Together with the younger prince, they constantly hoped and yearned for the day when their brothers, the rest of the islanders, would come to the realization that the only way to drink the waters was to do so without the influence and involvement of the outside world.

Only then could their morality once again be a beacon and guide; only then would the waters provide what they were meant to provide.

And so, they waited in silent agony and grief, yearning for the day that was yet to come.

The Story's the Thing

I t is late afternoon in the newsroom of the second-largest paper in Israel. The room is in a frenzy: journalists come and go, throwing the latest scoop on the desk of whichever editor they work for, then running off to get a drink from the cafeteria downstairs. Dvir Ninon, in a hurry as always, runs into the cavernous room, unstrapping his motorcycle helmet as he moves. Throwing out hellos and nods in every direction, he finally comes to a halt at the desk of the city editor, who, while yelling at someone over the phone and tapping an overflowing cigar into the nearest ashtray, motions Dvir to put whatever he had down on the corner of the packed desk. Dvir dumps the file down on the desk and leaves as quickly as he arrives.

The newsroom was a long, rectangular room separated out into cubicles, where the journalists sat and worked at their computers and traded tidbits of information with one another. A patch of carpet wound its way around the edge of the cubicles, setting them apart from the larger offices of the editors that overlooked the street outside. The senior editors even had a view of the Mediterranean from their windows, unlike the journalists, who had the pleasure of a bird's eye view of the polluted Tel Aviv street down below.

Although most of the offices were brightly illuminated, one office was mostly unlit. A small lamp at the edge of the desk lit up the blotter and a few newspaper cuttings; the rest of the room was dim. It was the office of Limor Senesh, known to one and all as the "queen of controversy." Since the sales of most newspapers correspond to the amount of controversy they manage to stir up, Limor was considered a highly prized cog in the paper's field of operations.

She had managed to stir up many a wasp's nest in her time. There had been the Ethiopian scandal, when she had uncovered an entire crew of influential people skimming off the Ethiopian refugees' funding. Then there was the scandal with the minister of communications and the illegal satellite dishes that he'd arranged to be camouflaged and scattered among private homes. That had caused him to be bumped out of his job. Limor Semesh was a feared woman, and she cultivated her reputation zealously.

But there was one group of people that she targeted much more often than any other: the *chareidim,* of course. They were prime fodder for her canons: naïve and simpleminded, following their leaders like mindless sheep. When something connected to *chareidim* came her way, Limor could never resist going for the kill. It was fun stirring up the entire country; whether about the money their politicians had managed to get for the yeshivos (after fighting tooth and nail), or the fact that so many young, eligible men didn't pull their weight as soldiers in the army. And when Limor took on a cause — watch out! She dug up dirt that had been hidden away for years, and phrased her pieces in a way that within no time at all the radio stations were all devoting air time to her topics and the country was up in arms, yet again. That was the secret of Limor's success.

The thing was, that nothing really juicy had come along for quite a while. As a result, the ratings were down, which in turn made the powers-that-be look at her with raised brows, as if pondering whether she had lost her touch. When she reached such a stage, and inevitably, it did happen periodically, she would retreat into the darkness to think things out and ponder a new topic for her column. As she sat, she skimmed through back issues of the paper to see what the hot news was these days, hoping that she'd be able to find something to tie into an issue that was already on the table.

As she skimmed, something interesting caught her eye, and she picked up the article to get a clearer look. The topic was *agunos*. Immediately, her antenna picked itself up and began to zero in on the action. It seemed that the husband of one of the country's celebrities had disappeared, and the rabbis were forbidding her to remarry so long as his whereabouts remained in question. She had known for quite a while that this particular issue was a waste of time, since the rabbis had very clear ideas about how they handled these cases. Usually, the nation went along with them, on the premise that laws of marriage and similar activities need to be overseen by the top rabbis of the nation.

This time, however, the scenario was different. Somehow, the rabbis had managed to offend the celebrity (one could argue that however they would have handled the situation she would have been offended). The press had been quick to pick up on the case and the public's sympathy definitely lay with the *agunah*. Which meant that Limor had a base to build on, a peg on which to stand. And Limor never let anything with that amount of potential out of her sight. The development would mean late nights for a while, until her research was complete and the piece was done, but the satisfaction when she saw her by-line in black and white was incredible, not to mention the check that would be deposited in her account.

Limor stared off into the distance as she contemplated how best to utilize her present information. She could see fellow workers scurrying around, as inside her brain a plan began to form. She would put herself into the mindset of an *agunah*. Not just the theoretical mindset, though... She would actually become an *agunah*.

She'd develop an entire case history for herself. She would verify the halachic ramifications of someone in her position, and she'd find a scenario that would cast the rabbis in an unjustifiable position. She'd invent a case where it seemed clear enough that her husband was truly gone, but which wouldn't be sufficiently kosher for the holier-than-thou rabbis.

Not that something like this was not without its risks. Limor remembered clearly a story of another journalist who had attempted something similar with devastating results. He had taken to the war-path with the intent of exposing the *mekubalim* of Israel as a bunch of frauds and impostors. Taking meticulous care with his appearance, the journalist had dressed up like a woman and traveled to the home of the Baba Sali to request a *berachah* for children.

Doubtless, he thought that the sage would be convinced by his deception and give him a beautiful blessing, which he would then hold up for ridicule in his column. He would decry the fraudulent society the religious were running in Israel: taking money from unsuspecting people and giving them nothing but a blessing in return. And, if Baba Sali would see fit to bless him that he have children, then what exactly was his blessing worth?

The journalist carried out his plan meticulously, making every effort to produce an exposé that would shock and disgust his readership. He reached the home of Baba Sali, where he presented himself in supplication, asking for a blessing for children. Indeed, he received a blessing from the holy man, that he merit the feelings of childbirth for the next nine months. The "feelings of childbirth" began from the moment he reached his home, giving him an endless amount of pain for the following nine months... Who would've believed something like that could have happened?!

◆　◆　◆

Limor chose a prominent Sephardic rabbi as her victim, due to her longstanding dislike of many of his policies. She would enjoy exposing him in her upcoming campaign. She planned her story carefully, rehearsing exactly what she was going to say. When she felt she had everything down pat, and she'd be able to present her situation in its unerring inaccuracy, she made an appointment. She awaited the inevitable with silent glee. There was no way that the *rav* would be able to give her a *heter* to get remarried, and when he refused to comply with her request, well, then the entire world would find out about it. There wouldn't be one person in the whole country who wouldn't read her piece and be influenced by it.

◆　◆　◆

She left her home at eight in the morning for her nine thirty appointment at the rabbi's home. She drove past the gatehouse of her kibbutz, turning left at the first intersection that would take her to the Tel Aviv-Jerusalem highway. As she drove she listened to Chopin on the car's system, reveling in the haunting melodies.

She hadn't wanted to overdo it by acting too much like the grieving widow, so she dressed in her normal style, toning it down just enough to give respect to the "holy man." There was no one as skeptical as a skeptical Limor Senesh.

The rabbi was sitting on the couch when Limor came in, learning from a *sefer*. An actress to the core, Limor immediately burst into tears and was quite unable to get her story out for the first five minutes of her visit. The rabbi waited patiently for her to calm down, and he listened attentively as she began her tale of woe. She spoke of her husband Shai, an officer in the army, who had "disappeared" some three years previously while on a secret mission in enemy territory. The rabbi heard her out sympathetically, and asked whether any of the soldiers who had been with him on that particular mission had seen him dead or could provide positive witness to something of that effect.

Limor had prepared for this question and had made sure to

brief Shai's "comrades" on what they should say if it would come to that. No, none of them would have seen Shai dead. The most they would be able to tell was that he'd been seen wounded, heavily wounded, with no chance of survival, especially not where the platoon had found itself in at the moment of the attack. Somehow, his buddies-in-arms had made it home alive, even as the bombs were exploding all around them. They had even brought a helicopter down with their hand-held missile launchers, but at the last moment, Shai had received a wound severe enough to have caused him to be separated from the rest of the boys. And that was the last time anyone had seen her Shai: critically wounded with almost no chance of survival, yes. But dead? No. That hadn't been witnessed by anyone there, which, in effect, made her an *agunah*.

She had thought that the army would discover Shai's whereabouts and he'd come home an army hero. But, the months and years had passed and there had been no sign of him. And now she didn't want to be an *agunah* any longer: could the *rav* help? A tear lay at the edge of each eye, and Limor waited in silence as the *rav* deliberated her problem in much the same way that he grappled with the scenarios that presented themselves to him on a daily basis.

Inside, Limor was hoping that the *rav* would return back from the halachic world he'd just entered and tell her that he would not be able to come to her assistance, that helping her was just out of the question. When that happened she would thank the rabbi for his time, and pretend to be utterly brokenhearted by this new development. And then she would drive on home. She would park her car and go upstairs and make her way to the computer alcove, where she'd turn on the little desk lamp and write a smasher of a story denouncing this rabbi and the entire ultra-Orthodox world along with him. In her mind's eye, she was already being interviewed by channel two of Israeli television, and she reveled in the upcoming glory which would be hers.

And then the *rav* looked up and he gave her his answer. It was nothing even close to what she had originally thought it would be, and it was extremely disconcerting, to say the least.

"Return to my home in two days," said the *rav*, "and hopefully I will be able to assist you." Limor was shocked! Was this the response of the most ultra of them all? Would he truly give a *heter* to someone in a situation such as hers? What on earth was going on here?! The matter, however, was not up for discussion, and after thanking the rabbi for his time, she left the apartment. Somewhat in a daze, she drove the rest of the way home, not to write up her story, but to wait two days, as the *rav* had instructed.

◆　◆　◆

Two days later, the husband of distinguished journalist Limor Senesh passed away in his sleep. He was still young. He left her free as a bird, and most definitely not an *agunah*.

As heard from Reb Meir Miller

So Different, So Similar

What can I say? This was one case where I was truly wrong! I know it now, but at that time I was convinced that the *Rav* was just... Oh, I'm running ahead of myself, but it is such an interesting story and it made such an impact on everyone who heard it! Whenever I remember the whole situation, I'm filled with admiration for both of them all over again.

"Okay already," you're probably thinking. "What's so special about this story?" Just hold on, and let me get through it at my own pace.

Now, you have to understand that when my brother Shuey got engaged, it was a tremendous *simchah* for the entire family. What made the *simchah* so much greater for all concerned was the fact that this was Shuey's second engagement. With much heartache, his first engagement had been broken, and so it was with great joy and trepidation that Shuey popped the question, received a positive reply, and unleashed a torrent of happiness on all of us.

Shuey and his *kallah* got along amazingly. Shuey and his in-laws, however, did not. They were forever calling to discuss this, dissect that, to make a change in this area, to improve somewhere else.

Shuey, as all who know him will testify, is a calm, serene, and funny individual, who never lets anything get to him. But a few days before the wedding, he received a phone call from his *shver* that shattered even his equanimity.

"Hi, Shuey," said the future *shver*.

"Hi." Shuey answered warily, bracing himself for whatever challenge was coming up.

"So, I was wondering," continued the *shver*, "who you were bringing to the wedding as *mesader kiddushin?*" He let the question hang in the air, and Shuey's mouth just about popped open in surprise. I had arrived home right then, just in time to see my brother at a loss for words. I waited to hear what was coming next.

"Um," mumbled Shuey, searching desperately for words and not finding any. "I thought I made it clear that my Rosh Yeshivah is coming to the wedding to be the *mesader kiddushin?*" Shuey's Rosh Yeshivah lived in a different state, which meant a fairly long trip for the elderly *rav*, but one that he had agreed to quite happily. He, more than anyone, knew what Shuey had gone through during that first engagement, and he, more than almost anyone, was looking forward to dancing at this wedding. It was the most natural thing in the world for Shuey to ask his Rosh Yeshivah to be the *mesader kiddushin* — and his *shver* knew that, as well! What on earth was going on here?!

"I know you mentioned something about your Rosh Yeshivah," continued the future *shver*, "but I would really like to invite my Ruv, and I was hoping that you would understand!" Shuey understood, alright! He understood that if he didn't put his foot down right now, at this crucial moment, he would never have any peace from this man for the rest of his life.

"Listen," said the *shver* before Shuey could say anything more (not that he knew what to say), "I have to run now and I'll call you back later. Have a good day." He hung up. Shuey did the only sensible thing that came to mind, he got right back on the horn and called his Rosh Yeshivah to ask him what to do.

The Rosh Yeshivah listened carefully to the whole saga, interjecting a question now and then to clarify a point, then he spoke. "From my point of view," he said, "I don't need the *kavod* and don't mind who is *mesader kiddushin*. However," and here there was a very long pause, "this is not about me! This is about you and the type of relationship you are going to have with your future father-in-law. In my opinion, you have no choice but to tell your *shver* that this something that you can't bend on. Do you understand me, Shuey?" asked his Rosh Yeshivah. "You must tell him this, but do it gently and with *derech eretz*. Let me know what happens."

◆　◆　◆

I watched the entire episode — from beginning to end — in fascination. I had yet to be involved in *shidduchim,* and I found myself almost completely disconnected from whole thing. My parents, on the other hand, were connected, and how! They wanted to pick up the phone, dial their *mechutan,* and give him a piece of their mind. I mean, one of the most elementary of *chasunah* rules is that the *chassan* gets to pick the *mesader kiddushin*! But, the phone was ringing again and Shuey answered his *shver* in his most congenial, nonconfrontational voice.

"Shuey," I heard the voice on the other end.

"Yes?"

"I was just by my Ruv," said the *shver,* and I could feel my heart jump with sudden worry.

"And?" prompted Shuey.

"And I told the Ruv that I am making a *chasunah* and I would like him to come." Shuey tried to say something, but the *shver* continued talking until Shuey grew silent. All this, while he was running around the dining-room table, being chased by my parents who wanted the phone, wanting to talk to the guy who was making their son a complete wreck three days before his *chasunah*.

"So what did the Ruv say?" asked Shuey.

"The Ruv said that at this point in his life he doesn't feel so well, but that if I'm inviting him for *siddur kiddushin*, he would try to come." He had done it! He had put my brother into the corner. My father turned red with anger, my mother turned white. Both reached for the phone, which Shuey dangled just out of their reach.

"I'm sorry," Shuey said, "but I'm going to have to stay with my original choice for *siddur kiddushin* and that means my Rosh Yeshivah. I hope you understand."

"Wait a second!" said his future *shver*. "The Ruv is an elderly Yid!"

"My Rosh Yeshivah isn't exactly a youngster," Shuey replied.

"Yes, but it's an *inyan* to be *mechabed* someone *chashuv* by the *chuppah*," he tried again.

"Right," Shuey said. "That's exactly why I want to honor my Rosh Yeshivah.

"But," said the *shver*, "the Ruv is a *talmid chochum*!"

"And so is my Rosh Yeshivah," said my brother. "I'm sorry, but this is the way it's going to have to be. Please try to understand." They said goodbye, everyone anxious over what the next few days would bring.

The *chuppah* room was magnificent. I watched from the sidelines as all the *kallah*'s brothers and sisters gathered in a semi-circle around her chair, posing for the pictures with artificial smiles and glitter galore. There was an endless array of combinations. The *kallah* with her mother, with her father, with each of her siblings, with special friends, with the children she worked with, with my mother, and on and on and on. Shuey, meanwhile, was ensconced at the *chassan*'s *tisch,* surrounded by his Rosh Yeshivah, our father, and great-uncle Shulom, who had arrived all the way from Hong Kong (don't ask me why he lives there).

Shuey was busy with his *tehillim*, and the rabbis were busy with the *kesubah*, and everyone else was busy eating. Eventually, they finished writing the *kesubah*, and the age-old chant was struck up. Shuey was escorted on either side by Tatty and his soon-to-be *shver*. They went in for the *badeken* and the singing was so loud that the air was vibrating. Shuey has like a thousand friends, and they were all there: singing, laughing, talking, and dancing — and the wedding hadn't even begun!

After the *badeken*, the mob made its leisurely way in reverse, back through the *kabolas panim* room, through the *chassan's* room and down the carpeted stairs in the direction of the huge hall where the *chuppah* was to take place. I was at the back of the crowd, and as we entered the beautifully decorated room, I shivered just for a second. This was it. This was final. In a matter of minutes, Shuey would be leaving the first chapter of his life. I couldn't help it; I was scared for his sake and I hoped that everything would work out.

As I entered the room, I noticed an elderly chassidishe Yid sitting in one of the middle rows, bedecked in a *kapote* with fur around the edges. There was no doubt in my mind: the Ruv was here, and he would be expecting *siddur kiddushin*. We were going to have some huge problems when they announced the honors and the Ruv found himself with a *berachah* alone. But there was no time to worry about anything. The *chassan*, flanked by the *mechutanim*, had already ascended the dais to the *chuppah* and was waiting silently for the *kallah*, all three of them davening with a *kavanah* so intense I could feel it all the way where I was, at the back of the room.

The three guys who were singing began their rendition of "*Mi Adir*," and everyone gradually began filing into their places. More and more people filled the room, until it was almost impossible for me to see anything, so I started inching my way up to the front. The guys finished singing and the *kallah*, flanked by mother and mother-in-law, entered the room. Everything was going like clockwork. As the *bachurim* sang, the *kallah* circled the *chassan*, and the ladies wiped away tears.

And then one of the brother-in-laws approached the dais, took hold of the microphone and began announcing the *kibbudim*. I held my breath. Who was going to get *siddur kiddushin*? Shuey's Rosh Yeshivah, or had the *shver* pulled a fast one and told him to call up the Ruv? I wasn't breathing, just standing there with my mouth open, waiting. And then I heard, "The Rosh Yeshivah from Yeshivas — *mechubad* with *siddur kiddushin*." I saw Shuey smile as his Rosh Yeshivah rose and began walking up to the dais.

At the next moment, everything fell apart. From one of the middle rows, an elderly man arose. A man clad in a beautiful, *choshuve*-looking *kapote* with fur around the neck and sleeves. It was the Ruv, and he was leaving the hall! I couldn't believe my eyes! "You old *ba'al gaiveh*, you!" I thought furiously to myself. "So that's the way it is? They don't give you *siddur kiddushin* so you get up and leave? Doesn't it mean anything to you at all that you are embarrassing both families and the *chassan* and the Rosh Yeshivah, who got the honor?! Who do you think you are?!" I was so angry, I was almost frothing.

The Ruv was making his way to the double doors at the back of the room as quickly as his ninety-year-old legs were able to carry him, when a voice rang out from under the *chuppah*; "The Rosh Yeshivah would like to honor the Ruv with *siddur kiddushin*." The entire hall waited, expectantly. You could have heard a toothpick drop on the other side of the door as the Ruv continued his attempt to get out of the room. But, from the front of the cavernous chamber came a second call that the Ruv could not ignore; "the Rosh Yeshivah would like to honor the Ruv with *siddur kiddushin*."

This was too much. The Ruv, who had been at the door, turned around and began shuffling down the long carpeted center aisle in the direction of the *chuppah*. And Shuey's Rosh Yeshivah smiled from ear to ear. "After all," I thought to myself, "why shouldn't he smile. The *shver* had been shown boundaries and the Ruv had received his *kibbud*."

The Rosh Yeshivah himself didn't mind one way or the other, and Shuey was happy as long as he was. The one person I didn't get was the Ruv. Ninety-five years old and still insisting on *kavod*! How ridiculous it seemed. How could someone so important, so holy, put an entire crowd through the experience we had just been through? It didn't make sense! And, as I looked around the crowded room, I could see that many people there were feeling the same way.

The Ruv said the *berachos,* and even I had to admit that there was something special about the way he said them. A tingle ran through the air, a certain elusive thread that can't be explained... Suffice it to say, the *chuppah* was something special, and it was because of him. That was clear. And yet...and yet...

It was a wonderful *chasunah* and I danced for what seemed like forever. From time to time over the next few days, I thought about the disturbing scene, but by the following week, it had been relegated to the back of my mind, to be pondered over when I had a free moment, which never came.

◆　◆　◆

It was a few months later when I finally learned the truth behind what I had witnessed. I was back home for a few days during *bein hazemanim,* and I happened to run into one of Shuey's old friends from yeshivah. He mentioned his regret at having missed what people were calling "the greatest wedding of the year," and he mentioned that the story behind the *chuppah* was one of the most amazing things he had ever heard!

"Yeah," I agreed, "the Rosh Yeshivah is truly special."

"Right," he said. "And the Ruv, forget it!"

I looked at him strangely for a minute and said, "What are talking about? What did the Ruv do?"

"What did the Ruv do?" he echoed me. "What do you mean? The Rosh Yeshivah came back from the *chasunah* all pumped up about what the Ruv did and what a tzaddik he is!"

"Okay, okay," I stopped him. "Why don't you tell me exactly what you're talking about."

"Well," he began, "the Rosh Yeshivah said something like this. He walked into the *chuppah* room right before the *chuppah* was about to start, and he noticed a *chashuve*-looking man sitting in one of the middle rows. Taking a wild guess, the Rosh asked the man if he was the Ruv. Not wanting to cause any mixups, the Rosh explained the background to the Ruv.

"He told the Ruv how the *shver* had called and pressured his *talmid* after he'd already asked his Rosh Yeshivah to the *chuppah*. He explained how he had felt there was no choice but for the *bachur* to insist that things remain as they were. The Ruv nodded in agreement, and he told the Rosh Yeshivah that he had thought that there was nobody else for *siddur kiddushin*. He had no problem receiving a *berachah* and nothing more.

"But then the Rosh began to demand that the Ruv indeed accept *siddur kiddushin*. He explained his reasoning as follows: He had no desire for the honor, and felt that it should really go to the Ruv. The only reason he had said otherwise was to prevent the *shver* from taking advantage of his *talmid*. But now that the *chassan* had gotten his way, there was no reason that the Ruv shouldn't be the *mesader kiddushin*!

"The Ruv listened to his esteemed colleague and agreed with him — except for one thing. He was not interested in the honor, either. He felt that it should go to the *chassan*'s rebbi. Back and forth they argued, and meanwhile the *chassan* was getting closer and closer. Then the Rosh had a brilliant idea.

191

" 'Listen,' he told the Ruv, 'you give me a *berachah* and then we'll be even.'"

The Ruv thought it over and agreed. They shook on it and the die was cast: the Ruv would be the *mesader kiddushin*.

"The Ruv, however, had no intention of taking the honor away from the Rosh Yeshivah. He waited until they announced the name of the *mesader kiddushin*, and he heard that it wasn't him. Satisfied that the *shver* hadn't gotten his way, he stood up to leave, and made his steady way to the door. His intention: not to take the honor away from the Rosh Yeshivah, and to break the deal they had made.

"The Rosh, however, was quick on the uptake, and he saw which way the wind was blowing. The second he reached the dais, he told them to announce the Ruv, knowing that the Ruv would then have no choice but to turn back and take his rightful place as the *mesader kiddushin*. He was right, for the Ruv did turn around, and the story ended happily for everyone concerned.

"But, just think about the *middos* of those two *gedolim*," my friend said in admiration. "All they wanted was for the other to receive the honor, for the other to be in the limelight. I'm sure you'll agree with me," he said, "that this is one amazing story!"

Of course I agreed with him. And it set me thinking about all the notions I had been brought up with, which were still so much a part of me. How I hadn't been able to bring myself to judge someone favorably, even though that someone was an elderly tzaddik and an obviously holy individual. It really made me think.

And you know something, that was the last *siddur kiddushin* that the Ruv ever did. He passed away two weeks after the *chasunah*. What can I say — we were very lucky, and I learnt a couple of lessons that would be with me for the rest of my life.

As heard from Rabbi Silverstein

Think Ahead!

Baruch was heartbroken. He was a man of standing: someone respected in the community, someone whose advice was sought after by one and all. But, none of the above mattered anymore. Every time he so much as glanced at his son, the son whom all had predicted would go on to become the next *gadol hador*, his heart skipped a beat. The black velvet yarmulke had gone, replaced by something different every day. Moishe's wardrobe, once home to rows of black pants and ironed white shirts, now contained an array of vastly different attire.

The clothes weren't what really bothered Baruch. He had grown up in a much more modern world, and he was not overly concerned by a few pairs of jeans and a couple of shirts from Burlingtons'. That wasn't the issue. He lay awake at night, tossing and turning, thinking about the changes he was constantly noticing in the *pnimiyus*, the inner soul, of his first-born son.

At first, Moishe had stopped davening with a minyan during *bein hazemanim*, blaming it on staying up too late "in the *beis hamedresh*." As time went on, however, Moshe made little attempt to hide the metamorphosis within. Baruch watched Moishe's friends change and language change, and he knew that he was on the road to the edge of the cliff. Baruch and his wife sat in the kitchen late into the night, drinking coffee and trying to decide what they should do. Sometimes they would see Moishe returning home and they would search for the words to talk to him — just to talk! But even that was proving too difficult.

◆　◆　◆

The Rav's beard was a lustrous white, his eyes held sparks of kindness and humor. Looking into that old, wise face, Baruch was finally able to open his heart to someone other than his wife. He could feel his shoulders beginning to relax, the tension leaving his neck, as the tears rolled down his cheeks. "*Rebbi*," he wailed, "why has this happened to us? We are good people, good Yidden, good role models. I've always learnt with my children and they've always seen me learning as well. Tzedakah and *chesed* play a big role in our home. What happened?"

The Rav leaned back in his chair and pondered the question. At length, he turned to his *talmid* and said, "Reb Baruch, let me ask you something. Did you spend a lot of time davening that your children should turn out well? Did you beg Hashem to allow you to see *nachas* from your children, or did you simply assume that everything would be okay and that *nachas* would be yours for the taking?" Reb Baruch hung his head; it was clear that he had been remiss. "Reb Baruch," the Rav said, "I want to tell you a story."

◆　◆　◆

During World War I, the whole of Europe was turned upside down. Parts of Hungary became Czechoslovakia and vice versa. Towns were ripped in half. What had been one neighborhood was now two countries. Families, friends, business partners, communities were now separated by barbed-wire fences and border police.

In our particular story, one of the biggest challenges was the fact that the town's cemetery was now out-of-bounds for half the town. But, the townspeople still had to bury their dead and families still needed to pray at the graves of their ancestors. What could they do? The town council held an emergency meeting, and they decided to approach the military commander of their zone. After great difficulty, they finally succeeded in making an appointment to see the general.

The day of the meeting finally arrived. The heads of the *kehal* donned their very best clothing. After receiving a *berachah* from their *rav*, they made their way to the general's headquarters.

Gathering all their courage, they entered the building, telling the sentry at the door of their appointment. They followed another soldier down a long, impressive corridor illuminated by countless lights in wall sconces. Finally, they arrived at an anteroom outside the general's office.

The general was lounging behind his desk, smoking a cigarette and looking bored. He didn't have the tough look they were expecting to see, and the delegation was surprised and pleased. As they entered the room, the general sat up in his chair and, surveying them one by one, he said, "Gentlemen, how can I be of service to you?"

Unnerved by the general's friendly tone, the delegation was silent. Finally, one of them gathered his wits and began to speak. He described the utter chaos which had resulted from the border change and the specific problem of the cemetery.

The general listened patiently, nodding imperceptibly from time to time. He heard out the spokesman, and when he had finished speaking, he told them that he would allow them across the border for funerals. All they needed to do was inform the officers that it was a funeral procession and they would be allowed through. The delegation thanked him again and again, and returned home jubilant.

◆　◆　◆

A month later, Yankel the shoemaker passed away. The entire town (at least the part that was on that side of the border) gathered together for the funeral. The rabbi spoke, the ladies cried, and the *chevrah kadishah* took care of their part. And when it was all over, the coffin was hoisted onto their shoulders and the procession made its somber way down the muddy street.

They arrived at the border and the *rosh hakahal* whipped out a letter from the general, granting his permission for them to cross. The order was given, and the crowd surged through the narrow area towards the next country, previously their home town. Through a misty drizzle they marched to the *beis hachaim,* where the *niftar* received a tearful farewell. Then the crowd reversed its tracks, making its collective way back to the "new country."

And so a rhythm was created in the city, and people were able to bury their dead without any problems. All until Berel the businessman came up with his brilliant plan.

Berel was one of those people able to turn every situation into a business advantage. While attending the next funeral, his agile mind arrived at a certain conclusion. For whatever reason, the general had decided to allow the Jewish community unrestricted border entry anytime somebody died. They trusted the Jews and would never suspect them of using a funeral for their own advantage.

The fact that the borders were closed created many a business opportunity for people like Berel. Needles and cotton, for example, were very expensive on one side of the border, while the price of sugar and tobacco was prohibitive on the other side. And Berel was getting in on the action. The next time somebody from the village passed away, before the *niftar* was laid into the coffin, Berel made sure to load in a decent amount of merchandise to be handed over to his agent on the other side of the border.

And that was what happened. The agent was met, the business concluded, and the money paid. Berel was a happy man (as they say, "one man's rain is another's sunshine"). But, "He who has one hundred wants two hundred," and Berel took his business to the next level. It was simple. If the police weren't checking the coffins, there was no reason to wait for a funeral to carry out a little business. He might as well fill up an empty coffin with merchandise and triple his money. And that was exactly what he did. The letter was shown, the Jews accompanying the coffin were allowed through, and the agent was on hand with his wagon to relieve them of their lucrative burden. Berel congratulated himself and the procession returned home, with Berel already making plans for the next funeral.

Over the next few months, Berel perfected his art. If the police wondered why there were so many Jews dying, they gave no sign of it, and Berel found himself more and more successful. But Berel made one mistake. He was so happy about his business, that he forgot to be sad during the funerals. Not only that, but his exuberance affected those around him. Even the *chevrah kadishah* forgot that there was supposed to be a dead man in the box, and they joked and laughed with one another. Before they knew it, the border police had grown suspicious.

The general was informed, and the next time a funeral was passing through, he put in a surprise appearance at the border crossing. As Berel caught sight of the posse of officers awaiting them, his face turned pale. He knew it was the end. As the procession reached the crossing, the general stepped out from the guardhouse, his face stern.

The group of mourners halted in their tracks, confusion and fear written on their faces. "You," ordered the general pointing at one of the delegation, "open the coffin!"

"But your honor," sputtered the man, "that would be a severe dishonor to the dead."

The general was unmoved. "Open the coffin," he said again, "or I will be forced to have my men open it up."

With no choice, one of the *chevrah kadishah* opened the coffin, revealing the piles of goods waiting to be handed over to the agent. Nobody enjoys being tricked, certainly not army generals, and this man was no exception. As he looked around him, he saw the crowd of Jews crying bitterly, as if they were taking part in the most heartbreaking of funerals.

Shaking his head at them he said, "If you wouldn't have been so happy, I would never have thought of opening the coffin. If you only would have cried when you were supposed to, this would never have happened."

◆ ◆ ◆

"Yes, Reb Baruch," said the Rav, "we have an obligation to daven for our children before they reach those moments where their lives could go either way. But we wait, thinking there is nothing to worry about. Not only that: we smile, we laugh, we enjoy life. We must daven from the very start, utilizing every *tefillah* for the sake of our children. If we cry now, hopefully in the years to come, we'll be able to laugh."

Forgiveness

Our mouths are potent weapons. With one word or action, one unexpected, thoughtless word or stupid deed, we can wreak havoc on people's lives. Once released, words are out of our control, gone forever. And then we might truly need forgiveness.

Forgiveness, though, is not always forthcoming. It can hide in the alleyways of the heart for decades, not wanting to emerge, ashamed. Forgiveness can run from the person pursuing it like the most fleeting of shadows.

The heart has the capacity to forgive, but it has the capacity to deaden itself as well, to become brittle and worn, to forget how to forgive. That happened to me.

I'm not so young anymore. Enough time has passed for me to tell the story and without feeling like a knife is stabbing me in the back. And it's a story I want everyone to know.

I was just twelve when my mother passed away. She was the glue that held our family together, and when she left us after a long illness, the entire structure fell apart. It tottered in the wind for a while and then, one day, the whole thing was knocked over like a house of cards. My father didn't have the strength to go on, and he was as much a broken shell as I was, as all the children were. And so, some of us children were sent to our grandparents, some went to cousins...it was a nightmare. True, what with my mother's illness our home hadn't been the warmest place to be for some time already. No soup on the stove, no cookies baking in the oven. No mother with a frilly apron to welcome us from school with a kind word and a welcoming smile. But it was home, and that means the world to a child.

In their boundless wisdom and endless care, the adults came to the conclusion that remaining in America would not be a good or healthy thing for me who was all of thirteen years old. And so it was decided to send me off to Eretz Yisrael, to the yeshivah run by our Chassidus. In the old days, I had dreamed of attending this exact place — but I hadn't dreamed that it would be at the tender age of thirteen! But there I was, being driven to the airport, a diminutive boy, swamped by a hat and long jacket, swimming eyes mercifully hidden behind a pair of glasses.

The day was gray and dark as we drove along the highway. Inside, I was cheerless and crying and scared. It began to rain. Fat drops of water splashed on the windshield, cascading downwards on the oil-slicked streets, where rainbows spread outwards in the water, only to blur out of focus. I was leaving and I didn't know when I'd be coming back. The worst part about it was that nobody cared.

The plane ride was a nightmare. If I fell asleep, there was nobody to tell the stewardess that I needed a meal. I was ignored by everyone I came into contact with and dozed my way through the flight, the mini cans of soda my only comfort. It seemed like forever, but before I knew it, we were landing. My ears were popping like balloons and I didn't even know if this normal or not. I swallowed repeatedly and clenched my teeth together so tightly that they felt like they were grinding to the nubs. And then, the wheels were down and the flaps were out and I saw land. There was a gentle bump and we had landed!

It was hot and sunny as we got off the plane, and I walked down the set of metal stairs and kissed the ground like I'd always heard that people do when they arrive in Eretz Yisrael for the first time. The tarmac had oil stains on it and I doubted that the people who had come all those years ago, had to contend with that!

The sights, the sounds, the smells! It was a brand-new world, one that I had the luxury of seeing for the first time while jet-lagged out of my mind. Somehow, I made it through passport control and out in one piece.

The warmth hit me as we exited the terminal, and my escort led the way to his car. I followed meekly. We drove to Yerushalayim and I fell asleep in the car, waking up as we ascended the curving road. The mountains were astonishing in their depths, the flowers' colors brilliant against the stark backdrop. The vehicle labored slowly up the hills, and then, all of a sudden, we were there.

We drove through the winding streets, filled with homes built closely together as if for comfort, where thousands of kids ran from door to door and played in the streets and laughed and cried, doing exactly what kids do. All I could think of was my own brothers and sisters and once again, tears rose unbidden to my eyes.

The car rolled into one of the neighborhoods and circled the streets, looking for the right address. We were given directions by a chassid who dressed much the same way that my family did. He was portly, with a large chest and self-assurance to match, and I wished that he was my father. We found the yeshivah building. It was old and worn out, and just a little on the tired side. The sounds of Yiddish filled the air, and from somewhere above came the sharp voice of a mother putting her children to bed. I thought of my own mother. It felt like a lifetime ago. The air smelled of Williamsburg, and the old men who walked the streets supported by canes and walkers could have been my Zeide's friends.

The driver sat there, tapping on the wheel, while I struggled with my bags and then there were people helping me. Before I knew it, I had been taken to the nearby home of the *mashgiach* and was being welcomed by his wife. She gave me chicken soup with *lokshen* and spoke to me in Yiddish and I wished she was my mother. The *mashgiach* spoke to me for a few minutes, and then he took me to the home where I'd be staying for a while before I settled into the dorm. I met more and more people and I couldn't concentrate, and they showed me a room and there was fresh bedding, and I simply collapsed. And then it was morning.

◆　◆　◆

Over the next few days I began to settle in. My *rebbeim* were very kind and caring, and the boys in my class treated me with kid gloves. Things began settling into a routine, and I found that life, while lonely, could look up at times. And then came the knock that would stay with me forever. It wasn't such a tremendous knock as knocks go, but to a sensitive little thirteen year old, it was too much to handle.

I had been sent to a building not far away from the yeshivah to meet someone who was to be my new tutor. I walked through the lively streets, now awash in the light of dusk, and found the building with relative ease. I entered and sat down on the lobby steps, waiting patiently for the tutor to come down. As I sat there, I hummed a *niggun* to myself and let my brain dissect my new life.

The door to the lobby came crashing open and a *bachur* came storming into the building. I vaguely recognized him from the neighborhood and was totally unprepared for what came next. He made a beeline for me and began yelling at me.

"Get off the stairs!" he screamed.

I thought he'd lost his mind. I stared at him, perplexed, not understanding what this *bachur* wanted from me. His eyes were open wide, spittle gathering on the edges of his lips, a wild look on his face.

"I TOLD YOU TO GET OFF THE STAIRS," he screamed at me and, raising his hand, he slapped me straight across the face, leaving a full hand mark in red on my innocent cheek.

I sat there in complete shock, incapable of movement. My cheek throbbed with the agony of the slap, and my mind simply wasn't capable of responding to what had happened. Why had he slapped me? Why had he yelled at me!? What was going on here? Had everyone gone crazy?

The *bachur* was still standing there, however, and his face was getting redder and redder. He was like a time bomb about to explode.

"I TOLD YOU TO GET OFF THE STAIRS," he yelled. "DO I HAVE TO SLAP YOU AGAIN?!"

I jumped off the staircase and ran for my life, all thoughts of tutors forgotten in my dash for salvation. Tears flared from my eyes and down my cheeks as I ran to the apartment where I dormed. I fumbled with the key and finally got the door open and ran to my room, avoiding anyone who might be around. I buried my face in the covers and cried and cried and cried. I cried the entire night, from start to finish, the wellsprings never drying up. I pummeled the pillow with agonizing gasps. I screamed silently and bit my lips until they bled and asked Hashem why this had happened to me.

It was because I didn't have a father to protect me from such people. It was because I didn't have a mother to comfort me. Nobody really cared about a lost thirteen year old with no parents who was alone in the world. I tossed and turned all night and, sometime deep in the darkest hours of the night, when the shadows of time kept the night birds company, I made a request of the One Above.

"Please, do not let this *bachur* get married," I begged Hashem, my fury piercing in its intensity. "Let him suffer like I have. Let him not get married forever!"

◆　◆　◆

The years moved on and I found my place in the society that I was in. I became known as a top-class *bachur* and I dived into the sea of learning with a growing *simchah* and *geshmak*. I was older now, and the *shidduchim* began coming. I was engaged within a month and married three months later. I was happier than I'd ever been before in my life. Every day had a rosy glow to it, every night beckoned with the promise of a delightful future. Life was beautiful. Eventually, we moved back to America and I found myself a *kollel* that was learning what I wanted to learn as well. My wife found herself a job, and all was well.

A few weeks after we had settled into the neighborhood, I went over to a friend's house to discuss something. He was in the middle of a phone call as he let me into his home.

"I will try," he said, to the party on the other end, "but the *matzav* isn't good. For one reason or another, everything that comes up for this *bachur* never works out. I am almost ready to give up on him! Anyway," he said as he began wrapping up the conversation, "if I think of something, I'll be in touch."

He sighed as he hung the phone, and I asked him what the matter was. He explained that he moonlighted as a *shadchan* and there was this *bachur* from Eretz Yisrael who was already twenty-seven years old and had never managed to find the right one.

"What's this *bachur*'s name?" I inquired offhandedly, not dreaming for a second that I knew him.

He told me the name. My jaw dropped. My head was spinning. My face was on fire. It was that very *bachur* from so long before. The *bachur* who had slapped me so hard, who had made me cry. The *bachur* whom I had cursed from the depths of my heart and soul.

My friend looked at me with concern. "Are you okay?" he asked me gently. I related the entire tale. How it was my fault that this *bachur* had never gotten married. How I had cursed him so many years before that he never get married, never merit the joy of walking down to the *chuppah*. How my curse had unfortunately come true. The *shadchan*'s face turned white in agitation. "This changes everything," he said.

"I don't know why," I replied and walked out of his house.

◆　◆　◆

The telephone rang the next day while I was home learning in my study. My wife was humming to herself as she did the housework, straightened the cushions on the couch, picked up the toys from the floor. The phone kept on ringing and I picked up the receiver, utterly unprepared for the voice which hit me from the other side.

It was the Rebbe! The Rebbe I followed, calling me from Eretz Yisrael. The *shadchan* had called him up, told him the whole sordid tale. The Rebbe wanted to speak to me, find out what could be done. Could I perhaps be *moichel* this *bachur*, who had gone through so much agony over the past years?

"Does the Rebbe want me to say that I'm *moichel* this *bachur*?" I asked through clenched teeth. "I can say that I'm *moichel* him, but what good would that do? I would have to mean it — and how could I mean it when he tore my soul apart with his callousness, his painful slap that sent me to my bed to cry that entire night! How can I be *moichel* such a person? Tell me how! How? I want to be *moichel* him, but I still feel the pain as if it happened yesterday! I feel like he cut me and stood, watching as my blood came pouring out! Show me the way!"

And the Rebbe did. He showed me how years of loneliness had come from my curse, and how that should soothe my wounded soul. He never tried to say that my pain was unjustified or that I should forgive just like that. We worked together for a very long time, me and the Rebbe, until I could finally hear, finally understand what he was telling me. Until I could finally forgive that *bachur* for the terrible past, for the endless pain that he had inflicted. And finally, finally, I was able to say the words and mean them, to be *moichel* this person and to really mean what I was saying.

Two weeks later, he was a *chassan*.

◆　◆　◆

That's it my friends. Think carefully before you speak. Before you scream at someone, certainly before you do something that could cause someone to be so hurt that he could come to curse you, *chas v'shalom*. That is my story, my friends. Please tell it to your friends and neighbors. Tell it to the people at work. Let them understand the power of their words.

As heard from Rav Shmelka Leifer

The Wheelbarrow

He sat in shul, watching the rabbi drifting off into his beard. The rabbi was old, there was no getting around that, and meanwhile, no one was getting what they needed from him. There was no warmth in the shul, no *bren*. The sizzle which had drawn people when the rabbi was young had long since disappeared, taking many of the younger members along with it. Now, only the core of older members were left, those with undying loyalty to the old man sitting at the front of the shul, and a few solitary guests who had happened in, but were sure never to return.

A shame, reflected the teenager, *that the rabbi had to go and get old. Didn't he realize how much work there remains to be done in the community!* The *gabbai* called the rabbi up for *shelishi* and he was roused with a start, an embarrassed smile creasing his dimpled cheeks. His warm, brown eyes still twinkled at his congregants; distant, now, it was true, but they would always feel his love. However, he was no fool. He knew more than anyone that he was no longer up to carrying out the job.

Motza'ei Shabbos, the rabbi called a meeting of the board. After a short speech, in which he thanked the board for allowing him to lead them all these years, he regretfully announced that now it was time to step down. The shul's president stood up to respond. He thanked the rabbi for all his years of devoted service — thirty-two, to be exact — and asked him to please stay on as rabbi emeritus. "You, more than anyone, will be in a position to instruct and help ease in the younger rabbi who will come to take your place. We would appreciate your staying on in this new position."

The rabbi acquiesced, and the table was cleared for the new discussion; namely, the idea that now they were in the market for a new rabbi. It was a novel idea to the members, but one they quickly warmed to.

Over the next few months, a succession of rabbis arrived at the shul to try out for the job. There were young rabbis trying their hardest to grow in a wispy beard, and older rabbis with years of experience and many children. There were thin rabbis with pleasant voices, who made the davening come alive, and there were rabbis with thick glasses whose speeches were funny enough to bring the house down.

Some were charismatic, some were boring. Some articulate, some always searching desperately for that elusive word. Some had class, their suits the latest word on the fashion scene, while others arrived on Shabbos morning still tucking in their shirttails. A kaleidoscope of rabbis, an entire collection of men who wanted to inspire and be inspired in return. And then there was Rabbi Menashe Kahan, who came, saw, and conquered.

◆　◆　◆

The boy would never forget how Rabbi Kahan strode into the sanctuary like an unstoppable whirlwind. There was something so alive about him, so rich; like a golden fountain. And those eyes. Deep blue, the deep blue of the ocean's depths. They turned stormy blue-grey when he was passionate about something, and they carried a special hint of green when he found something humorous. He made his way to the rabbi's seat, two young sons in tow, like toy boats in the wake of a wave. There was a sudden electricity which took hold of the shul, and even old man Cohen, who hadn't stirred since the previous Rosh HaShanah, sat up and took notice.

He sang with luster. He davened with *heartz*. He was quick with a joke and even faster with a word of condolence and empathy. But all of those things were just jewels in the crown of his speaking skills. His first speech stole the shul's collective heart and held onto it forever.

"There was a young man named Pedro," the rabbi began. "A young boy just out of his teens, not much older than some of you sitting here this morning." His eyes sought out the youngster sitting ten rows in front of him and he smiled. "This Pedro had talent. He could walk across the world on a wire if he were so inclined. He balanced like no human could balance.

"He could have made his fortune in his native Spain," continued the rabbi, "but he felt that his homeland was much too small for a man of his talent. He was resolved to get out to the big, wide world to seek fame and fortune on a scale that his small country could never provide. And so, he traveled to America, land of endless opportunity.

"He arrived in New York on a Wednesday afternoon and, after some thought, boarded a bus in the direction of Buffalo. After checking into a cheap motel, resting, and buying something to eat, Pedro was ready to check out the world-famous tourist attraction located in Buffalo: Niagara Falls.

"Home of the most awesome waterfall in the world, Niagara Falls attracts millions of tourists every year. They come from all over to do the sights. Some ride the *Maid of the Mist*, others go hiking in the man-made tunnels behind the falls. Some pay a visit to Sea World, while others run to Ripley's Believe It Or Not. But everyone strolls along the waterfront at some point or another. And that was exactly what Pedro was waiting to see.

"Sunday morning dawned bright and sunny, with not a cloud in sight. The air held the chill from over the Canadian border, but the wind was as quiet as he could hope for. Pedro set out from his motel towards the waterfall, his equipment sitting snugly in the huge bag he pulled along behind him. As soon as he arrived at the falls, Pedro swung into action. Along with the two professional tightrope walkers he had hired for the occasion, he began setting up his rope. Pedro was going to walk over the falls in the middle of a Sunday afternoon, a time calculated for garnering the most publicity possible.

"As the thick rope stretched its way from one side of the river to the other, the crowd began humming in anticipation. It was rare, they knew, to find a performer both talented and foolhardy enough to attempt such a feat. But Pedro was doing it. As the crowd slowly began to swell along the surrounding gates, Pedro took his first step off the ledge and out onto the rope, nothing under him but the mighty waves cascading down and away in huge circles of triumphant spray. The rope swayed slightly for a second and the audience gasped as one, but Pedro righted himself instantly. There was no doubt in anyone's mind that the little man from Spain was capable of doing exactly what he had promised.

"There and then," continued Rabbi Kahane, "began the event of a lifetime. The media arrived in all its glory, cameras on hand to film the madman who dared do something so incredibly stupid. As the wind began picking up strength, the figure on the rope twisted and danced on nimble toes, reading the wind's mind and keeping one step ahead of its grasping arms. Step by step he moved along, light as a butterfly, stepping delicately along the rope, nimbly evading certain disaster.

"But before they knew what was happening, Pedro had made it to the other side and was stepping off the last bit of rope onto the ledge, his hands raised upwards in a triumphant gesture of victory. The crowd went wild. Hats were thrown up into the air, people roared their approval of the man who had braved such a challenge and emerged victorious. Pedro stood on the ledge, hands still raised above his head, the bright lights of the media on his face. He screamed above the noise. 'Who's the man?' The entire crowd roared in unison: 'Pedro!'

" 'Who?' he asked, raising his hand to his ear. 'Who?' he asked again. 'Pedro!' they replied, and Pedro felt the meaning of fame.

"Then, without a word, he turned around and started making his way back onto the rope, returning to the other side of the falls. The crowd couldn't believe their eyes. Was such a thing possible?! What kind of a person was this Pedro?!

"But Pedro danced his way right back onto the rope, the wind much stronger now, the froth and chill from the river more stinging than before. He moved swiftly along the rope, destination true and clear. The crowd was totally swept up in the frenzy of the performance, and the bets were on as to how long Pedro would be able to stay on the rope.

"But stay on he did. Through the wind and the spray came a man who rose above it all. Pedro was obviously not disturbed by the windy skies overlooking the swirling waters and, to the applause of the world, he finished his return trip over the falls.

"Pedro raised his arms to the overcast sky. 'Who's the man?' he screamed, his voice hoarse. 'Pedro!' came the reply, loud as a clap of thunder, thousands of voices combining as one.

" 'I can't hear you!' he yelled. 'Who?'

" 'Pedro! Pedro! Pedro!' Like a mantra it rose and fell, merging with the sound of the river's echo."

◆　◆　◆

The shul was utterly silent now, everyone intent on the rabbi and what he was saying, everyone wondering where on earth he was going with this. Rabbi Kahan paused for breath and continued his narrative.

"As soon as Pedro lifted his arms for silence, the crowd was quiet. The tremendous noise was instantly replaced by a tense and expectant silence. Pedro looked at the crowd. 'You all saw me cross Niagara Falls twice today,' he said. 'I will now prove to you all my total supremacy when it comes to balancing on a rope.' There wasn't a sound.

"Pedro looked around at his audience. 'I will now cross the falls wearing a blindfold.' The roar that greeted those words extended into the very clouds and reverberated back at them.

" 'Yes, my friends,' he said, pleased at the reaction. And Pedro proceeded to do just that. One of his assistants wrapped a thick piece of black material around his face, completely obstructing his vision, and he was then helped onto the rope to start his suicidal mission. The audience waited with bated breath as Pedro took first one step, then another along the rope. Every step took an eternity, and every movement caused them to gasp anew.

"There he stood, a solitary figure, surrounded by nothing but air...and he triumphed over all odds. Defeating the wind and light drizzle, Pedro completed his trek in one piece.

"Once again he went through the ritual.

" 'Who's the man?'

" 'Pedro, Pedro!'

" 'Who?' he screamed, cupping his hand to his ear, 'Pedro,' they replied, drawing out the thunderous sound of the rushing water spilling over the falls.

"His hands raised for silence, Pedro said in a quiet voice, 'I will now cross the falls blindfolded, and pushing a wheelbarrow!' Nobody breathed. Would this brilliant performer really sacrifice his life to the rushing waters beneath him?

"With the eyes of the entire world upon him, Pedro, still blindfolded, took control of the wheelbarrow that one of his assistants had wheeled onto the platform. Then, wheeling the unwieldy thing, he began what would ever be remembered as a legendary feat. He danced like a raindrop, swerved through the fog like a particle of dust in a ray of sunlight.

"And somehow, he and the wheelbarrow made it across in one piece. Nobody knew how, but everyone knew what they had just witnessed. The crowd wasn't waiting for him this time. They were celebrating their hero with song and dance. 'Pedro! Pedro! Pedro!' came from one side of the falls and bounced back to the other side, with the help of the river's mighty echo.

"And finally, Pedro raised his arms for silence once again. 'For my next feat,' he began, 'I will cross the falls blindfolded and pushing a wheelbarrow — as you've all seen me do. You all know that there is nobody in the entire world who can do what I have done here today in front of your very eyes.

" 'And now,' he paused for breath, 'I will perform the ultimate trick. Before you all, I will now push the wheelbarrow across the falls with one of you inside it. Who will volunteer to climb inside my wheelbarrow and be pushed across the falls?' "

◆　◆　◆

The shul had never been so still. Rabbi Menashe Kahan stopped dead center of the podium and looked his future congregants straight in the eyes. "We are no different than those people," he said. "Every day we say in davening '*Ani ma'amin be'emunah sheleimah* — we believe in You Hashem. *Shema Yisrael Hashem Elokeinu* — We believe in You Hashem.' You are the King, we proclaim, You are the King. And, we even believe it. But who among us all is really ready to go out there, step over the edge, and get into that wheelbarrow?"

Just Part of
the Plan

Friday Encounter

I t's great to get engaged, and Yossi's enjoyment was no exception to the rule. Yossi looked around the hall, happy to see everyone he knew having a terrific time at his very own party. Listen, it was high time this happened — after all, almost all of his *shiur* had already taken the big step. It was time that he, too, joined the club of holy matrimony. The boys were dancing up a storm, except for the guys who were busy sampling the mini potato knishes or making sure the egg rolls disappeared as quickly as they were put out. The photographer was snapping away at anything that moved, and Yossi had a permanent smile plastered onto his face.

The *vort* moved along, with everyone doing what everyone does at *vorts*. The *chassan*'s musical friends pounded away at their instruments, the guests enjoyed the abundance of creative food masterpieces and the *rabbanim* spoke with gusto and charisma, detailing the couple's many fine attributes. In short, the evening was a success. As the evening drew to a close, Yossi's father called him over to the side of the hall and extracted a thick white envelope from his pocket, which he handed over to Yossi.

"Yossi," he said, "here is five thousand dollars for you to buy your *kallah* her ring and another special piece of jewelry. Just take good care of this envelope, alright?" Yossi looked at his father and told him that he'd do his best. And he really intended to do just that.

The next day was a Friday, and Yossi headed into Manhattan, determined to get a good look at the sales going on in a few of the major department stores. The money was safely ensconced in his inner jacket pocket, and he checked on it every so often, trying hard not to belie his nervousness at carrying so much money at once. He caught an inner window seat and looked at the view from the subway car until they entered the darkness of the city-bound tunnel. The lights flickered on and off as the train swayed to and fro, the monster rushing into the blackened entrance of its cave. Yossi was relieved when they emerged at his stop, and he untangled himself from the crowd of commuters and pedestrians surrounding him.

The money was still with him as he climbed the stairs up to the city streets, and within a very short time he was staring in awe at the skyscrapers that stood proudly all around him. He checked out some of the latest in stereo systems and picked up a shirt at Macy's before beginning to make his rounds from one jewelry department to the next. He was in for a disappointment. First of all, none of the sales were even half as good as the stores had suggested in their ads, and the items on sale were not even close to what he'd consider buying for his *kallah*. And even when he finally found a store with a truly decent sale going on, they were missing the style of ring that he knew his *kallah* wanted. Either they only had Tiffany cuts, or the diamond was too big, or it was rectangular when all he really wanted was a teardrop shape. All in all, it wasn't the most successful shopping expedition he'd ever undertaken.

But it was getting late and Shabbos was approaching; it was time to head back to Brooklyn. So, brushing aside his chagrin at not being able to present his *kallah* with a beautiful piece of jewelry in the near future, he left the store and headed in the direction of the Brooklyn-bound subway station and his grandparents' home, where he would be spending the upcoming Shabbos.

His problems didn't stop when he stood on the platform, unsure which train would take him back to Brooklyn. The hour was steadily closing in on him, and a feeling of nervousness was quickly taking over the pit of his stomach. Yossi began to berate himself. How he could have been so cavalier as to take such a time-consuming trip on an *erev Shabbos*?

It took him some time but, after studying the subway map carefully, he eventually figured out what the map was saying. Yossi stood off to the side, tapping his feet and glancing at his watch, sighing in relief as the train roared into the station. He boarded the train, finding a seat in the corner of the crowded car and waited to hear the conductor's voice announcing the familiar names of the upcoming stations over the PA system. He waited in vain. The names — when they came — were not in the least recognizable, and what was more, they were few and far between. After about twenty minutes, Yossi plucked up his courage and began looking for help.

Across the aisle, two black men were carrying on a conversation. Timidly, Yossi interrupted their heated exchange with an "Excuse me sir but could you help me out?" The men looked at him and Yossi could see the wheels turning in their minds as they asked themselves why on earth this Jewish boy in a hat and jacket was riding their line.

"Whats a mattar man?" one of them finally spoke up.

"Well," said Yossi, "I was just wondering if you could tell me which line I need to get back to Brooklyn?"

"Brooklyn?" said the second man with a heavy Bronx drawl. "You on de totally wrong train, man! Dis train goin to de Bronx, no goin' t'Brooklyn. You on de wrong train, man!"

"Not only dat, man," interjected the first fellow, "this train, she an express train. No stoppin' for de next ten minute at least."

Things were going from bad to worse to schlocky. He had just taken the train in the wrong direction and had gone about forty-five minutes out of his way. He had to get off the train, get back on a different one heading the other way, and make it to Brooklyn with enough time to stash his pile of gelt in a secure place for Shabbos. Glancing out the window, Yossi had a top view of some of the Bronx's finest burnt-out buildings. A cloud of smoke was rising off in the distance, and down on the street two teenagers were in the process of dismantling a car that had foolishly strayed into their territory. What was he doing surrounded by strangers, on an express train heading deeper into the urban sprawl, with five thousand dollars in his pocket?

When many long minutes later the train finally came to a halt, Yossi was the first one out the door. He ran down the length of the platform, up the stairs, around the bend and down an identical flight where he waited anxiously for the train that would return him to familiar ground. Halfways down the platform a sad-looking man sat, slowly strumming a banjo to a tune only he could hear: perfect welcoming music to this relic of a neighborhood.

Yossi glanced at his watch for the thousandth time that day. It was almost five thirty. Shabbos would arrive in less than an hour and a half. He sighed with relief when he felt the vibrations of the incoming train approaching. It was the right train this time, and Yossi wiped his sweaty forehead as the doors slid closed behind him. Sinking down onto one of the few available seats, he bade the Bronx a silent farewell, hoping never to see the place again. It was incredible to think that only fifty years before, the Bronx had been one of the most Jewish neighborhoods in NY City.

This time it seemed that things were going smoothly. The train chugged along making record time, and within half an hour they had arrived at Forty-second Street, where Yossi was to change to a Brooklyn-bound train. This, too, arrived right on schedule, and swallowed him up into its mammoth insides. Nothing — not even the rush hour congestion — could bother him at this point, with his destination so close. But then, just as the train was spanning the bridge that would take him into Brooklyn and his grandparents' home, there was a grinding of brakes. There, mid-bridge, the train slowly pulled to a halt and sat there, sweltering in the late June sunshine.

All around, people grumbled of road works and collisions and turned another page in their newspapers, but Yossi's heart started pumping wildly. This was too much! What was he going to do? By the time the train started moving again it would be too late to take it all the way to his grandparents. He would get off as late as possible, but he would have a major walk to look forward to. And he still didn't know what he was going to do with the money burning a hole in his pocket. He sat, silently counting the seconds as they moved on relentlessly.

The sun was sinking slowly over the New York skyline, and Yossi's heart descended along with the setting orb. What was he going to do with all the money in his pocket? Should he just hand it to someone on the train and beg them to hold it for him? Would they give it back to him? Stories of *gedolim* from the past came to his mind: all those Rebbes riding into town, asking the innkeeper to hold onto their money for Shabbos. The old man on his left began nodding off, his sweaty, balding head lolling onto Yossi's shoulder and Yossi looked heavenward in despair.

Suddenly, amidst a sigh of relief from the crowd, the train jolted into movement. The old man straightened with a *harumph* and turned to the next story in his paper. Yossi got up and stood near the door, calculating the absolute latest he had to exit the train. He had just over twenty minutes.

Fifteen minutes later the train pulled to a halt a few stops into Brooklyn and Yossi alighted, dodging pedestrians, bumping into men with attaché cases and, ignoring the escalator, raced up to the street. There were five minutes left.

As twilight descended over Brooklyn, Yossi found himself in an alien world. In desperation, he looked at the assortment of stores all around him, wondering where he should deposit the money for the weekend. All around him were stores of varied description, multiple languages scrawled boldly across their awnings. Many of the signs were written in Chinese. There were Italian tailor shops and Polish delicatessens with smoked slabs of meat hanging in their front windows. A dinky beauty parlor shared a front with a barber shop, its vandalized pole swinging pitifully in the muggy evening air. Never before had Boro Park felt so far away.

There was no more time to waste. Clutching his bundle of money in his hand, Yossi turned and entered the shop closest to him — a wine and liquor shop run by an old Korean couple. The man looked up suspiciously when Yossi came bounding into his shop, keeping his hand under the counter while sizing him up with a ferocious glare.

"Yes?" he finally inquired, and Yossi knew, he just knew, that this wasn't going to work.

"Mister," Yossi said, "could you do me a favor?" The man looked as if he was going to bite his head off but Yossi strode manfully on. "You see," he continued, "in a matter of moments my Sabbath will commence." He stopped in confusion, not knowing if the man knew what that word meant. "Sir, would I be able to leave this bundle of cash with you here until tomorrow night when I will be able to return?"

The man's face had taken on a violent shade of purple. "So you're from de police, you are," he said, "trick me into handling bad cash, catch me with bad money, put me in jail for ten years, take away my store... What will happen to my wife and kids and my nephew Momo still in Korea still wanting to come here to the States! How will it ever happen if I'm stuck in jail?" His voice had risen, his eyes were dilating, and Yossi was scared he was going to have a heart attack!

"GET OUT OF MY STORE!" the man shouted at Yossi. "I'M AN HONEST MAN! DON'T YOU TRY GETTIN' ME IN TROUBLE, YOU HEAR!" Yossi heard. He turned and ran for his life down the street, as dusk drew closer and the sounds of the boom boxes gradually took over the night. And then he knew that he would try once more, do his *hishtadlus* and hopefully Hashem would help. Otherwise, goodbye five thousand dollars. It wasn't a comforting thought. But *ein mah la'asot*. Nothing to do.

And so, without missing a beat, Yossi turned and strode across the street, pulled open the door to Marvin's Convenience Center, and walked inside.

◆　◆　◆

Two little bells hanging over the counter tinkled gracefully, announcing Yossi's arrival. An older man stood at the counter, talking in quiet tones with a customer. His hair was very gray and it curled over his shirt collar and down his neck. He was wearing a T-shirt with some slogan scrawled across the front, barely legible now from years of going through the wash. He looked like any one of the myriad nationalities that made up the neighborhood.

Yossi strode up to the counter and waited impatiently for the guy to finish counting out some change for the customer before him. As soon as he was out the door, Yossi turned burning eyes on the older man and said, "Mister, you have got to do me a favor." The man stared at him as if he was from outer space but replied, "What exactly do you want me to do?" This was the funny part. How would it sound to this *goy* when Yossi told him that he wanted him to hold onto five thousand dollars for him until the next evening. Yossi told him what he needed him to do. He expected the guy to stare at him like he was totally crazy, or to at least laugh at his naïveté in trusting an absolute stranger with such a huge sum of money.

But the man did none of the above. Wordlessly, he held out his hand for the money. The man slid the money into his cash register and told Yossi that he would see him the next evening. Only as he was walking out of the store, faced with the madness and intensity of the weekend all around him, did Yossi face the idea that he would be walking for the foreseeable future.

◆　◆　◆

That Shabbos was one of the strangest Shabbosim he'd ever spent. On one hand, Yossi was very proud of the way he'd handled the *nisayon* that heaven had thrown at him. On the other hand — and this was a big hand — it sickened him to realize that he'd basically taken five grand and thrown it away into the wild blue yonder without so much as a goodbye. He highly doubted that the money would be waiting for him when he'd return. He told no one the whole story, playing down his lateness, keeping the dull heartache to himself. Suffice it to say, his *tefillos* that Shabbos were of a very high caliber indeed.

Motza'ei Shabbos, Yossi borrowed his *zeide*'s car and drove the half hour downtown, finally pulling over near the convenience store. He got out of the car, steeling himself for the upcoming encounter with the owner, who would for sure deny that the story ever happened. He pushed opened the doors and walked inside, outwardly cool as a cucumber, while shaking like a leaf on the inside.

The man with the gray hair seemed not to have moved from the spot since he'd last seen him. The same T-shirt adorned his bulk, the same poker look sat on his face. But there was something in those eyes, something that hadn't been there before. Yossi greeted the guy and asked him how his weekend was. "Fine," the owner replied. Then he flipped open the cash register and removed the five thousand dollars. With a flourish, he handed over the envelope to the astounded young man.

It took him quite a while, but Yossi finally recovered enough to ask the man why on earth he'd been so honest! What made him return the money just like that!? The man went over to the fridge, took out a can of Coke and handed it to Yossi. He then took him over to a few chairs by the wall and they sat down, side by side. "I'll tell you why I gave you back the money," said the man. "It's because I'm *frum* like you."

Yossi's mouth dropped opened and he waited for the man to continue. "Yes," the man continued in a sad voice. "When I moved into this neighborhood thirty-five years ago, I was as religious as you are today. I, too, would never have dreamed of carrying money on Shabbos, and I kept every single mitzvah in the book. But slowly I began to change. The little things went first, and slowly, slowly one thing led to another. As the years passed by, I found that I was getting less and less religious and it bothered me, but I couldn't muster up the energy to change.

"Until yesterday, that is. When you walked into my store, eyes aflame with worry about our precious Shabbos, not knowing who was going to hold your money for you, or whether you would even get it back, for the first time in years I felt the pain of what I had dropped. But when you asked me to hold your money because you had absolutely no idea that I was a Jew, I knew that I had gone way too far! That I should look like a *goy*! What had happened to me? How low would I sink? It was at that moment that I came back to my previous self. It will take me time to really get back to where I once was, but this Shabbos I realized where I need to go, and I hope to get there sometime soon."

Yossi bade the man a warm goodbye and got back in his car, happier in more ways than one.

As heard from Yaacov Yisrael Babad, who heard it from
Yossi's grandfather one Friday afternoon

The Weak Against the Mighty

Way back in '92, when the *kever* of Yosef HaTzaddik was still accessible to the Yidden of Eretz Yisrael, and the yeshivah of Od Yosef Chai was alive and well, and thriving in the city of Shechem, in close proximity to the *kever* of Yosef HaTzaddik, a large group decided to donate a new *sefer Torah* to the yeshivah. The *hachnasas sefer Torah*, welcoming the new arrival, was to take place on the first night of Chanukah at the yeshivah in Shechem. A beautiful idea and their hearts were certainly in the right place, but there was one tiny problem: the Israeli army was determined to prevent it from happening.

They would set up roadblocks, they would stretch metal teeth across the roads, and they would ensure that the Arabs who lived in Shechem and its environs would not *chas v'shalom* be disturbed by the rejoicing that invariably accompanies such an occasion. In short, no one wanted to antagonize the Arabs — those same Arabs who would later destroy Yosef's grave with their bare hands and dance upon its roof as they torched the ancient building.

Obviously, the army's orders could not be obeyed in this particular case, and preparations for the celebration took place in defiance of the law. Jews have been defying governments for thousands of years, and this event would be but one more link in the chain which spans our history.

So it was that I found myself sitting comfortably in my neighbor's Mitsubishi on that first night of Chanukah back in 1992. My neighbors, the Kleins, were die-hard Chevron and Shechem supporters; of course they would be putting in an appearance that night. And I was joining them for the ride.

It was one of those delicious winter nights. The sky was a velvet blanket with little stars sewn all over it, the wind rushed up and down the darkened streets, and a feeling of excitement filled the air. As we began the drive, Mr. Klein explained the game plan.

"There are two main ways to approach Shechem," began Yitzchak Klein. "One passes through Kfar Tapuach, the second bypasses Kedumim. Most of the people who will attempt to attend this evening's festivities will travel through Kfar Tapuach, where the army will almost certainly be waiting to stop them. We, on the other hand, will take the Kedumim route, which will hopefully have far fewer roadblocks, thereby ensuring our arrival at Kever Yosef in time for the *hachnasas sefer Torah*, which will be attempting to break through from the other direction. That's the plan. What do you say?"

"Yitzchak," said I, "whatever you say is fine with me." And away we went.

We drove out of our settlement, past the guardhouse and onto the winding roads of the Shomron region. We made good time and soon we were swinging to the right, which led in the direction of Kedumim, a mere five minutes away. As we approached the well-lit road that led up to the settlement, the soldiers standing guard on the side of the road motioned us to a halt. Yitzchak ignored them. Only when the soldier nearest us aimed his gun at our wheels did Yitzchak swerve to a short stop.

The young soldier was very upset as he ran over to the van, smashing his rifle's butt on the thick anti-rock windows and yelling at us. "Why didn't you stop?" he screamed at Yitzchak. "I almost fired at you!"

"Why didn't you look at the color of my plates, they're yellow!" Yitzchak yelled back. Eventually, they both calmed down, but it was obvious that the soldiers were on a high level of alert and were very edgy.

We continued on, threading our way along the narrow highway past the beautiful homes of Kedumim, which looked down at us from their perch high atop their mountain. Orchards bordered the road's perimeters on either side, and ancient olive trees abounded, their gnarled trunks twisted with old age.

As we drove, we noticed an interesting trend. Many of the Arab cars we were passing were driving with one headlight on and one off. Yitzchak explained that this was a system used by the Arabs to let their brothers up on the hilltops know that they were Arab and not Jewish, and so avert a possible attack on their vehicles. After driving for another fifteen minutes, we arrived at a more serious-looking checkpoint, complete with barrier and soldiers.

"Uh oh," said Yitzchak. "Now the fun starts." He rolled down his window and gave the soldier a questioning glance.

"Sir, I am sorry but you cannot continue driving past this point tonight," said the soldier.

"How can that be?" said Yitzchak. "As you can see, I have a van full of kids and I need to get to Eilon Moreh (a settlement located past Shechem). I need to get my kids back home. What am I supposed to do — drive back to Tel Aviv and book three rooms at the Dan Panorama just because the Israeli Army decided that they won't allow a *hachnasas sefer Torah*?"

Yitzchak was getting really steamed up, working himself into a serious temper.

"I'm sorry," said the soldier, "but these are my orders. You know what, let me see your I.D. card. If it says that your family lives in Eilon Moreh, I will be more than happy to let you continue."

To which Yitzchak quickly countered with, "I don't have it here with me."

To which the soldier shrugged in response and refused to let us through.

To which Yitzchak requested to speak to the soldier's commanding officer.

The soldier escorted him into the guardhouse and called the officer on the phone. I do not know what Yitzchak said to that officer. All I know is that he emerged from the guardhouse smiling, with permission to continue on his tour of the Shomron. Shaking his head in exasperation, the soldier pulled back the barrier and we were on our way, into Indian country.

The road became very narrow, with towering mountains on either side. As we drove, we listened to music and talked and laughed. We were having a merry old time when we suddenly underwent an attack. Something that felt as strong as a cinder block hit the van with astounding force, leaving us unsure whether we'd been hit by a burst of gunfire or by a very heavy rock thrown off the top of the mountain. Needless to say, Yitzchak stepped on the gas, putting us out of the immediate range of fire and then, pulling over to the side of the road, he reached under his seat and removed a very effective looking gun from its holster.

In a matter of moments he had checked the gun for bullets and put it into user mode, handing me the holster to hold at eye level for the benefit of any passerby who might harbor somewhat nefarious ideas. Without a doubt, it was the most exciting entrance I'd ever made into a city. Because suddenly, there we were, entering Shechem, ancient city of war between brothers. Unlike those sickly and feeble moments in the past, Shechem was alive and kicking.

Businessmen were rushing from here to there in three-piece suits and silk ties and many stores were still open, despite the lateness of the hour.

After driving for a few minutes in the direction of Shechem's Casbah, which is basically the town square, we ran into a patrol of army police on duty. I was extremely happy to see those policemen, since I'd never seen so many Arabs before in my life, and it wasn't the most pleasant sight in the world. Remember what occurred just a few years ago in Ramallah, and you'll begin to understand what I was feeling.

We greeted the men with a "*Chanukah sameach*," and were answered in kind by the policemen. Then one of them pipes up: "I hope you aren't headed over to Kever Yosef. It's totally off-bounds to anyone tonight."

"Of course not," Yitzchak replied. "We wouldn't dream of going to Kever Yosef on a night like tonight. We're actually heading in the direction of Eilon Moreh, and you gentlemen should go and have yourselves a beautiful holiday."

And with that, Yitzchak pressed down on the gas and we surged forward into Shechem's busy streets, unmindful of the pedestrians passing us by on either side of the van's windows.

Now, for some reason, the policemen had not been totally convinced by Yitzchak's professed destination and so, when we pulled up at the street corner which leads to Kever Yosef a few minutes later and got out of the van to stretch our legs, we received military visitors almost instantaneously. And they were mad!

You see, for some odd reason the policemen hadn't truly believed Yitzchak when he told them that he was taking the little *kinderlach* straight home to bed. They had a sneaking suspicion that he wasn't being 100 per cent accurate with them. And they happened to be right. They had followed us across Shechem to see where we would end up and, what do you know, we were by Kever Yosef — the last place we were allowed to be right then.

Left with no choice, Yitzchak got dramatic. He knew that if the soldiers made us leave right then, chances were we'd miss the *sefer Torah* when it arrived. After all we had been through that night, we deserved to be there for the Torah's arrival. So Yitzchak told those soldiers that I was an American who had come for a short visit and that this would be the only chance I'd have to daven at the grave of Yosef HaTzaddik — and how could a Jew deny his brother a chance like that?

But the soldiers had their orders and weren't about to give in so easily. They told Yitzchak that there was absolutely no way they could let me in to the grave. We'd have to leave right away. So Yitzchak insisted on talking to their *mefaked*, their commanding officer. I was impressed! The man was proving to be real good at getting what he wanted.

The soldiers escorted him past the roadblock, complete with soldiers in full battle gear, and down the winding road to the guardhouse where the phone was located. I took the opportunity to strike up a conversation with one of the soldiers; he had just arrived from Gaza, where he'd been on patrol for the past half a year. He showed me the crack in his tooth where he'd been hit by a rock in the narrow streets of the Gaza slums. I could only marvel at his courage.

Fifteen minutes later, Yitzchak returned triumphant, shoulders squared and thrown back, like a man who had taken on the might of the entire Israeli army and emerged victorious. I would be allowed in, he said, for ten minutes, and then we'd be on our way. And hopefully, by that time the settlers with the *sefer Torah* would have broken through the army's defenses and would be here with the *sefer Torah*. Then we wouldn't have to leave, and joy and holiness would reign in Shechem...at least for a while.

And so, I was escorted down the tiny street by my soldier friend, who continued our discussion until we reached the *kever*. There, I spent the next twenty minutes saying *tehillim* and davening at the grave site of one of *klal Yisrael*'s purest tzaddikim ever. By the time I got back to the "Kleinmobile," the soldiers were really rushing us out of there, which made us wonder if perhaps the Torah was arriving right then. But with no choice, we said our goodbyes to the friendly group of soldiers and drove off in the direction of home, taking the Kfar Tapuach route this time, hoping to meet up with the *sefer Torah* making its way to its future home.

We drove out of Shechem into the dark and unfriendly country, and pretty soon we reached a roadblock. It was manned by a number of soldiers in white knitted *kippot*, who were in a very jolly Chanukah mood. We continued on our way and, as we drove, we began to notice groups of Arabs walking along the road in the direction of Shechem. First one group passed, then another, and then we realized that they weren't Arabs at all. They were Yidden — and they were walking briskly in the direction of Shechem! They were going in, soldiers or no soldiers! We passed group after group, some singing, others dancing, and we stopped and got out of the van to get a better look at the festivities.

Of course, it didn't take too long before the soldiers found out about the surprise coming straight at them. They quickly formed a human chain, stretching themselves across the road, attempting to block the people from going through. Time after time the people pushed up against them, forcing the chain apart. Time after time the soldiers would run forward, regroup, and form a human chain once again. (Funny, the soldiers who were not religious had no trouble keeping the chain unbroken. I guess our soldiers weren't trying that hard.)

They placed rows of metal teeth in the road, and suddenly we were boxed in: on one side there were the teeth and on the other there was a huge traffic jam. And so, there we sat, while more and more groups of Yidden passed, intent on bringing in their *sefer Torah* with song and dance. The group bearing the Torah finally arrived as well, and we watched as the men held it aloft, their faces shining with joy.

And then, after sitting there for an hour, when everything had almost become quiet, an ambulance, siren wailing, drove past us headed in the direction of Tapuach junction. Knowing that this might be our last chance to emerge from this jam, we drove right behind the ambulance as it threaded its way through the cars and emerged in the Tapuach junction, where a lively party was in full swing. A stage had been set up, there was music and dancing, and they were giving out jelly donuts. Life was good. But the *sefer Torah* didn't get through that night.

They tried again a few nights later, and this time the soldiers weren't friendly. Not at all. In fact, they were hostile, and they had no trouble at all holding the line against the crowds surging up at them. The *sefer Torah* was pushed and shoved as soldiers battled the crowds. "*Ribono shel olam*," I thought to myself, "how can Yidden push Your *sefer Torah* with such impunity!" But push it they did, and again the *sefer Torah* did not get through.

At this point, one of the army generals had had enough. Aside from the fact that it was costing the army a serious amount of money every time they had to ship their soldiers in to the region, he just couldn't see the point of refusing to allow the *hachnasas sefer Torah*. So let the Arabs get a little upset! And so, taking the initiative, he announced on the radio that the army was allowing the *sefer Torah* to be brought in on *zos Chanukah*, with singing and dancing. All were invited.

This statement, which had not been authorized by army headquarters, brought the general much flack from as high up as the army commander-in-chief, Yitzchak Rabin. But he took it in stride and the party went on. The *sefer Torah* finally arrived at its rightful home (at least, until the yeshivah was evicted from Shechem a few years later). At the *hachnasas sefer Torah*, the rabbi spoke. "Everything has a *mazal*," he said, "even a *sefer Torah* in the *heichal*. The proper time for this *sefer Torah*'s arrival was right now, and not a minute earlier."

The Spark Within

What is a best friend? I can think of a few definitions. Best friends can be spiritual or physical guards for each other; they can be the other's alter ego; and they can be like brothers. Having a best friend means having someone on your side who truly cares about you. In short, there is a spark which exists in both your hearts, connecting the two of you in an everlasting bond of friendship. You might not talk to each other for years, but when you do speak it's as if no time has passed at all.

I know of someone who is just such a best friend. He possesses a spark within which burns so brightly that it attracts the goodness in everyone. Almost anyone who comes into contact with him feels that spark, relates to it, and is inspired by it.

This genuine and sensitive person, whom I'll call Mordechai for the story's sake, wasn't rich. He owned no car and, besides, at the time of this story he lived in Manhattan, where owning a car can be a most unpleasant experience (unless you happen to be in the underground parking lot business, of course, in which case having a car is a terrific thing). Anyway, being without a car but still having to get around, meant that Mordechai took the train a lot.

On this particular evening, as he rode the IRT through Manhattan, the train's clientele would have given any lesser being heart failure. Mordechai, however, was completely relaxed. He was just sitting there, probably reading a *sefer*, when two boys of Spanish persuasion decided to join him. Juan and Pedro saw the boy — he was sitting by himself and he looked harmless. In short, an easy mark. I wasn't there, but I can picture the scene. Juan sidles in on one side of Mordechai, Pedro takes a stand on the other side, the edge of a nasty-looking switchblade peeking out of his pocket. They begin with their usual tactics, probably threatening him, maybe pushing him a little. They're surprised to see that Mordechai is completely calm. He smiles at them and, suddenly, the spark within is there for them to see, to feel. It's like nothing they've ever experienced before. Something totally foreign to these tough Spanish boys, who were probably beaten before they even learned to talk.

And suddenly, amazingly, they find themselves talking, really pouring out their hearts to this Jewish boy whom they had been about to mug. They're not cursing, they're expressing raw emotion that would earn them everlasting contempt if they were overheard. But with this Jew-boy their secrets are safe, and they know it. They talk for half an hour: two Spanish toughs in black leather jackets and metal-toed boots and the gentle yeshivah boy in his white shirt and dark suit. Finally they say goodbye, asking him for his phone number before they part!

Now that you have a little taste as to what Mordechai and his spark are all about, I'm going to relate to you the story which showed me the extent of his power. Again, it was late at night and Mordechai was traveling back to his school. The subway car was entirely deserted. Now, Mordechai is a musical kind of guy, although he didn't normally show it off. He plays the harmonica. And now, in the emptiness of a New York City subway car, he pulled his harmonica out of his jacket pocket and began playing a tune on it, a tune that was soulful and poignant and full of life all at the same time. There he is, sitting and playing his harmonica, when the door at the end of his car opens and this huge black man walks in and makes his way over to Mordechai.

The train is approaching Harlem and it's late at night, and this giant of a man sits down across the aisle from Mordechai, listening to his music. When Mordechai finishes the song, the man says, "You know, I also play the harmonica."

"Really?" Mordechai replies.

"Yea I do, and I have it here with me. D'you mind if I join you?" asks the man.

"Not at all," Mordechai replies, and there they sit companionably, the mountain and the small yeshivah *bachur*, playing harmonica together as the train rumbles along towards Harlem, sharing the spark within.

Mit a mul, they arrive at a station somewhere around 125th Street, right smack bang in the middle of Harlem. The man tells Mordechai that this is his stop and asks if he would like to get off with him and maybe take a walk. Mordechai agrees. (I could only stare at him in silent amazement when he told me that; how could he have accompanied this man off the train into the middle of Harlem?) They get off and continue playing their harmonicas together as they stroll through the streets of Harlem, past burnt-out storefronts and abandoned buildings. Then the guy tells Mordechai that he's the leader of the Black Panthers. Now, for those of you who may not know, the Black Panthers was a militant anti-government group in the 60's, who protested the government's policies towards the black community. This guy is involved in running all their operations.

As they're walking along, they come across a huge group of Black Panthers, who stop dead in their tracks and gape in wonder at the sight of their leader just strolling along, deep in conversation with some white Jewish kid. The man just smiles reassuringly back at them and signals "He's my man, boys" and that was that. As they walk along, side by side, Mordechai asks him why he felt they had to blow up buildings to further their cause.

The man looks at him, dark black eyes smoldering with fury. "You think I don't try the other way?" he roars. "I wait for hours in them offices trying to get some clerk's attention so I can maybe get some support for all the programs that I run to try to help my people! I tutor kids for free every afternoon, trying to convince them to work hard enough to be able to get into college. But the only way to get the government's attention is to bomb it! Only then do they listen!"

He walks Mordechai to the next subway station and makes sure that he gets safely on the train.

A few weeks later, Mordechai read in a paper that the big, big black man who had cared so much for his brethren had blown himself up while assembling a bomb. And it saddened him.

As heard from Mordechai Leeder

The Bird

Based on a True Story

There they were again, whole flocks of them circling the air, jawing at each other with a mockery so intense one could think they were almost human. They migrated through the country every year, flock after flock, heading to places unknown. They themselves probably had no idea where they were traveling, but the call of nature was strong inside, and they followed that call across the world.

There were so many types of birds to see: she kept track of them all. The graceful warbler, twittering from bush to bush, cocking his head just so at his mate, inquisitive look as clear as if he'd actually voiced a question. The plover, with its striking black and white markings. The timid dove, always giving way to the other birds over the crumbs she put out under the giant tree and at the splashing competitions held in the kiddie pool during the summertime.

Mostly, she sat and watched them from her porch. Years before, when the kids were still very young and the backyard was a tangle of grass, weeds, and all sorts of remnants from the glorious outdoors, her husband had constructed the porch — the better for them to keep an eye on the kids as they played outside. Over the years, however, the porch had become her personal oasis. Made from beautifully varnished wooded slats, measured to the exact centimeter by her husband the perfectionist, and repainted every season by the older boys, the porch was the perfect spot for a delicious heart-to-heart talk, a contented afternoon with a good book and a glass of iced tea, or just to steal outside for a few minutes to take in the air and hum a song under her breath.

There, too, she got to know her feathered friends. To those not in the know, all birds look the same, but she could tell them apart with a glance. She addressed them by the nicknames she'd given them and held long, delightful conversations where she did most of the talking and they responded in their own perfectly genuine ways. Her family accepted her need for solitude and, once in a while, if a child had been especially good, he was allowed to join her for a mug of cocoa on an early-morning bird-watch. Those were the good days, the days when the land although never completely peaceful, was not the dangerous place it would soon become. And when that happened, it would never be the same again.

◆　　◆　　◆

As the world looked on in admiration, two white-haired men stood on the lawn of the building that housed the most powerful person in the world and joined hands with a murderer. The Oslo peace process had begun, and terror waited in the wings.

I would hope that those who masterminded the experiment for "peace with our neighbors" had some regret when what any simple schoolchild could have predicted would happen, happened. Alas, I fear they do not regret. I fear that they sleep as well as they did back then, when the idea first became a reality. But that is neither here nor there. What is to the point is that the situation in Israel changed almost overnight, especially in the later years of the "Oslo experiment" and during the second intifada that followed a few short years later.

The effect on the people of the land was catastrophic, especially once they began bombing the buses. Just reading the newspaper or turning on the radio became an exercise in bravery. Pain floated through the air and the people hurt. But the men with white hair still jetted around the world, basked in the admiration, and didn't think of relenting, of retreating back from the brink of the abyss to which they had led their people.

She first noticed it a few days after a bus bombing in Tel Aviv had claimed the lives of twelve, wounding fifty. The pictures in the paper made her retreat to the porch, like a wounded animal who finds a quiet spot to lick its bloody welts and wait for the healing to begin. She knew that her healing lay amid the smell and sounds of nature, and she headed to her refuge with a soul ripped asunder from the grief of a nation torn in two.

It was early morning when she made her way out onto the porch, together with her little boy Zechariah, known to one and all as Zach (at eleven years old, he was technically too old to be called little, but there it was). Balancing a cup of tea, a book, and some peanut butter for the birds, she was struck by the strange sight that greeted her. Normally, the garden was fairly quiet at that time of day, with maybe a few birds gathered on the bird table. But today she was greeted by a crowd of newcomers she had never seen before. Not only that, but the fluttering birds had absolutely nothing in common with each other. They weren't of the same family, and not even the type of birds one would expect to see clustered together.

She looked on in amazement, cup of tea forgotten on the wooden railing, and stared at the strange fraternity. A old and withered dove shared a moment at the fountain with a young and adorable little sunbird. An impressive-looking bee-eater, color surrounding its chest, flitted amid a pile of bread crumbs. She pointed all this out to Zach and then they settled down, fascinated, into their regular seats on the porch.

She took a seat on the swing her husband had hung for her on one of the porch's sturdy beams. Swinging peacefully back and forth, she perused the paper, reading the current events with interest, discussing some of them with her astute eleven year old. When she reached the third page, however, she was greeted by pictures of the victims of the latest suicide bombing in Tel Aviv. Young and old, men and women — there was no apparent system to those who had been killed. A Russian soldier, all of twenty years old, was right beside a sixty-year-old woman who worked as a cleaning woman. A thirty-five-year-old computer programmer shared his line on the page with a fifteen-year-old girl who had been coming home from high school, whose eyes would forever sparkle with the glow of youth. It was painful, too painful, to look at the pictures and see how lives had changed so drastically from one moment to the next.

As she read the small print, it got harder and harder for her to see. She looked up, trying to blink back the tears, only to notice that she had been joined by some of the birds from her garden, who were sitting peacefully all around the porch. It was strange, but there was something human about the looks on their faces, as if they knew something and were expecting her to figure it out as well. And in those faces she could just make out the face of the forty-year-old rabbi and the sweet face of the six-year-old girl, staring at her knowingly from the eyes of a nightingale.

"It's like even the birds know what's going on," she remarked to Zach. "Look," she went on, "they're acting totally out of character, hanging out together like this when they have nothing in common with one another. Maybe they're uniting against a brutal world, coming together to a safe place." Seeing the way the birds acted around his mother, Zach agreed with everything she said. They spent the morning with the birds, and it felt good for them all. They spoke to them, she and Zach, and she read out loud from her *Tehillim*, noticing how still and calm the birds grew when she did. And, despite the fact that they talked not a word, she learned from them, as well.

◆　◆　◆

The months passed and it seemed like her garden was reflecting the country's situation. It was as if this was the spot where they all came after their brutal exit from the world. Sometimes she castigated herself for thinking such nonsense. She told no one of what she felt to be true, partly since she knew they wouldn't believe her, and partly since it was something so precious to her, so very private, that she didn't want the world to know about it. Thus life went on.

The days shortened and became colder, and the long, dark nights of winter set in. The weather didn't really allow for long visits to the garden; the porch was wet and the winds were sharp. From time to time, she caught a glimpse of a different set of birds, that belonged together no more than the first group, and she knew. But life in the country had reached a level of horror that had never been felt before.

The streets of the land were besieged. The people were afraid to venture forth. Almost daily came news of another kamikaze who had sacrificed his life on the altar of hell, taking many innocent people along. And the people reacted by closeting themselves into their homes, retreating from the stench of the battlefield like frightened mice. And who could blame them?

It became so she found it hard to look at them. At whoever they were out there, coming to her garden. Why they had chosen this spot she did not know, but it was too hard! How could she be so darned happy in her own life when a world filled with such raw pain existed just a few feet away, in her own backyard? But then she'd be filled with remorse. After all, someone had sent these souls to her, hadn't they? So she'd go outside and spend some time among the birds, holding out bread crumbs softened in milk, feeling their feathers scratch her skin in thanks for the comfort she provided.

And then, after a long and terrible time, things began to calm down. There was still the odd skirmish: rocks were still being tossed at fifty miles an hour through car windows, rockets were still going off. Still there were madmen and glassy-eyed youth who thought it the greatest privilege to blow themselves up — but now they were the minority. And everyone felt able to take a breath of the fresh air.

The long months of that terrible winter were drawing to a close. The sharpness in the air became less urgent. The first petals of spring were beginning to poke their slender necks above the sweet-smelling earth. Coffee shops were full with people having the odd espresso and pastry, and the restaurants had customers once again. Real customers, with credit cards, who didn't hesitate to tip. Maybe life could return to normal. And yet, some held on to the opinion that this was a momentary lull in the action, and they barricaded themselves in their homes just as they had before. And who knew who was right?

◆　◆　◆

Spring was here. The sound of crickets chirping joyfully in the nighttime air, the smell of freshly mowed lawns, the thud of soccer balls thumping into the net. The sun, back to itself after a long wintertime hiatus, in which it had vanished for days at a clip, was now visible for long stretches, smiling down at the earth as if it alone was in possession of secrets worth dying for. Springtime stirred up the exploration juices in boys of all ages and would see them heading off on their forays out into the wilderness, enchanted with all that nature had to offer.

Living as they did on the outskirts of the city, they were not far at all from the wide-open expanses of a boy's ultimate expedition grounds. There were caves hidden in the mountainside foliage (usually invisible, unless one knew where to look). There were flowers of all kinds, and trees, oh boy, were there trees. Tall trees with thick trunks that soared into the far-off sky, and short, bumpy olive trees gnarled with age and still giving forth a bumper crop year after year. The kids hiked those mountains and paddled in the shallow streams that ran through the wadis, still full of winter's leftover rain. The kids loved it out there in the wilderness. They'd come home, cheeks red from the wind, sparkle in their eyes, and eat as if the house was on fire. The energy they burned during that season could have powered a city.

Zach was a born hiker if there ever was one; he lived for the outdoors. It was an experience to empty out the pockets of his pants in preparation for the washing machine. There were old bird's nests in there, along with pieces of string and whatever type of card he was currently collecting. There were perfectly round pebbles, empty snack bags, and, sometimes, a frog or two.

He was one of those kids it was fun to have around. One you could carry on an intelligent conversation with, one mature beyond his years. The children understood this instinctively, and Zach was the leader of the pack without ever having attempted to take control. They asked his opinion and they followed it — and that was that.

The few days after Pesach but before school started were prime time for adventure, and Zach planned a nice long hike through the wadi for two days after *yom tov*. Zach had been reading maps since he was nine, and he was very responsible. They weren't going to any dangerous places, and Zach had done stuff like this many times before. And so, she waved them off early that morning with a smile, no qualms about letting them go off by themselves. As she looked at her son, filled to bursting with the generous breakfast she had just prepared for him, the happy feeling of motherhood surged through her. He waved back carelessly, and she watched as they walked down the street. She watched as they arrived at the bus stop, where they would catch the bus that would take them to their hiking area. She watched as the bus turned the corner and they disappeared from her life. She'd remember that last little halfway wave as long as she lived.

◆　◆　◆

She knew why they had come before they told her. The year before, the son of someone from down the road had been brutally wounded in a terrorist attack and she had seen them standing at the door the same way they stood now, stiff and unsmiling. There had been a doctor, as well, to give the injection, and the rest of the day passed in one giant pain-filled haze. Nobody had to tell her what happened. She just knew.

There had been a bus bombing. Nothing more had been needed to be said. Nobody had had to explain to her in what state they'd discovered the boys. As it was, they left her under sedation, dead to the world but not dead enough to avoid suffering when she woke up.

Many months passed before she was ready to face the world once again. Even when things were beginning to get back to normal, her garden was still off-limits. She couldn't bring herself to go out to her little hideaway, to sit and commune with the world around her, to appreciate nature the way she always had. And, most of all, she couldn't bear to see the birds, for seeing the birds meant being forced to remember...and that was something she wasn't able to do. So she stayed in the kitchen, drank her tea there, read the paper, listened to her music, and crept back into herself.

◆　◆　◆

It was early Sunday morning when she came downstairs to fix breakfast for herself. She toasted a bagel and put the coffee maker up to percolate, and she was just washing off a knife in the sink when she noticed it. A warbler was sitting on her windowsill, looking at her intently with its piercing black eyes. And she knew, she just knew... She knew the look in its eyes.

The bird hopped onto the window ledge, opened its little beak and chirped sweetly. She watched it for a minute before she went off to finish making her breakfast. It stayed in her mind as she went about her daily tasks and, although she still couldn't face them all out there in the garden, a little part of her, somewhere deep inside, was hoping that the little bird was going to come back. And it did.

She stood at the kitchen window, talking to the little bird, the look in its bright eyes tugging at her heart. Eventually, they graduated from the kitchen window to the porch. Sitting and swinging back and forth, right in the place where Zach used to sit brought her a quiet joy, an intense feeling of belonging to the world. And perched on the edge of the swing, its alert eyes more searching than ever, sat the bird. Finally, she brought herself to say the words she thought she'd never speak again.

"Hello, little bird," she said, and with those few words she transcended to a place where her fractured soul would begin to come back together again.

The Rabbi of Caracas

T here are Jews all over the world — and it's your job to find them." That was the way the *rav* who gave me *semichah* began his speech on the day I officially became a rabbi. I spent my formative yeshivah years in a place that encouraged active participation with the Jews of the world. With that in mind, after I spent a number of years studying in *kollel*, my wife and I decided to move to Caracas, Venezuela, where I become rabbi of the Ashkenazic community. The overall community comprised about fifty thousand Jews, and my shul had around three thousand families. So we moved to the land of guitars, steaks, and intense corruption, and life was never boring again.

A few years into our stay in Caracas, we decided to take a few days' vacation, to get away from the intense pressures of my job. We chose to go to Aruba, an island in the Caribbean under the jurisdiction of The Netherlands. And so, I booked a suite for our long-awaited vacation. It seemed, though, that things weren't so simple. When we got to the airport, the airport clerk pointed out that our visas weren't valid, and that we wouldn't be able to return once we left. The fact is, he was right. Our visas were not valid in the least, since they had been purchased by someone in the Caracas community.

Once we left, it really wouldn't be that easy to return. I bent over towards the clerk and talked in a low voice.

"I know that there are problems with my visa," I said, "and I'm impressed with your vigilance and sharp eye." The clerk smiled at my open flattery. "However," I went on, "I've heard that it is possible in special cases to purchase an emergency visa at the airport which will allow us to return after our vacation, if you understand what I'm saying."

The clerk smiled at me. A wide smile, revealing a happy mouth of rotten teeth.

"This is true," he confirmed in a quiet tone. "But, alas, I regret to inform you that such special visas cost *mucho denaro.*" He spread his arms and looked very sad at being the bearer of such bad tidings. He had been born for the stage. It was a crying shame that he was wasted here in the departure lounge of the airport instead of performing his craft in the grand theater in the center of the capital.

"How much money are we talking here?" I asked him, preparing myself for the worst.

"The visas are one hundred dollars American per person," he informed me with tears in his eyes.

I leaned even closer across the counter and whispered: "But I heard that they cost thirty dollars and no more, is that not so?"

"Forty-five," rejoined the security clerk in the Caracas International Airport, and forty-five dollars it was. A minute later I witnessed a man arrive at the very same desk where he ceremoniously presented the clerk with two bottles of Johnnie Walker. His passport was stamped then and there with a flourish. Well, I had learned a lesson for the future, one that I wouldn't forget. Oh, and our vacation was wonderful.

◆　◆　◆

As a spiritual leader in one of the biggest Jewish communities of the land, it was my "privilege" to take part in a meeting with the then-newly elected president of Venezuela: Mr. Hugo Chavez, who stormed into office after days of brutal fighting in the capital's streets. It was not a time to be outside and, in fact, nobody left their homes. After he was sworn into office, however, and the situation had quieted down to some degree, Mr. Chavez wanted to meet with the country's religious leaders. I was invited, along with the chief rabbi of the Sefardic community.

We took our seats along the table, sitting side by side, and we spoke about matters pertaining to both of our communities while we waited for Chavez to put in his appearance. When he arrived, he took his place at the rostrum and began to deliver a powerful speech to his audience. Now, I am not a native Spanish speaker, but after dealing with people in that language for a while, I'd become somewhat fluent. Fluent enough that is, to sense that Mr. Chavez's use of the language was grammatically incorrect, and I found that idea very strange. Wanting to clarify my doubts on the matter, I turned to my colleague and discreetly inquired as to whether I was imagining things, or in fact Chavez was speaking like an uneducated boor. He confirmed what I had been thinking, but explained to me that the people loved the man and didn't care that he was inarticulate, badly spoken, and that his colloquialisms made no sense. "This is South America. Get used to it," he said. And I did. But some things took a little longer to get used to than others.

◆　　◆　　◆

As I mentioned, my community numbered in the thousands, but among all those people, very few were actually *shomer Shabbos*. That being the case, I became very friendly with the members of my shul who attended services on a regular basis, our relationship far surpassing the normal rabbi-congregant connection. That was why the disappearance of Mr. Kellman caused me a lot of worry. When a number of days had gone by and Kellman still hadn't shown his face in shul, I approached another member of the *kehillah* who was friendly with him, and I asked if Kellman was in the hospital or something.

"No," the man answered. "Kellman's been kidnaped!"

I was very shaken up by this information, although the other members of the shul didn't seem overly worried. And, as it turned out, they were right, for Kellman was back in shul a few weeks later, looking tired and thin, but otherwise none the worse for his experience at the hands of the kidnappers.

I approached him after davening and asked him what had happened. He made light of the whole thing. Apparently, armed men had abducted him along with his wife from a crowded public building and had taken them to a hiding spot deep in the South American jungle. There they had been kept locked away until the ransom was put together by his business associates. Kellman was in the gold industry, and kidnaping was pretty common by the look of things.

"Anyway," he said, "as soon as the robbers received their money they brought us back to civilization, and here we are — whole, healthy, and thankful to Hashem."

"But weren't you worried that things would get rough out there in the middle of the jungle?" I asked, incredulous.

He laughed. "No," he said. "I wasn't. You see, this is the third time I've been kidnaped, so I have come to learn what to expect. The first time was very scary. But now, it's just part of business! It's just the life of the South American businessman!"

◆　◆　◆

And then there were the encounters that really shook me up and which I think about until this very day. One morning, I was approached by one of the wealthier members of the community. He explained that the family had just purchased a brand new home on one of the nearby islands in the Caribbean and would I be available to travel down to the island and put up the many mezuzos that were needed?

You have to understand that every society has their comparisons, their monetary way of showing off. In some places it might be where you spend your Pesach or summer vacation, in others, it's what type of car you drive. In Caracas, keeping up with the Joneses meant owning a huge mansion on one of the nearby islands. That's just the way it was. I gladly accepted, and he told me how many mezuzos he would need. (On every trip that I took to Eretz Yisrael, I made sure to bring back as many mezuzos and pairs of tefillin that I was able to.) We agreed on a day, and he told me to be at the airport at nine o'clock, where I would take his private jet to the island. (A private jet is also a necessity in Caracas. How else would you transport your guests to your island mansion when you make a bar mitzvah or bris?)

Well, we flew down to this island, and it was a beautiful day with the sun glinting off the ocean below. South America is a beautiful land and the sights are magnificent. A place truly worth seeing — if you have guts. Anyway, we arrived at the island and I exited the plane and went through customs, carrying all those mezuzos in a large bag. The customs officer took a good look, and I did my best to explain to him what they were and how they were used.

It's an interesting thing, but during my entire stay in South America, I experienced no anti-Semitism in any shape or form. Here, too, the officer simply examined my passport and luggage and I left the airport, making my way to the nearby taxi stand where I would take a taxi to the home of my friend.

So there I was, soaking in the sunshine and taking in the most amazing coastline I had ever seen, when I was approached by an elderly woman wearing a straw hat, whose eyes were covered by a giant pair of shades. She looked bewildered and confused, and that might explain why my first reaction to her query was: "Run that by me one more time." What she actually asked me was, "What day does Pesach come out on this year?"

Now, before you ask me what is so strange about a question like that, I will explain. Simply speaking, the woman didn't look Jewish. I am pretty good at sniffing out Jews (coming from Caracas you can get a lot of practice doing just that), but in her case, I would have never dreamed that she was a Jew.

Her story was fascinating. She had gone through the war. She had been in the camps, and had been liberated by the American army. She was one of those people standing at the fences with paper-thin arms and expressionless faces. And this one American soldier picked her out of the entire crowd and decided that he was going to marry this Jewish girl. Unfortunately, he was not a Jew and she, having just survived the war, wasn't in any position to argue with this handsome American soldier, who came from a well-to-do family back home, and who wanted nothing more than to marry a Holocaust survivor. Go figure.

The one thing this young man insisted on was that she keep her faith a secret from everyone she met for the rest of her life. A small thing to ask, right? After experiencing the Holocaust, it didn't take much persuasion to convince her that that was the best course of action. He took her out of Europe, introducing her to his family as his "European bride." And she never told anyone that she was a Jew. Children were born to them, and they had no inkling that they were Jewish. She was an active member of her community for many years, and nobody had the slightest clue. She had married the soldier, and she respected their agreement — for better or for worse.

The years passed and they moved to Miami, Florida and then to this island in the Caribbean, where they intended to spend their golden years in peace and tranquility. And for all those years, she had never mentioned a word about being a Jew. Not to her husband, their kids, or her relatives. It came to the point where she had almost forgotten that she actually was a Jew. All of a sudden, her husband got sick and, a few months later, he passed away, with she, his loyal wife, standing at his side until the very end.

And then she saw me. I was so very clearly a Jew. Big black yarmulke. Tzitzis. A respectable-looking suit. Clearly a Jew. And suddenly, it all came flooding back in a wave of memories. She remembered that she was a Yid. She remembered her life in pre-war Europe. But so many decades had gone by since those years! What remained for her to do? And she thought of the time of year and she realized that it was springtime and that meant Pesach. So, a woman who hadn't given Judaism a thought for the last fifty years, asked this obviously Jewish man when Pesach was going to arrive. A spark had been kindled on a flame long extinguished. We spoke for a while and I gave her my card and begged her to call me if there was anything at all that I could do for her. Then I took my leave and went to put up the mezuzos. After all, the mansion had to be ready for its family.

And then there were the dangerous moments. I was sitting in my office one morning, eating breakfast, when there was a knock on the door. The door opened, and a giant of a man entered my domain. He introduced himself as Rabbi X from Israel and explained that he worked as a *shaliach beis din*, a messenger for a particular court of law. He had been sent to Caracas on a mission of mercy: to track down the husband of an Israeli woman who had been missing for quite a few years. He had been sent on his tracks and, after sifting through tons of mud, had finally hit solid rock. He had discovered that the husband had escaped to Caracas. Would I help him track the man down?

I told him that I would do my best but, the fact is, I had never even heard of the man. Obviously, he didn't count himself among my congregants. I asked the *shaliach* to give me some time to find out more. I took down all his particulars: his name, where he had last been seen, and his physical appearance. Then I told the man I would be in touch.

Later that day I emerged from my office for *Minchah* and, as I walked through the building towards the side room where we prayed during the week, my mind was churning with possibilities! What should be done? Who should I talk to? How does one go about tracking down someone so elusive in a sprawling country like Venezuela? Besides, so much of the land is jungle, the people savages. What was I to do?

I entered the sanctuary and began davening, and then the solution came to me. It was simple! After davening was over, I approached one of my regular congregants. You see, this particular man was in charge of the Venezuelian equivalent of the American Secret Service, the government body which protects the president, whose officers are some of the most intensely trained personnel out of all law-enforcement branches. And this man was their boss. If there was any one person who had access to the type of files I so desperately needed, it was he. I pulled him aside and explained the problem. He asked me for the man's name, and he told me to give him two days to find out.

Two days later he was back with the information. The man was living deep in the jungle, in an Indian village surrounded on all sides by hostile natives. He was an arms trader by profession, and he had the reputation of being a tough guy. It seemed that many Israelis were involved in this type of work. Now we would simply have to take a little trip down to the middle of the South American jungle to track this man down.

"How will we get there?" I asked my friend.

"No problem," he replied. "You'll take my plane."

The morning dawned, blustery and gray. Not my kind of morning at all. But the plane was reserved for us, and I met the *shaliach beis din* at shul, where he joined me for the trip to the airport. The *shaliach* was a mountain of a man, which provided me with a little feeling of security, and I glanced at him from time to time to see how he was reacting to the whole thing. Apparently, he was used to chasing errant husbands across the globe. His face was unreadable, and he looked ready to take on anything that we'd encounter.

We flew over mountains and valleys, rivers and forests. South America is very beautiful, and I never tired of staring at the view. It is the land of the Amazon, the land of minerals and natural wealth and oil — and that was exactly where we were headed. To the Venezuelan oil fields, smack bang in the middle of the jungle. Finally, after around three hours, we landed on the runway that had been built for the oil fields, and the next thing I knew, we had rented a four-wheel drive and were headed in a direct course for the village where our friend, the Israeli arms dealer, lived with his non-Jewish wife.

The roads were not paved. We bumped over every rut we could find — and they were bone shattering! The driver was a taciturn, middle-aged Indian man, who smoked like a chimney and asked no questions. He simply drove us to the village we had requested and consented to wait while we took care of our business there. It took us about forty-five minutes to get there, bumping the entire way, and our bodies felt pretty sore by the time we had reached the place.

It was like we had stepped back two hundred years in time! The village was just that: an Indian village. Little children clad in rags played in the mud, and the smell of baking bread wafted along the dirty streets. The housing was primitive, and the sanitation department would have had a field day. But, we weren't there on a government mission, we were there to help a Jewish woman in distress, and so, we kept on asking everyone we met for directions to the home of the arms dealer. It turned out that he lived in a colossal mansion at the edge of the village, and the Indians directed our driver to his home, where we instructed him to remain outside, waiting for us. He was to go nowhere. After all, you never know what to expect from a person. Least of all from an arms dealer.

We knocked on the door. The word had obviously spread that we were in the neighborhood, looking for him, and the guy came to the door and opened it himself. He had a long, black ponytail that cascaded down his back, deep-set, chocolate-colored eyes, and the most cunning and crafty look that I had seen on anyone's face for quite some time. He eyebrows were thickset and close together, and he scared me. He invited us into his living room and inquired as to why we had come. The *shaliach*, his imposing bulk squeezed into one of our hosts' smallish chairs, explained to him exactly why we had come.

The man looked us in the eye and said, "I don't know if you have realized, but I'm very far from the Jewish religion. In fact, I don't care for anything you have to say, and there's no way I'm going to give my wife a *get*! I don't even consider her my wife any more. From my point of view, once I left her she isn't my wife. I don't care what happens to her!" Hearing his raised voice, his Indian wife peeked into the room. She looked afraid.

The *shaliach beis din* stood his ground. "Listen to me," he said. "I came this far to find you. I tracked you down in South America. I took a plane here and then a jeep ride through the jungle. Do you realistically think that I'm going to get up and walk out of here? Not a chance!"

Through this whole friendly exchange, I was expecting the arms dealer to get up, go to the closet where he stored his weapons, pick up some fifty caliber colt and aim it in our direction while telling us to leave. But he didn't. They both sat looking at each other in stony silence. The huge *shaliach beis din* and the stubborn Israeli weapons man. They stared and stared at each other, hatred written on one face, impassiveness on the other. Hours went by. The little sunlight which had filtered in through the overhanging trees became watered down, and here and there lights began to flicker, as the village started getting ready for night. And still they sat, wordless and frigid, engaged in a silent war. No side was willing to give in. He because it went against his principles, we because this was our only chance to ensure the continued purity of our nation.

Five hours passed this way. Five hours of heated stillness. Five hours of silent debate. Suddenly, the arms dealer lifted his hands in a gesture of defeat and said very grudgingly, "Okay, I'll sign, then get out of my house!"

That was more than fine with us. He signed the document that the *shaliach* produced, and we both signed on as witnesses. The *get* would be delivered to his ex-wife, and she would now become a divorced woman, with the opportunity to remarry and have a normal life once again. And we said goodbye, returned to our jeep, drove the return route through the jungle, and took our plane back to civilization, thankful that Hashem had been on our side, allowing us to fulfill this mitzvah.

As I said, I'm the Rabbi of Caracas, and I do all I can to bring all those Jews back to where they belong. I think that the man who delivered the speech which inspired me all those years ago would have been proud.

As heard from the Rabbi of Caracas

Mind Versus Body

I always thought that all those stories that I'd heard about mind over matter were just that: stories. I remember reading about a family that went traveling cross-country and were involved in a car accident. Their vehicle ended up balancing on the edge of the cliff, hanging in there by a thread. The family was thrown from the vehicle and lay scattered across the area. But the youngest, the baby, had somehow come to be trapped under the car, out of the mother's reach. When the distraught mother realized this, she summoned up superhuman strength: she lifted up the car and pulled the baby out from underneath.

An amazing tale, and I was duly impressed. I had come across other stories of this type, but after the first amazement had passed, I'd find myself regarding them with a healthy dose of skepticism. I found it hard to believe that the mind was able to influence the body. I mean, either you had the ability to pick up a car or you didn't! And no mother I was acquainted with had such an ability.

I imagine that the reason I took such a strong line on the matter was because the whole concept pertained to me in a pretty direct way. You see, from the time I was a little boy, I had had all sorts of problems with my feet. I was a fairly regular occupant of the children's ward, and I found myself fascinated by all things medical. I was in constant need of physical therapy, and I had to exercise constantly just to keep myself in the bare minimum of order. But in my mind it was a simple equation: the more I exercised, the healthier and more supple my lower body would become. And it had nothing to do with the mind, nothing at all! In my opinion, it was sheer physical stimulation that I needed, and that was what I was determined to pursue.

◆ ◆ ◆

During a routine checkup with one of my therapists, she informed me about a certain book that was a must-read for anyone with my condition. The book had been written by a man who currently worked as a physical therapist for wounded Marines at the Quantico military base in Virginia. It is especially frustrating for a young soldier who has devoted his entire life to the service, who has gone through "hell week," and has graduated the course, when something unforeseen happens, like pulling a ligament, or worse. Injured soldiers want to get up, ignore the pain and go straight back into battle. It is this therapist's job to make sure that they are eventually ready to do so. He wrote a book based on his approach to therapy, and I found it fascinating. In fact, I was so impressed with the man that I went the extra mile, and I decided to get in touch with him.

On the back cover of the book, there was a little paragraph listing his many accomplishments and his e-mail address, and I sent him an e-mail from a friend's house. I told him that we don't have internet at home and would he please call me at my home. He called me back a few days later.

"Barook," he said after I had told him my name, "I'm very glad to speak to you. It makes me very happy to know that people out there are reading my book and making changes for the better!"

"Yes," I told him. "I found your book tremendously helpful for my physical development and, in fact, my therapist was the one who recommended it."

"Really?"

"Yes," said I. "In fact," I continued, "I would really like to meet you, maybe have a session or two. Do you think that something like that is a possibility?"

"Hold on, let me think for a second," he said and I could hear him mumbling to himself. "See, the thing is, most of the time I'm on the base. The rest of the time I'm home, and that's Chicago, which I can't imagine is a place that you're planning on visiting in the near future." I admitted that I hadn't been planning on it.

"Wait a second," he said suddenly, as if he had been struck by a brilliant idea. "Hold on," he told me, and I was left holding the phone while he went off to take care of something. I waited for about five minutes before he came back on the line.

"Well, it's settled," he said.

"What's settled?" I asked.

"You can come here to Quantico." You could have knocked me down with a feather. I mean, this was post 9/11 and security was tight like a brand new Swiss watch. This was the last gesture that I was expecting.

"Wow," I said, not knowing what else to say. "Why are you doing this?"

"I'll explain," he said. "I was born with a serious foot condition, which caused me constant agony and which set me aside from the rest of my family. My great-great-great grandfather served in the American army during the Civil War, and it's been son after son in the armed forces ever since. My father currently serves as a general in the army and my brothers are military police. But I wasn't able to do anything.

"I couldn't be in the Air Force since I don't have perfect vision. I couldn't be in the Navy since I get seasick while on the ocean. Basically, I wasn't cut out for anything military. But I didn't take it sitting down. I went through strenuous therapy, killing myself until I was able to pass the most rigorous tests the army had been able to devise. I became a Seal (standing for sea, air, and land), the cream of the American armed forces.

"I had become one of them, one of the elite. I subjected myself to the most grueling exercises in the world. I, who had started off not being able to walk very well, was swimming in the ocean with forty pounds on my back and crawling through barbed wire and sandbags. It was unbelievable! I had gone through hell week — and I was a Seal! And that, Barook," he finished, "is why I would love for you to come down here to my base for a few days. I want to meet a young man who really wants to help himself!"

He went on to tell me that the Seals had been so impressed by his determination that he had been given a scholarship to West Point, which he accepted. That was how he had been commissioned the youngest lieutenant in the Seals demolition department.

I probably would have gone anyway, but after hearing a speech like the one he delivered, there was no holding me back. So I drove the two hundred miles from my home in N.Y. down to Virginia, enjoying some of the most picturesque scenery I had ever seen along the way. It was mid-autumn, and the leaves were swirling in the fierce breeze as if driven by some inner force. The drive did me good, and I arrived at the base with cheeks red from the fresh air, my spirit filled with a wild and unrestrainable sense of freedom.

The base was impressively secure. The Marines guarding the place looked like they could chew me up for breakfast, spit out the bones, and then start again, easily. I was assigned a military liaison, whose job it would be to make sure that I didn't get into anything I wasn't supposed to, and to protect me from myself. I loved the base, but I was very happy that I wasn't staying there; I had accommodation in the nearby Jewish community.

I met my new friend, Doug, and was extremely impressed. He explained to me that as much as he wished he could devote the majority of his day to me, that was not going to happen. The first day he would be spending two hours with me, the second day he would do the same. On my third and final day on the base, we would spend a much larger chunk of the day together (we ended up spending sixteen hours together).

The first part of my therapy consisted of Doug telling me all about his home-spun philosophy. He explained his approach and I found it very similar to the mind/body ideas that I had been rejecting all this time. He, too, tied together mind and body: that the mind takes the body to the next level, and stuff like that. And even though this was coming from Doug, someone I respected, I still had a hard time agreeing with him.

He didn't bother arguing about it for long, merely ordering me to get out of my civilian attire and transfer into military fatigues. This added an additional seven pounds to my concentrated body weight, ensuring that I would have a harder time walking than previously, adding to the foot therapy that I would be undergoing. Doug then told me that I would be subjected to tests from some of the soldiers. Some of the tests would be obvious, others would not. I was to be prepared for anything that might happen to me. I smiled. I had never felt as prepared for anything in my entire life! I was ready for the challenges and hoped for the best. And I got them in spades!

They had me running around the camp till I couldn't move another inch. They put me in a pool with surf that pounded away at you with more power than anything you have ever encountered at the beach. When I couldn't move my feet any longer, Doug ordered me out of the pool and told me to explain myself! I simply told him that my strength had all run out.

"Okay," he said, "try this." Then he wound some sort of steel weight around my legs and threw me back in the water. "You can't use your feet anymore, right?" he asked me. "So use your hands instead!" The exercise lasted for so long I thought I would faint, I felt like I was going to collapse, like my body just couldn't go on any longer. But Doug wouldn't take no for an answer. He just kept on pushing me way past what I had considered the extent of my stamina.

Other soldiers put me through rigorous water tests as well, keeping my head under water for as long as I was able, then pushing me back underneath when I tried to emerge! It's amazing what they were willing to do to show me what the human body is capable of. And the funny thing was, the more they kicked me around, the more abuse my body was able to take, until I was able to revel in the action, despite everything my body was incapable of doing.

◆　◆　◆

It was my second day at the base when the action really started. The day began normally enough: I davened at the nearby shul and then drove the short ride to the base. Upon arrival I hooked up with my liaison officer, who introduced me to the soldiers who would be putting me through my therapy for the day. This was followed by hours of harsh and stimulative exercise — in the pool, weight room, and on the running track. It was as I was returning from my morning exercises that I heard the sounds of a fight.

Even from afar I could hear the sounds. A crowd gathering, the soldiers combative and restless, egging the combatants on with shouts and screams. The air was thick with the aggression and restless energy of armed men, men who spend their every waking minute preparing for war. There was a mini-war going on at that moment, and no soldier worth his salt was prepared to miss a moment of it. There they were: a crowd worthy of a fight, or a wrestling match (which was really what they were doing). Many of them stood crowded around a ring. Red hair and blond, tall and short, broad shouldered and stocky: this was entertainment and they were taking full advantage.

I maneuvered my way into the crowd, making my way between two brawny marines, sweating despite the cool air all around. I slipped through the next few men and then passed another, so intent on the match that he failed to notice who was pushing past. I could hear the thud of body hitting mat, the grunt of expelled air when knee collided with sternum, the muffled shouts of surprise when one or the other got the drop. I inched my way through and found myself standing at the front of the crowd.

There was a giant ring surrounded by a low fence. The floor of the ring was covered in purple-painted matting. In the center of the ring stood two powerful Marines, and they were wrestling. One was black, the other white, balding, with a mustache. Both were absolutely huge, with biceps that strained and flexed as each tried to overcome the opponent. The crowd was entranced, fascinated by their fighting prowess. I wondered how long it had taken for these men to learn how to fight like that.

Suddenly, one grabbed the other and put him into a choke hold. He was promptly flipped over his friend's back, landing in a heap on the matting. He was up a moment later, sailing through the air at his opponent's throat. He was evaded with a head butt. I watched in open-mouthed astonishment. They were being bruised and biffed, kicked and smashed...yet I could see that they were enjoying the match! And then, one of the soldiers put the other into a head lock and, try as he might, he was stuck and couldn't disentangle himself from the other's grasp.

Slowly, slowly, the victor began lowering his vanquished onto the mat, where he would count to three and officially be declared the winner. But, right at the moment when victory was there in his grasp, everything changed. Suddenly, I received a tremendous shove from behind me, as two guys vied over a place in the action. I found myself flying through the air, into the ring, and straight into the two combatants. The force of the shove was so great that my body hit them hard, sending them both flying, and effectively breaking up the match! The soldier who had been on the losing end was now free, and the would-be winner was, literally, frothing at the mouth.

I took one look at the soldier, and I knew that he meant to kill me. He opened his mouth and a stream of obscenities the likes of which I'd never heard before came pouring out (and I'm from Far Rockaway)! When I looked at him again I saw that he had taken a knife out of a little leather case that was clipped onto the side of his pants. He lifted it up and it glinted in the sunlight. Suddenly, I knew the meaning of fear.

"I'm going to kill you," he screamed in a terrible, hoarse voice. I jumped out of the ring and ran like I've never run before or after. The soldiers around us parted like water and I took off like an arrow in flight. I was running for my life and I knew it. It seemed like forever, but it was probably closer to ten minutes. Behind me was a continuous bellowing of curses and the sound of heavy footsteps chasing me for what seemed like a tour of the entire base! And then I realized something. I realized that here I was, someone with a walking problem, who was being chased by a soldier in top form. There was no reason in the world why I hadn't been caught by now...unless I wasn't supposed to be caught.

I slowed down, turned around. The sweat dripped down his forehead, but my pursuer was smiling. He slipped the knife back into its sheath. He approached me and held out his hand.

"That was pretty good runnin'," he said. I thanked him, and waited to catch my breath.

"So it was all a test, right?" I asked him.

"Yup," he replied.

"How did I do?" I asked.

"Well, let's take a look and see," he said and motioned me to a lounge, where we sat down in front of a VCR for a special showing of "Barook's Flight." I hadn't had the faintest clue that they were taping me, but there I was, in full army gear, running for my life as if demons were chasing me. And there was the marine: running after me, yelling, making me think that the world was coming to an end! And they showed me my speed and the sheer beauty of my running and how I had run smoother and with better coordination than someone on a basketball court. Then Doug came in, and he, too, watched the video from beginning to end.

When it finished, he let out a long whistle and turned to me. "Well, Barook," he began. "There it is. My theory has been proven correct." I hadn't the foggiest clue as to what he was going on about and I told him so.

"Don't you see, Barook," he said. "There was no way that somebody in your physical condition should have been able to run as fast as you just did! The only possible way that the marathon you just ran could have occurred was because your mind took over the game and your body obeyed the orders it was getting without question.

"Don't you see," he went on. "Without the fear that you were experiencing, there is no way that this whole episode could have taken place.

"This should prove something conclusive to you, Barook," he ended off. "Without the mind being involved in the body's every move, the body is a lost case. But if the mind decides to take over the body's development, then there is no limit to where a person could go."

And finally I understood what I had been missing all these years: a true understanding of the role that our minds play in every facet of our lives. Suddenly I knew that it wasn't just about our physical lives, about our normal existence. I knew that the same idea, the same "mind over body" concept could be applied to the Torah, as well. If our minds just made the concrete decision to become the scholars and better Jews that was in our body's power to become, then it would truly happen. It is up to us to make that decision and then to see it through: not to wait for monumental fears or terrible calamity, not to wait for horrible pressure or the knowledge that it is too late for what we want to accomplish. Now was the time, and it was up to me to choose where to place my mind. And then, I knew, my body would follow.

As heard from "Barook"

Window to His Soul

We called him Max. He was old and bent over, and he always wore a beat-up gray felt hat that long ago had become one with him. We, the kids, looked at him without too much thought; to us he was just Max. He was there in the morning, sipping scaldingly hot tea through a sugar cube and chopping a *shtikel* herring after davening, and he was there at night, sitting quietly, right next to the window in the corner of the shul. In front of him would be a *Mishneh Berurah* or an *Ein Yaakov*, which he studied until the final evening service, after which he'd shuffle out of the shul, leaning heavily on his walker for support.

I remember once on a Shabbos morning, when I happened to pass next to him on the way to the candy man, he pulled me over and said excitedly, "Look, Zevi. Look outside! Do you see the sunshine?" But that had really been the extent of my connection with him. What he did between the morning and the evening I didn't know, and I didn't wonder about it, either. After all, Max was just Max. Part and parcel of the shul. No one to worry about.

Then one morning, I arrived at the shul and glanced around at the benches, casually taking in the scene. Everything looked the same, except for one thing, and I couldn't put my finger on what it was. That feeling persisted the entire davening, bothering me, giving me little jabs. I tried to ignore it and get into the davening, but I found it really hard, I was bothered. I left shul shaking my head in exasperation, knowing deep inside that something in my normally orderly life was out of place.

That morning just wasn't the same as usual. The *gemara* we were learning went in one ear and out the next. My *rebbi* chided me all morning for my lack of concentration, but no matter what I did I couldn't concentrate. And then, in the middle of *Navi*, while learning about the wicked King Achav and Queen Izevel, the answer came to me.

"Max!" I said out loud without meaning to, and the entire class laughed.

"Zevi," said Rabbi Shain, using that powerful *rebbi*-stare on me, "are you alright?"

"I'm fine," I replied, finally realizing what it was that was disturbing my equilibrium. Max hadn't been in shul that morning. But Max never missed *Shacharis*; he was always there! He was more dependable than the rabbi! You could just about set your clock by him!

If Max wasn't there, then something must have happened to him. The thought of something happening to old Max suddenly made me sadder than anything. I have absolutely no recollection of what happened to the royal family of Achav; the rest of the lesson I spent deciding what I had to do. If Max wasn't at *Ma'ariv* that evening, I finally concluded, I would have to find out where he lived and go visit him.

◆　◆　◆

After supper that night and homework, I walked quickly down the block to the *shteibel*, arriving just at the end of the *daf yomi shiur*. At this time of night Max was always in shul, sitting in his corner next to the window, waiting for *Ma'ariv* to begin. This time, however, he wasn't there. My worst fears were confirmed.

My father only arrived home from work in an hour's time, and I knew that if I went home and waited for him my mother would never let me out later. My father would probably just shrug in typical adult fashion and say that Max would be there in the morning. But I knew that Max needed help and that it couldn't wait.

Luckily, the shul had had a directory of all the members. Max Yarris was way down at the bottom of the list. He lived on a street called Bocanmask Road, known far and wide and with little affection as "Brokenglass." I looked around the shul, hoping someone was still there whom I could ask to accompany me, but they had all left to their warm and comfortable homes. So I set out into the night, a young boy listening to nothing but the pull of his heart.

The closer I got to Brokenglass Road, the faster my heart thumped. I watched as the neighborhood slowly changed from well-tended homes and gardens to ramshackle and dirty tenements and run-down clapboard houses. Many times I thought of turning and running away, but something made me go on. And then, at the end of the road, sat the lonely little house whose basement Max called home.

As I approached, I realized that the basement's one and only window was broken and boarded up. I wondered how a man like Max, who loved looking outside at the world, could survive in such a place. How could he ever see the sunlight? How was he able to get up in the morning, to pull himself out of bed, to face another day, living as he did?

I knocked on the side door, but there was no response. Over and over I pounded on the rough wooden door until I heard a sound which might have been a "come in." I pushed open the door and walked down the rickety wooden staircase into Max's basement. On one side sat a huge boiler, making horrible noises and emitting foul-smelling smoke. On the other side of the dismal room sat a bed, a small burner, and two chairs. There was also a bookcase which was full to overflowing with books of all kinds, and a small table. The books were obviously well read and loved, and the table held stacks of *sefarim* in orderly piles. The room was dimly lit by a tiny night-light, that illuminated the figure of the broken man sitting despondently on the bed.

"Max," I said, "what happened to you?" He looked up, as if noticing for the first time that there was someone else in the room.

"Zevi," he stammered, clearly embarrassed that I was witness to his humble abode, but too overcome by what life was throwing at him to really care. "What are you doing here?"

So I told Max that I had noticed that he wasn't in shul and I came to see what the problem was. Suddenly, he was bawling; no simple crying for Max. The tears were spilling down his thin face faster than he could wipe them off. I went over to the broken man and put my arms around him, encircling his frail shoulders in my embrace.

"Please, Max, tell me what happened!" Max tried to pull himself together, and slowly his wracking sobs began to subside.

"Zevi," he began, "do you see my window?" I looked in the direction of the window, where slivers of sharp-ended pieces of glass hung viciously from the frame. The wind was seeping in through the cardboard and plastic bags, whistling through the tiny apartment. From outside the tiny apartment came the sounds of shouting, cursing, and shattering glass. Max dried his eyes.

"You see, Zevi," he said choking on his own words. "I'm an old man, with no *kinderlach* to keep me company, and no money for comforts. There is the shul, but that's only in the morning and at night. The rest of the day I'm all by myself, with nobody to talk to and nothing to do. I'm not complaining, *chas v'shalom*. This is my life and I accept it. But this morning, I woke up and saw that my window

— my one source of real light, my hope for a brighter future — was shattered.

"You must understand, Zevi," Max continued, "this is my only source of light. It not only gives me a way to read, it allows me to look out of my miserable world at the lives of other more happy and fulfilled people. I can see toddlers learning to walk and big kids riding bikes. I see the tree on the other side of the park, and sometimes a flower or two that manages to grow in the dirt outside my house. And this morning, when I saw that my only source of joy was gone, well, I just couldn't bring myself to get up and go anywhere. I just did my best to fill the space with whatever *shmattes* I had, and I accepted that this was the end."

Max finished his story and I found that my cheeks were wet with tears. Without a word, I took off my jacket and helped him into it, resisting all his questions as I led him to the door. Together, we climbed the stairs to the windy street outside.

We walked for what seemed like forever. As we reached my block, I looked around at all the beautiful homes lining the spacious road, whose windows afforded us an occasional glimpse into the light and joy of the lives of all those happy families. My house, too, was all lit up; the family was gathered together in the living room. I suddenly realized how worried they must have been when I hadn't arrived home from *Ma'ariv* as usual. How angry would they be? We walked up the path to a friendly house of red brick, whose windows not only allowed us to see the glorious things outside our home but also sent friendship and warmth out to the street in return.

I knocked on the door and there stood my mother and father, their relieved faces soft in the dim hallway light. Without a word, they hugged me tightly to them. Then they saw Max, and all I knew was that my father invited him into the house with a warm handshake and a smile, while my mother took me into my room for a little interrogation as to what had taken place that evening.

Today, our Max still goes to shul in the morning and evening, and he still looks out the window. But, you see, it's a different kind of window from the one he had before, because this one reflects both ways. It takes the tremendous sights of the outside in to us, providing Max with no end of enjoyment, and in return we send out our happiness to everyone out there. Our happiness which wasn't complete, we now realize, without the addition of an old man's smile. An old man named Max.

All Because of the Snow

It started off with a fever that just kept on rising. Whatever we did and whatever medicine she took, it simply wasn't going away. In the middle of the night I would wake up to the moans of pain coming from her bedroom, and then we would hold her in our arms and comfort her and promise her everything she might conceivably desire if she would only get better. But she didn't.

We were finished with the local medical clinic and had become frequent visitors to the children's ward at the nearby hospital, where she had to undergo oh-so-many tests. She smiled through them all, while we cried like babies, and then went back for just another test and then another...

Finally they had an answer for us. And we came down to the hospital with dread in our hearts and fear written across our faces. We walked liked space creatures through the familiar hallways of the dreaded building until we reached the office of the consultant. He was waiting for us; young, not overly compassionate, not a very humble man. He could've taken a lesson from the exemplary behavior of a little girl many years his junior. He informed us that the best his staff could come up with was that she was suffering from some illness with a long name that I'd never heard of, and that we should travel to New York to meet with the team of physicians who were the acknowledged experts in this particular field.

Chanukah vacation was rapidly approaching, and we made reservations for the entire family to fly to America right away. I can still recall the shuttle ride to the airport, how we all sat huddled in a silence so unlike our lively family's normal exuberance, and how all the kids felt the need to touch her, their little sister, to reassure themselves that she was still with us. I can see the frost gathered on the window. I remember the songs playing on the radio, and the driver's cheerful voice as he bantered playfully with the dispatcher.

It was freezing cold in Israel when we left, and it was freezing cold in America when we landed, and it had been freezing cold on the plane. That's what happens when your heart is freezing cold.

There had been a giant snowstorm a few days before, and the roads around the airport were covered in a slushy layer of gray, dirty water. Welcome to America.

The hospital was located a short distance away, and Monsey was the nearest *frum* community, so it made sense to make it our base. The people were amazing: there was an apartment waiting for us when we arrived, with plenty of food and clean bedding. The first thing on the agenda, of course, was a trip to the clinic, where the experts were all lined up to examine our little girl. All thoughts of the future flew out of my mind. No more was I thinking about my job at the yeshivah and who I would find as a replacement. I stopped thinking about the need to find schools for all the kids. I stopped thinking, period.

We waited anxiously, reading from a *tehillim*, gazing with unseeing eyes at a magazine. And then the doctor came out and he said, that yes, after studying all the test results they knew enough to make a diagnosis. We went into his office and he told us that she was a definite carrier of this sickness. She would need immediate surgery, and she would then have to be monitored for about half a year.

To me, signing the forms for an operation seemed so final, like stamping my consent to the decree. I needed more time. It was Thursday afternoon, and I told the doctor I'd be in touch with him on Sunday with my answer. It was time for a break, time for Shabbos. We had just the place to go: to my parents in the holy city of Boro Park, home of Amnon's Pizza, the Bobover *beis medrash*, and Thirteenth Avenue.

Since I was not as familiar with American highways as I would have liked, we decided to begin our journey on Friday morning. This would give us more than sufficient time to reach Brooklyn before the onset of Shabbos. But I hadn't counted on the snow...or the traffic.

In Israel, the slightest snowfall is enough to put an entire city out of commission. The nation takes one look at the falling snowflakes and runs for its collective life. Vehicles head for their cozy parking spots, and pedestrians run to the nearest bus stops, hoping to get home before public transportation ceases to function.

In America, however, people are not afraid of the snow, and they do continue to drive. And so, on this Friday, the roads were as crowded as I'd ever seen them — and it was only getting worse. As we sat in our spot on the unmoving highway, the snowflakes began changing from small, cute little guys to big *zetzers*. Like the sky was involved in a snowball fight against us without giving us anything to throw back at them.

We sat on that highway for hours and moved almost not at all. It went from twelve to one almost without a whisper, and the clock was nearing two when the traffic finally opened just a little. But the snow was falling much heavier now, and the cars were crawling along just because they could barely see five feet in front of them.

And there we were, a car full of hungry, tired, and upset kids, and a driver who didn't really know where he was, and Shabbos fast approaching. A recipe for one big mess. Then, just as we were nearing the stretch of highway which would take us in the direction we needed to go, there was an accident, and once again the road locked down and traffic came to a standstill.

By now, Shabbos was about two hours away, and we still had a long way to go. But, there was no way we could continue, seeing the condition the roads were in. With no choice, we decided to leave the highway at the first opportunity and find the closest Jewish community. Once there, we would find a place to crash for Shabbos. This was easier said than done. The roads were completely clogged, and there was no way for us to exit. So we waited, inching along through the snow and the hail, as the molten sky grew darker and more threatening, and Shabbos was less than an hour away.

Finally there was an exit sign a short distance ahead, and we aimed for it. But there was snow on the ground and the car kept on getting stuck. The wheels churned helplessly and, eventually, we gave up the fight right there on the shoulder. I parked the car as best I could and then, removing as many of our possessions as we were able to carry, we set off for civilization. It turned out that we were fairly close to the Lower East Side of all places (don't ask me how we ended up there), and as we traipsed through the snowy streets, weighed down by all our things, by heavy coats and snow-laden shoes, all we wanted was a warm place with a mezuzah on the door where we could rest our weary heads.

And then, as we were walking down a freezing avenue, I caught sight of a large building with Hebrew lettering over the doorway! In the middle of the icy desert we had found a yeshivah, and we were overjoyed. As quickly as possible, I rushed my crew past a coffee shop, a dry cleaner, and a mini market and into the warm confines of Mesivta Tiferes Yerushalayim or, as popularly known, MTJ. The kids were shivering with cold. Some of the younger ones were crying, and I settled them down on the nearest chairs I could find and went to get them all a hot drink.

On my way to the coffee room I bumped into the *shammas*. He had been busy putting the *beis medrash* in order for the upcoming Shabbos and was very surprised to see my entire family huddled together next to the coat room. Upon hearing the whole story he graciously invited us to stay with him for the entire Shabbos. We grabbed at his invitation with both hands and followed him through the chilly New York streets to his simple, yet warm and welcoming home.

We were given rooms with fresh linen and then a warm, yummy meal for the younger kids who hadn't eaten more than a couple of sandwiches all day. When I left them to go to the yeshivah for davening, they were playing a game on the living-room floor, while both wives were chatting away like they'd always known each other. Leaving this cozy and comforting scene, we headed off to the yeshivah for *Kabbalas Shabbos* and the familiar feelings that Shabbos invokes.

◆　　◆　　◆

It was a wonderful Shabbos: uplifting and serene. If I hadn't been so worried about my little girl I would have enjoyed the privilege substantially more. After *Minchah* on Shabbos afternoon, I was invited to eat *shalosh seudos* in the home of the Rosh Yeshivah, HaRav Moshe Feinstein, *zt"l*.

I entered his simple apartment, so empty of material things, so full of *sefarim* and holiness. I was in awe. I sat and studied the visage of the elderly man sitting at the head of the table. I could not believe that here I was, sitting at the table of the *gadol hador*, the leader of our generation! And then Reb Moshe turned to me, and with the genuine love that he showed every Jew, inquired as to how I had arrived at his yeshivah. I told him the whole story.

I told him how my daughter needed special medical care that was available only in the States, and how the entire family had come in so we could all stay together for the many months of treatment. I told the Rosh Yeshivah how we had left on Friday morning and had spent the entire Friday on the road, arriving in Manhattan right before Shabbos began. I related my story in detail, and Reb Moshe listened deeply to every word.

When *motza'ei Shabbos* rolled around, I asked Reb Moshe's grandson whether I might bring my daughter over for a *berachah*. This was already near the end of the Rosh Yeshivah's life and he was very weak. But I was given permission to bring in my little girl for a short while. I flew home on gossamer wings! Reb Moshe was going to give my little girl a *berachah*! We ran back to the house, and Reb Moshe bade her to come close to his bed. He gave her the most warm and tender *berachah* imaginable, almost as if he was giving a *berachah* to his very own grandchild. The sight touched me in a way nothing had ever done before. And I felt the raw power of the *berachah* that he gave her.

We left the presence of greatness and, sheltered deep inside our coats, walked into the bone-chilling New York winter night. Upon arriving at the home of our host, we put all our things together and prepared to leave the warm and caring home we had been privileged to spend time in. While standing together at the door for a final goodbye, my host pulled me aside and whispered that he had a daughter who hadn't been home that Shabbos and who was in desperate need of a *shidduch*. Would I perhaps keep her in mind if I met any suitable young men?

I smiled at him, this *shammas*, this prince among men, and I told him that I would definitely keep her in mind. After meeting the father, I was sure that the daughter was extra special, and I would love to help him any way I could. We left their home. Our car had probably been towed off the highway and it was the middle of the night, so we took a cab back to Monsey. As the yellow taxi sped through the deserted Manhattan streets, I waved a silent goodbye to the island of hope that had been my home for the last twenty-five hours. Then we crossed the bridge and soon enough found ourselves in the suburbia of Monsey.

◆ ◆ ◆

We had an appointment to see the doctor on Sunday morning. This would be the final checkup before the operation, which was scheduled for the following day. We were ushered into the spacious office and the doctor gave my daughter his stethoscope to play with while he gave her an all-around and very thorough examination. His brow was furrowed, and every few seconds his eyebrows lifted upwards as he checked his data and made little notes on her chart. We waited, tense.

He checked the test results we had brought from Israel, and he looked over the results of the tests administered only a few days before. And then, his eyes lit up in a way that made our hearts jump for joy.

"Never," he began, and it sounded as if he was suspiciously choked up, "never have I seen such a miracle! I mean, it was only three days ago that we gave her an examination and she was in definite need of an operation!"

Yes, I thought to myself, *but that was before she came in contact with Reb Moshe, the gadol hador.*

He was going on and on. "I've been a doctor in this particular field for twelve years," he said in a somewhat dazed voice, "and I have never seen anything so amazing! How on earth did this happen?! She was so sick! It's incredible! She's completely healed! It's like the disease was never even there!"

We simply smiled and joined him in a *l'chaim* from a bottle that he produced. I wasn't about to go into detail about what had transpired over the weekend. That was between us and the Rosh Yeshivah.

◆   ◆   ◆

A few days later we found ourselves happily ensconced on the plane for our return voyage back to the holy land, the entire family healthy and of sound mind. And, to the satisfaction of everyone involved, two weeks later we celebrated the engagement of my oldest nephew, who was learning in an American yeshivah, to the daughter of our Shabbos hosts. What can I say? Sometimes getting caught in a snowstorm is a wonderful thing.

About the Author

Rabbi Nachman Seltzer is the author of the bestselling novels *The Edge* and *The Link*. *Stories with a Twist* is his second book of short stories, following *In the Blink of an Eye*. He is a frequent contributor to *Hamodia* magazine.

Rabbi Seltzer learns in the Mir and teaches at Yeshivas Netsach. In addition, he runs the Shira Chadasha Boys Choir, which is based in Jerusalem. He lives with his wonderful wife and *kinderlach* in Ramat Beit Shemesh.

Other Bestselling Books by Nachman Seltzer. .

An ancient secret
must be protected.

One man will do anyth
to destroy it.

One man will do anyth
to hide it.

Only one man has
the power to reveal it

A brilliantly crafted, captivating novel of the deadly battle
between larger-than-life powers: men who, if defeated,
stand to lose much more than their lives.

Palma de Mallorca, 2003

The sparkling blue waters of the ocean, combined with the brilliant whiteness of the island's immaculate beaches, caused all who visited here to stop and gaze in wonder. However, not all who were arriving on this particular morning had sightseeing on their minds. Tall, imposing men, who radiated power even from afar, they were picked up at twenty-minute intervals by chauffeur-driven four-wheel drives with dark-tinted windows, and whisked off to their meeting place, a Spanish ranch-house villa perched upon the edge of a cliff. As each passenger was delivered, each chauffeur took up his designated place of watch, Uzi submachine guns in hand.

Inside the villa, the men were shown to the conference room and seated at a long, gleaming, mahogany table surrounded by eight chairs. The chairman of the group arose and began the meeting.

The chairman gave a cursory update of the group's successes and failures in different parts of the world, while the seven men listened to him in silence. He spoke of some of the major problems facing their organization, and detailed the recent efforts undertaken by those who opposed them, bringing dark looks to the faces of his colleagues. In view of the situation, drastic measures were called for, continued the chairman, and he proceeded to outline exactly what these measures were.

At the closure of his remarks, the chairman raised his hand to quiet the babble of voices which were raised, some in favor, others in protest.

"We will now take a vote," he said. He turned to the man seated on his right, and began to take a count.

"Little John?" "Yes."

"Gilbert of the White Hand?" "Yes."

"Will Scarlet?" "I don't think we're ready—" The chairman cut him off in mid-sentence, "Yes or no?" "No."

"Friar Tuck?" "Yes."

"Much the Miller's Son?" "No."

"Alan-a-Dale?" "Yes."

"Will Stutley?" "Yes."

"That's five to two in favor, and I, as your chairman, Robin Hood, will now add my yes to yours. The measure stands."

The meeting was over. As the sun slipped down beneath the edge of the cliff, the villa's lights came on one by one, until the grounds resembled a fairy's palace. When the time to depart arrived, the four-wheel drives were ready and waiting. They carried their passengers away, one at a time, at intervals of twenty minutes, until the villa was left alone, quiet and deserted, as it had been just seven hours before.

THE EDGE

a novel
Nachman Seltzer

It's his final race. . .and he's racing. . .to the edge.

A gripping novel of danger, turmoil, and discovery as a world-famou
sailing champion is led onto a life-changing adventure completely
different from any life-course he could ever have imagined.

Eilat

Hold it, I said to myself. *What's that guy doing wearing a leather jacket when it's seventy-eight degrees outside?* He was quite bulky under that jacket too! The situation made me a little nervous. It was time to notify security and find out what this guy's deal was. I pressed the button that was supposed to put me in contact with security and waited for them to reply. Meanwhile I watched as the blond-haired man entered the gate without being stopped. I pressed the button again. No response. There seemed to be something wrong with the security radio system; I wasn't getting through to anyone!

I told myself to calm down. What I saw was probably nothing anyway. So what if he was wearing a leather jacket? Maybe he didn't want to leave it on the bus. I called someone else into the office to take over for me and mentioned that the call button wasn't working and should be fixed. Then I made my way down to the front gate, keeping an eye out for the blond guy the entire way, hoping that I wasn't making a terrible mistake by not sending security after him.

The blond-haired man was perspiring. He reached a hand up to this forehead to wipe away the perspiration, then quickly pulled it back as he remembered that he was smearing his makeup. He wished that he didn't have to wear the heavy leather jacket. Well, it didn't matter, he told himself; soon he would be in paradise where it was cool as could be, with the fountains of water forever flowing. He derived comfort from that delightful thought as he sat down on a bench to get his bearings.

His instructions were to locate the most heavily populated area in the aquarium and then to blow himself up. His mind filled with images of the white-bearded *imam* whose eyes flashed with the zeal of a true believer: "The more infidels you take with you, my children," he would say, "the greater your reward will be." Soon, soon it would happen; he would be a martyr and Arab children the world over would sing his name in praise forever.

Zack and I entered the underground observatory. Down there, beneath the ocean, yet apart from it, we were in an exotic world with rainbow-colored inhabitants. We were both overcome by the it's grandeur and majesty.

And then, as I was saying something to Zack, I saw him. I reached down to the walkie-talkie I had put on when I left the office and quickly spoke into it. "All security to the Tower. I repeat, all security to the Tower."

He was still wearing his heavy leather jacket and he was sweating. As I looked a little closer, I realized it was not sweat; it was makeup. And, in the areas on his face that the makeup was coming off, darker skin showed underneath. I glanced at his eyes — they were glazed.

Our security instructors always said, "If you look at the eyes and they are blank or glazed over, with no emotions showing, then you're in trouble."